Described by *The Times* as 'a pioneer . . . a true jazz original', Graham Collier is an internationally renowned jazz composer, whose work has been favourably compared to that of his three jazz composer icons: Duke Ellington, Charles Mingus and Gil Evans. He has released nineteen CDs, is the author of seven previously published books on jazz, including the highly praised *Interaction: Opening up the Jazz Ensemble,* and for twelve years was artistic director of the jazz degree course at the Royal Academy of Music in London. He currently lives in Greece, where he continues to compose, travelling from there to present concerts and workshops around the world.

the jazz composer

moving music off the paper

Graham Collier

Northway publications

Published in 2009

Northway Publications
39 Tytherton Road, London N19 4PZ, UK.
www.northwaybooks.com

The publishers acknowledge with thanks the kind permission of
Karlijne Pietersma to reprint the photo on the back cover of this
book.

Cover design by Adam Yeldham of Raven Design.

A CIP record for this book is available from the British Library.

ISBN 978 09557888 0 2

Printed and bound in Great Britain by Cromwell Press Group,
Trowbridge, Wiltshire.

Dedicated to Herb Pomeroy (1930–2007), who influenced my music in a way that few others have done, teaching me that it is the musicians in front of you who are important, not the rules, or even the notes that you have written.

With a sense of irony, Coleman Hawkins recalled his intention to try to learn his own solo on 'Body and Soul' from the recording because it was requested by audience members . . . . In the end, his creative instincts prevailed, however . . . . 'To this day I never play 'Body and Soul' the same way twice.'[1]

The success of a jazz composition can be best determined by what the players do at that point in the performance when there are no black dots to play. In essence, one listens to the quality of the improvisations as a way of judging the merits of a composition. If the soloist is not inspired, all the black dots in the world won't compensate for this deficiency. And if the soloist is inspired, just a few black dots – or none at all – will suffice.[2]

CONTENTS

TAKE TIME OUT TO LISTEN

INTRODUCING THE JAZZ COMPOSER

Within the past twenty-five years or so years, Toshiko Akiyoshi, Sammy Nestico, Bob Florence, Maria Schneider, and Jim McNeeley are among those who have extended the idiom of big band composition.[1]

That quote is from an article in the *Jazz Education Journal*, the house magazine of the now defunct International Association for Jazz Education. Few jazz educators would presume to argue with the statement: the writers named are very popular in jazz education, are among those whose arrangements are regularly commissioned and performed by big bands around the world, and whose claim to such fame would seem to be without question. But, as the title to this chapter says, 'take time out to listen'.

Listen to those writers who, at the start of the article, are among those named as being part of 'a glorious tradition of original composition for large ensembles, or big bands': Don Redman, Duke Ellington, Gil Evans and Gerry Mulligan. Apart from finding the omission of Charles Mingus rather curious, I have no argument with those and the others named. They are all good writers for the jazz big band – as indeed are the ones named in the opening quote – but the important difference is that Ellington, Evans and the others listed with them are also true *jazz composers*. In pursuing their art they *have* 'extended the idiom of big band composition' and in doing so have kept it in its rightful place as part of jazz composition. If we take time out to listen to McNeeley and Nestico compared to Ellington and Evans, we can see that they, and those named with them above, seem to have lost sight of the idea of 'extending the idiom of big band composition', perhaps pursuing sales instead, certainly continuing to use writing styles that are now well out of date, definitely not realising that jazz composition, and big band composition, has moved on. (The fact that they may not see that jazz composition and big band writing *should* move on is one of the arguments I discuss below.)

The dichotomy between these approaches is at the core of this book. The phrase jazz composition can be applied purely to big band writing but, in addition to this, jazz composition can be regarded as something which attempts to join the two words together, creating an entity, with its own meaning, which adds up to more than the sum of its parts. Ellington knew this, Charles Mingus knew it, Gil Evans knew it. But, sadly, many others don't. In the words of my title, take time out to listen.

As the painter Clyfford Still said, 'How can we live and die and never know the difference?'

Jazz composition can be seen to encompass many different areas. But there is a vast difference between pieces such as 'Blue Monk', a twelve bar blues by Thelonious Monk, and Wynton Marsalis' hour-long *Blood on the Fields*. In the way of such things, Monk's blues has become a staple of the jazz musician's repertoire, while Marsalis' composition, which was given a Pulitzer prize (something denied to Duke Ellington, as we shall see), attracted very divergent critical reactions, and is now rarely performed.

Leaving such differences aside for the moment, can writers such as Sammy Nestico, Jim McNeeley, and the others named above, whose scores are in constant use around the world, be called jazz composers when they are, in the main, using formulaic *arranging* methods common over the past fifty or more years? Does classical composer Mark-Anthony Turnage become a jazz composer when he writes *Blood on the Floor* to feature jazz soloists John Scofield and Peter Erskine with the contemporary music group Ensemble Moderne? Does Gershwin become a jazz composer when his tune 'Summertime' becomes the basis for a great Sidney Bechet performance? Does Gil Evans become a jazz composer when his arrangement of 'Summertime' for Miles Davis recomposes it, adding a succession of constantly changing textures to support Miles' solo?

In a word, yes. In so far as the world sees the term, they are all jazz composers in their own different ways. This will be discussed later, as will the fact that many who are called jazz composers are using styles and ideas firmly rooted in the past. In doing so, they ignore the real potential of the music. This potential, and its culmination in works of high art, can be seen in the work of the acknowledged big names of the genre: Duke Ellington, Charles Mingus and Gil Evans. It can also be seen in the work of many other jazz writers around the world, far less known, who have followed their example.

Before taking this argument further – and possibly irritating even more people in the process – it is necessary to discuss what jazz composition *means*.

Take time out to listen to one of Bach's solo cello suites. The way that the single line is developed is quite staggering, a feat similar to that achieved in Gregorian chant. Listen to one of Bartók's string quartets, or those of Beethoven, Ravel, or Debussy, where the power and complexity achieved by just four voices are amazing. Listen to a Shostakovich symphony for the colours, the weight, the sheer power. Or try any of the sixteen symphonies by the little-known Swedish composer Allan Pettersson.

In comparison, it might seem that almost everything written in jazz is simple, naive and childlike. Many jazz compositions contain a great deal of straightforward repetition and simple transposition over some very basic chord changes. Perhaps Leonard Feather's comment that 'C-Jam Blues' is 'a trifle, even a child could have written it', is true, not only about that very simple tune, but about jazz tunes, jazz compositions in general.

So why do jazz composers make the effort? Take time out to listen to a solo by Ben Webster or John Coltrane. Although they are, in theory, playing the same kind of instrument, their sounds are totally distinctive, as are their approaches to the tune in question. Additionally, the different colourings and shadings of almost every note, and the rhythmic and harmonic subtleties that are constantly on view, are incredibly complex. Allied with the development of musical ideas, they present a staggering vision of what, ostensibly, one person is capable of doing. Not, of course, that it is just one person. Take time out to listen to the interplay of the supporting rhythm section. The intricacy of their interlocking roles is a true miracle. And one that happens over and over again.

The sound world inhabited by jazz musicians presents an entirely different landscape from that inhabited by the music of Bach or Bartók or Shostakovich, and it is this difference that creative jazz composers want to incorporate into their vision of the world. Take time out to listen.

No book such as this can pretend to be exhaustive, and this is not my aim. Nor is it my aim to discuss jazz composition in technical terms. In fact, I am not sure that it can be discussed in this way. When I see an extensive three-page analysis of Billy Strayhorn's 'U.M.M.G. (Upper Manhattan Medical Group)' in Walter van de Leur's Strayhorn biography *Something to Live For*, I can only marvel at the detail, but wonder why there is no mention of the performances that the tune inspired, apart from the routine comment that 'the Ellington orchestra made a number of excellent recordings of the piece.' In terms of jazz composition, what happened in the performances is a far more interesting and important matter than which chord resolves to which other chord. In writing about jazz, in appreciating jazz, even in playing jazz, what needs to be appreciated is that, more than any starting point, more than any chord voicing, more than any particular texture, it is the *performance* that is paramount.

Here, reference is, of course, made to related books and recordings. Where possible, current details of recordings mentioned are included in the text; two or three relevant books are listed with editorial comments at the end of each chapter, and full details are given in the bibliography. Where possible, references to tunes and records are to well-known material such as 'Stella by Starlight' or *Kind of Blue.* Where it is necessary to use less famous material, additional text will serve to make the argument clear.

While it will be easily seen that most of the examples I have chosen are American, there is an obvious reason, and a caveat. The obvious reason is that most of the best-known jazz musicians and composers are American and will therefore be the ones most likely to have been heard of, and be available to be heard, by the reader. The caveat is in the word 'known'.

As I say elsewhere in this book, there are many non-American composers whose work I greatly admire – Australian Paul Grabowsky and Austrian Christian Mühlbacher, my joint 'classic advance arrangements' in chapter twelve, DON'T BE AFRAID . . . , for example. But their work will be unknown to all but a relatively small handful of jazz critics and fans. And one would hazard that most of those who know of them will be from the composers' own countries. For this reason, to attempt to list comprehensively similar creative jazz composers from around the world would be beyond my knowledge, and outside the remit of this book. However, some names do occur here, and, on my website *www.jazzcontinuum.com* there is a list – very much a work in progress – of those writers whose work I particularly admire.

The book is aimed at all interested parties, in particular those who enjoy jazz without understanding much about it. Therefore a lack of musical knowledge is no bar to understanding my arguments. The book will also be of value to those who play jazz or may be involved in the music at a deeper level. In keeping with one of the subjects under discussion in chapter sixteen, 'PLAY A RAT PATROL SOUND', there are many levels present in the book. One of these is the titles and subtitles of the separate sections, the meanings of which, like RAT PATROL, will be revealed in due course. Another level will cover some of the history and chronology of the title 'jazz composer', while others will be based on my views of how the term has been treated, and my ideas of what *can* be done with jazz composition.

Interwoven within these are some comments and anecdotes showing parts of 'a jazz composer's life', as lived, by me, in real time, once. I must admit, however, that there is sometimes a sense of *déjà vu* when it seems as though one is constantly reliving the problems which are inherent in being involved in an unrecognised art. At times one feels like one of Malcolm Lowry's characters whom we will meet at the end of this book, 'repeating this process, to the irreducible logic of which he appeared eternally committed'. But, as Raymond Chandler said: 'Two very simple rules. a. you don't have to write. b. you can't do anything else. The rest comes of itself.'

But I do realise that being a jazz composer beats working in a factory. To quote my own personal motto when waiting for the phone to ring, 'Anything can happen. And probably won't.' The fact that something *might* happen is what keeps me going.

As does John Lewis' comment that 'the reward for playing jazz is playing jazz.'

§ *Many years ago, coming back on the underground from a gig, with my string bass on my back and feeling a little depressed, I was approached by a young man who said 'Mr. Collier? I just want to thank you for some wonderful moments in jazz.' At which he walked off, leaving me thinking that, despite my lifelong atheism, there might be a God after all.*

It is inevitable that in these discussions I rely on recordings. However much we say that jazz is a live art, the fact is that, for the majority of people, most of the jazz they hear exists on record. As I say elsewhere, 'would we want to be without our recordings of Louis Armstrong, Duke Ellington, Miles Davis?' And it must be remembered that these are records of performances, whether live or in the studio. Not of the definitive performance, but of a moment in time which captures what the musicians were doing. It's when we regard records as immovable objects, setting the performances in stone, never to be surpassed, that the danger comes in.

Generally, my examples are drawn from older recorded material. This is because they will stand a better chance of being known to the majority of readers than if I had chosen more contemporary examples. Another reason is that the opening up of the music in the 'revolutionary decade' between the mid-1950s and the mid-1960s, which I rely on for much of my argument, has meant that everyone can do their own thing. In reality, of course, some have continued doing the old thing, but those who have taken advantage of the potential that was unleashed in that time, have produced a body of work which it would be impossible to cover in any book, let alone one of this size. What this book does is point to *some* of the ways that some composers since that revolutionary decade have realised this.

Whether we like all of it or not is a matter of personal taste. As art critic Clement Greenberg, something of a mentor of mine in matters of criticism, said: 'When it comes to aesthetic experience, you're all alone to start and end with. Other people's responses may put you under pressure, but what you then have to do is go back and look again, listen again, read again.'[2]

The main emphasis in the book is, perhaps not surprisingly and despite any caveats I raised at the start of this introduction, on writing for larger groups. This is because, in the main, small groups usually work from a tune, often using the traditional theme-solos-theme as the overall form. When the group is larger than the conventional jazz quintet or sextet, more possibilities are opened up, and more writing, be it arranging or composition, may be needed. However, I would not, could not, argue that a jazz composition *needs* to be for a large group, or last a long time to be any good. Charles Mingus' 'Self-Portrait in Three Colors', from *Mingus Ah Um* (CBS), written for an eight-piece group, and a fraction over three minutes long (and, interestingly, containing only one bar of improvising), is proof enough of that.

There is, as I have pointed out, a crucial distinction between the tune as such and the performance it generates. Appreciating this will move us into understanding what a jazz composition is *for*. It's there to provide the basis for a performance, nothing more, nothing less. It doesn't mean anything when it's just on the paper. As this book's subtitle implies, it needs to be *moved off the paper*, made into a performance by the musicians concerned. As the chapter on performance says *jazz happens in real time, once*. Which is why 'Stella by Starlight' in the performance Miles Davis recorded on *The Complete Concert, 1964* (Columbia Jazz Masterpieces) is a great jazz composition. As is 'Flamenco Sketches', even though there is no tune, no chords, only five scales of seven notes each. And why Mingus' 'Self-Portrait in Three Colors' is jazz, even if it only has that one bar of improvising.

At the heart of this book, both literally and figuratively, is *Kind of Blue* (Columbia/Legacy), the record from which the Miles Davis performance of 'Flamenco Sketches' comes. Critic Gary Giddins' comment that 'hardly anyone recognised it for the insurrection it was' has much resonance, and will be discussed further in INFINITE POSSIBILITIES. Although I will often use *Kind of Blue* as a shorthand to signify the period, when speaking of it I don't mean just the record, though every reader, in fact everybody, should own it (sales are now said to be around twelve million copies, so there is still some way to go). I mean the ideas behind the music: the concepts developed by many different musicians between the mid-1950s and mid-1960s which opened up the potential of jazz in a very radical way.

Jazz composing can be said to exist in three overlapping areas: tune, arrangement and composition. Tunes, in their pre-*Kind of Blue* manifestation, are, like 'That's a Plenty' or 'C-Jam Blues', something written to provide the basis for improvisation, setting a mood and establishing the form and chord progression on which the subsequent improvisations take place. Others are written, or borrowed in many cases, so they can be improvised *with*. Bechet's

'Summertime' (*Refreshing Tracks,* Blue Note), for example, takes the Gershwin tune and changes it into something very personal by virtue of the performance and the improvising. These aspects of the jazz musician's art are discussed initially in the first three chapters: the tune in SOMETHING BORROWED, SOMETHING NEW; the performance in JAZZ HAPPENS IN REAL TIME, ONCE and improvising in WELL MAN, WE JUST BLOW.

These ways of performing jazz, and writing for such performances, still continue but since *Kind of Blue* jazz musicians have been empowered to transform the tune away from being solely a starting point for improvising, as we will see in chapter eleven, NO MORE BLUES?[*]

Arranging – determining 'who does what when' – can exist without being written down, but it generally refers to the art of writing specific parts for each musician in a specific pre-determined group. Before *Kind of Blue*, much of this was decided in terms of the practical function of many larger groups as dance bands. This led to formularised methods – essentially block voicings in the various sections or the whole ensemble – that are still in use today. However, post-*Kind of Blue* arrangers have, as with the tune, been empowered to change the parameters. Composition, on the other hand, has developed as a separate path.

By composition, I mean a way of writing where there is some development of ideas, some sign of an individual being in charge and, most importantly, an essence of integration between what is written and what is improvised. These ideas were developed in jazz during the twenties and thirties, chiefly in the work of Duke Ellington and Jelly Roll Morton. Their work differed from the

---

[*] The question mark, like that in WHY WOULD WE WANT TO REPEAT IT?, is in the title of the chapter, and not meant to connect with the material in the previous sentence. As will be explained later, it heads a chapter that deals with the newer ideas that are happening in jazz tunes, and recognises that some of these do indeed still use the blues form.

norm of their time, when 'jazz composition' was seen as something solely related to the tune and the arrangement. And it was the thinking behind the changes of the fifties and sixties that allowed other jazz composers to take advantage of the seeds sown decades earlier by Duke and Jelly Roll (although, as sometimes happens, Morton has largely slipped off the radar in this regard).

Without doubt, Ellington is the acknowledged genius of jazz composition. An unconventional composer, and untrained, except by doing it, he was once described as a 'compiler' rather than a composer, a comment that, as well as being true in much of his work, connects in a very real way with the methods of some contemporary composers. Ellington, as befits his place in the pantheon, has two chapters dedicated to him in this book.

Whether or not jazz should have a pantheon – or a canon of acclaimed works – has roused much controversy, not least because, lately, that pantheon seems to have been exclusively designed by (and for?) Wynton Marsalis. Naturally, I have no argument with the inclusion of Ellington in any such list, but should point out at this early stage of the book, that this is one of the very few areas of jazz on which Marsalis and I *do* agree. For many jazz musicians, myself included, Marsalis has become a little too prominent in defining what jazz *is*. His stewardship in New York of the Lincoln Center, and his significant involvement with the Ken Burns *Jazz* television series, have given his views an apparent importance that many of us strongly disagree with. This will be examined and explained in various places throughout the book, but suffice it for now to say that some years ago I overheard guitarist Jim Hall saying his next gig was at the Lincoln Center, and adding 'I think I'll take my pedals and annoy Wynton.'

The first chapter on Ellington, deals with his work as a *compiler*, borrowing and using what he had around him, while the second looks closely at the areas he chose to compose in. I came across THINKING OF A BETTER WAY, the title of that chapter, while researching this book, and feel that the phrase has enormous resonance for composers in jazz. It is, I believe, behind 'jazz form', a somewhat laissez-faire approach* to how jazz is structured *in performance*, which has been part of my subconscious thinking for many years. Explaining how jazz works will never be easy, but accepting that a philosophy of jazz form – created by 'thinking of a better way' – exists, does, I believe, help explain some of the mysteries, and will be covered in several of the later chapters.

Ellington's influence on jazz has been immense. In fact, so immense that criticism of him and his work is rarely allowed (and may well result in a visit from the Ellington police, of whom more later). Underlying that influence, and rarely alluded to in these terms, is a very simple fact: Duke realised what jazz composition was about, what it could be about, what its potential really was, long before *Kind of Blue* showed the same thing. Put simply, jazz and jazz composition are about the performance, *which is created by the people playing it*. The fact that Duke took tunes and parts of tunes from his musicians, that he used their ideas in making up his arrangements, that he would change the parts and the players around in rehearsal because, in Billy Strayhorn's words, 'the man and the part weren't the same character', prove that he realised this.

To isolate one simple but deeply meaningful example: It's not how Duke Ellington voiced his chords that's important, though it has provided the main focus for many books about him. It is that he chose specific musicians, with their individual voices, to play each of the notes. The first is a technical, angels-on-the-head-of-a-pin, matter. The second is a way of life, and proves a deeper

---

* A dictionary definition of laissez-faire – 'a deliberate refraining from interfering in the freedom and choices of others' – may seem to contradict the various ways that a composer controls a performance of his music, but I fall back on the idea that such control is not interfering, rather assisting.

understanding of what jazz really is than a boatload of critics have ever realised.

§ *'Why compose if you're relying wholly on improvised solos for impetus and character?'[3] That remark, coming as it did in a review which started by saying that 'Graham Collier is widely celebrated as one of those problematic beings a "jazz composer",' could be said to raise important issues. My response, if I had been allowed one, would have been that, like Ellington with 'Cottontail', I and other jazz composers need our soloists. What is written is the starting point for the soloist's addition of 'impetus and character'. (In the interests of full disclosure I should also add that Philip Clark summed up the album, the otherwise highly praised* The Third Colour, *as 'resolutely mediocre'.)*

Tune writers and arrangers have to decide whether or not to take the changes of the late 1950s on board. Composers, in the real sense of the word, should not have that dilemma. The lessons of Ellington are plain, and have only been deepened by the example of *Kind of Blue* and the rest of the 'new thing', now as far away from us as the beginnings of jazz were from it. Sadly though, as we shall see, there is still a problem, exacerbated by the overlapping of terms, perhaps, but also strongly affected by writers (musicians and critics) who still misunderstand what jazz is capable of.

A discussion of those changes, and the potential they have opened up, make up the remainder of the book. The first chapter in PART THREE, *REDISCOVERING THE POTENTIAL*, discusses tradition, asking, in a paraphrase of the words of Miles Davis, *WHY WOULD WE WANT TO REPEAT IT?* The second, *INFINITE POSSIBILITIES*, contains the central point of the book: that jazz underwent a sea change in what I have called the revolutionary decade, and cannot, in any real sense of the word, ever be the same again. In acknowledging that the roots of the change lie in the music of Duke Ellington, it reminds us that jazz is a continuum. That it can also be an art – at times – is the subject of the third chapter *DEEPENING THE GAME AMID THE BACKGROUND HUM*. The final chapter in this section, *IT AIN'T WHO YOU ARE (IT'S THE WAY THAT YOU DO IT)*, deals with the sociological aspects of working in a music that is long claimed to be the sole province of black, American, macho, males.

PART FOUR, *SKINNING THE CAT*, looks at the various ways contemporary jazz composers have approached their art. Although I have, of necessity, spread my net wider, it is interesting to realise that each of the broad aspects of contemporary jazz writing can be seen in the work of Gil Evans, and, proving my point above, almost all of them can be traced back to Ellington.

It was Gerry Mulligan who, using an anagram of Gil Evans' name, called him Svengali, an apt title for someone who was able to transform almost everything he touched into something different, and usually much more interesting. Evans' fingerprints can be seen on *Kind of Blue*, which although ostensibly 'just a set of tunes', produced a series of great performances, which, as we will see throughout the book, is what a tune should be there to do.

Gil Evans also had the ability to redefine the term jazz composer, which is illustrated in the way he transformed, *recomposed*, his chosen material. He also opened up the instrumental possibilities of arranging. These are both aspects of the jazz composers' art, which will be discussed in chapter twelve, *DON'T BE AFRAID . . .* , a chapter whose ironic title is explained later. *I HEAR A SYMPHONY* looks at how some composers have tried to do more than just write, or arrange, a tune, with Gil Evans' 'Saeta' (*Sketches of Spain*, Columbia) being a fascinating example of what can be achieved. The final chapter of *PART FOUR*, *TAKING A CHANCE*, deals with those contemporary jazz composers who rely on very little written music, or none at all, to achieve their aims, an area in which, late in his life, Evans was also involved.

Which, while it just about covers all the bases of contemporary jazz composition, leaves Charles Mingus, the other great mover and shaker in jazz composing terms, somewhat on the sidelines, a matter which will, of course, be rectified below.

The final section, DIRECTING 14 JACKSON POLLOCKS, (another title which will become clear in due course), is a case study of my own music and, at the same time, a summation of the book. In it I will show, as I have said above, that tradition is important, that there is a continuum connecting the authentic music which is happening now back to Ellington, and that the concepts used by some contemporary jazz composers reinforce basic premises which have become obscured in recent years.

The first part, ROLLED STEEL INTO GOLD, looks at how some of the sounds which are created are developed by the musicians concerned. As Ellington once said, the music is a basis for change. And, as the overall title of this section has it, the musicians are important. They are the equivalent of Jackson Pollock, artists with their own strong identity, and it is the jazz composer's job – as Ellington showed – to use and develop those identities while following his own art.

The penultimate chapter, 'PLAY A RAT PATROL SOUND', looks at three concepts of jazz composition – space, levels and jazz form – which, one could say, 'just happen'. They can be pre-planned, but by taking advantage of what jazz *is*, they can happen spontaneously. They become elements that happen *because of the performance* and in this they become part of the whole that makes jazz composition the art it is, an art that is very separate and different from classical composing.

THE FINAL WORD, RECOGNISING THE VIBRATIONS, returns us to Clyfford Still's words. We must 'know the difference'. Not easy in what, in art, has been called 'an age of deep pluralism'; an age that in jazz seems dominated as never before by the market and the media. But there is a lot else happening. Take time out to listen.

References are made throughout the book to a website dedicated to this book and its contents, *www.thejazzcomposer.com*, and the audio examples used in the two penultimate chapters will be found there. The website will, as far as possible, be interactive, carrying updated material and new thoughts, as well as extracts from reviews and comments from readers, who can contact me via the email link. One of my other websites *www.jazzcontinuum.com* includes recommendations for tracks to listen to from other jazz composers I respect, while *www.grahamcolliermusic.com*, a site dedicated to my life and career, contains audio and MSS examples from all my records, including other examples relevant to this book

Released to coincide with the book is a double CD, *directing 14 Jackson Pollocks*, a concert recording of two major compositions which inspired one concert-goer to coin the phrase which names the CD, and which is used in the last section of the book. The CD also contains *The Alternate Third Colour*, a different recording of a piece that illustrates my maxim that jazz happens in real time, once. Its title points up that what I am trying to do is find the third colour which exists between what is composed and what is improvised.

My thanks are due to poet and critic Stephen Middleton, to saxophonist and educator Frank Griffiths, and to pianist and composer Roger Dean who took time out from their own busy lives to read early drafts and make some invaluable suggestions. As always, I should thank John Gill, my partner of over thirty years, for his suggestions on the text, and for his sub-editor's eagle eye, which has corrected many of my mistakes – but of course any that remain are my own. The final link in the chain has been Ann and Roger Cotterrell of Northway Publications who not only agreed to take on the project, but who have expertly shepherded it through the necessary processes on the way to a finished product.

The dedication of this book to Herb Pomeroy, whose passing was announced while I was revising the last draft, is a reflection of his influence on my formative years when I attended Berklee School of Music (now College). A good friend and mentor, and an inspiring teacher, Herb taught me a lot and it was he who had first taught me the lesson that has stayed with me ever since: that regard for the individual is what really counts in jazz.

I would also like to thank those who have supported me throughout my career, mainly of course, all the musicians who have given themselves to my music while retaining their own identity. Some of this music was recorded, some is still in the memory. Some may not have worked as well as one expected perhaps, but most, I hope, was good, and served to add something to the development of the art form that is called jazz composition.

Graham Collier
Skopelos, Greece,
January 2009

PART ONE

DEFINING THE SITUATION

1

SOMETHING BORROWED,
SOMETHING NEW

REPERTOIRE

dedicated to Barney Bigard

If I use familiar shapes I can put any colour in the world in them.[1]

Dedicating a chapter on jazz repertoire to someone best known as a clarinet player with Duke Ellington may seem perverse. Why not George Gershwin, who wrote 'I Got Rhythm', 'Summertime' and many other standard tunes on which jazz musicians base their improvising? Why not Thelonious Monk, a highly regarded jazz composer and pianist whose tunes are considered to be among the very best jazz standards? Why not Ellington himself, the writer of such great songs as 'Sophisticated Lady' and 'Prelude to a Kiss' and, in most people's opinion, the greatest jazz composer ever? All these are better known as writers of tunes, and all have written many more tunes. So what exactly has Bigard done to warrant my accolade? Isn't his chief claim to fame in composing based on the story that he, not Duke Ellington, wrote 'C-Jam Blues'?

Without having much proof on my side – apart from the fact that in September 1941, four months before Ellington's first recording, Bigard had recorded the tune as his own 'C Blues' – I am willing to accept that Bigard *did* write 'C-Jam Blues'. It fits in with many stories of Duke 'borrowing' material from his sidemen. As we shall see later, this is very much part of how he worked.

And, being cynical – a jazz musician's prerogative, I sometimes feel – one could say that Duke purloining Barney's tune was a kind of rough justice for the times Duke's own tunes were supposedly 'co-written' with his manager Irving Mills.

But why single out 'C-Jam Blues' as worthy of mention? In essence it's a simple melody based on a repetitive two note rhythmic figure, played over a basic three-chord blues progression. Ellington himself called it 'one of our more or less trite things.'

But, simple though it is, 'C-Jam Blues' has inspired many great jazz performances. In fact it could be argued that 'C-Jam Blues' is the epitome of the perfect jazz composition. It suggests and fulfils the main purpose of the genre: the provision of a strong and memorable framework which reflects the composer's thinking, while stimulating and informing the improviser, who, ideally, is inspired without being inhibited. That statement, with one important proviso, is as relevant to a long complex piece as it is to a very simple blues.

The proviso is, that even though the melodic, harmonic and rhythmic material of the tune stay essentially the same, and even though the structure of the long complex piece may remain, the performances will have been, and should continue to be, essentially different.

This openness to change is the common ground of most jazz compositions. And their reason for being. That this can be seen in something as simple as 'C-Jam Blues', is a crucial pointer to what makes jazz composition a different art. So much is dependent on performance and improvisation that a jazz composition doesn't exist on paper. It needs the performance, it needs improvising and, at times, it needs arranging. One can even say, as I did in the introduction, that Miles Davis makes 'Stella by Starlight' *into* a jazz composition by means of a particular performance. As does John Coltrane when he transforms the seemingly totally unsuitable 'My Favorite Things' into a jazz masterpiece.

But before going down those paths we need to establish what the starting points might be, those elements which are on the paper or, in the case of something as simple as 'C-Jam Blues', in the memory.

THE BLUES

The starting point in 'C-Jam Blues' is the form, the three-chord twelve bar blues form, a staple of jazz since its very beginnings, and in common use in all popular music. After the melody is played, usually twice, the twelve bar form is repeated over and over as the basis for solos, before the tune is played again at the end. How many times the form is repeated, and any deviation from it, is either decided in performance, or is the province of the arranger, using the term in its broadest sense.

Inside the blues form, the three strongest chords of a key – the tonic, subdominant and dominant (C F and G7 in the key of C) – are used and altered in various ways to underpin the melody and any subsequent improvisations. These three chords are the basic pillars of what is known as functional harmony. The progressions formed using these chords and their substitutions are the basis of a large part of jazz and popular music. In essence, the progressions are tonally based (although the tonality can change within a tune) and use what are called 'cycle of fifths' harmonies (G7 to C for example).

The melody of 'C-Jam Blues' is, as we have already seen, very simple. A two note rhythmic cell is repeated twelve times against a steady pulse. There is a fairly minor rhythmic change in the fourth, eighth and twelfth repeat which also marks the only melodic variation – the resolution of the repeated G, the fifth of the scale, to its tonic, C. Nothing to it, yet its success as a jazz composition is based on those very points: its simplicity, its repetitiveness, and its rhythmic drive.

There are some further points of interest in this simple tune. After the rhythmic cell is repeated three more times, there is a gap, a little shorter than the duration of the four motifs. This allows the melody space, room to breathe, before the next phrase, a repeat of the first, enters. That space will normally be filled by the accompanying rhythm section, but it could also be filled with a written or improvised phrase. What's written, what's improvised, to fill that gap could be anything, but we would normally expect it to relate in some way to the written motif. This 'call and response' device, which became a strong factor of jazz in the swing era, originally came from African music, and not only illustrates the continuum of jazz, but also the concept, vital for jazz, of integrating what is improvised with what is written.

In all these aspects – a repeatable form, functional harmony, a simple repetitive melody, rhythmic drive over a steady pulse – 'C-Jam Blues' offers a basic example of what a jazz musician uses as a starting point. It shows some of the devices they look for when writing their own tunes, or when borrowing tunes from elsewhere. Broadly speaking one can see that the tunes used in jazz fall into two main areas: those to be improvised *from* and those which can also be improvised *with*.

'C-Jam Blues' falls firmly in the first category. Its rhythmic drive means that it is usually played more or less 'as written' (although its simplicity means that it was probably never even written down in the first place). Other tunes, usually less rhythmically based and often slower in pace, can be improvised *with*. One of the joys of jazz is what instrumentalists and singers do with a borrowed melody such as 'My Funny Valentine' or 'Stella by Starlight'.

BROADWAY BORROWING

As those examples illustrate, much of the jazz repertoire is borrowed from popular music. Today the net is drawn much wider than before, but there is still a large core of songs, known as 'standards', often taken from old musical shows, which most conventional jazz musicians are expected to know. A mainstream jazz evening might well include, along with a few tunes based on the blues, some or all of the following: 'I Got Rhythm', 'Body and Soul', 'All the Things You Are', 'Summertime', 'My Funny Valentine' and 'Stella by Starlight'. All taken into jazz from outside and, possibly, all played from memory by the musicians concerned.

My past experience as a gigging musician led me to list those particular tunes, but I found later that all of them (except 'I Got Rhythm' for reasons I explain below), are in the first ten on *jazzstandards.com*. This is a listings website where 'a composition is ranked highest because it has been included most often on currently issued CDs by the greatest number of jazz artists . . . [those] whose main body of work is jazz, not pop artists who have dabbled in jazz.'

One thousand songs are listed. Most of them are from the thirties and forties, and brought into jazz from outside. As might be expected 'Body and Soul' is the most popular. The most recent song when I last checked was from 1980(!), and of the ninety-one tunes composed since 1959 when *Kind of Blue* was recorded, three ('All Blues', 'Blue in Green' and 'So What') come from that album. Less than half of the others come from people we might regard as jazz composers. I have no way of judging the accuracy of these statistics but, looking at them, one might say of the normal jazz repertoire that 'much has been borrowed, with not a lot being new'.

Looking more closely at 'I Got Rhythm', the first tune on my list, one can see that it has many things in common with 'C-Jam Blues'. Its form is repeatable and uses a chord progression, which although not as simple as the blues, has its basis in the same functional three-chord harmony. There is a steady pulse and the melody, reflecting the spirit of the title and the lyrics, has a rhythmic drive to it. That melody, although again not as simple as 'C-Jam Blues', is based on repetitive phrases.

The form underlying 'I Got Rhythm', like almost all borrowed standard songs, is thirty-two bars long (there is a two-bar tag ending in the original, but this is rarely used in jazz). That thirty-two bar form is, almost always, divided into four sections of eight bars each, illustrating the necessity for repetition in the tune's origin as a Broadway show tune. 'I Got Rhythm' follows the most common division, AABA, where the first eight is repeated, something new happens in the third section (known as 'the bridge' or, somewhat erroneously, as 'the middle eight') before the first eight is repeated again. Although there may be some variation in the repeats, this repetition of material is seen as a plus by jazz musicians. There is less to memorise, and more opportunity to build a solo constructively.

There are literally thousands of standard tunes which have been used in jazz but, what has been common practice, and is among the defining aspects of a large area of jazz composing, is that *parts* of the standard song are borrowed to create new material. The parts used are those which more closely serve the jazz musicians' purpose: the thirty-two bar form, which, as well as having internal repetitions, can be repeated many times during a performance, and all, or just a section, of the underlying chord progression. Such borrowings allow composers and improvisers to add something new while continuing to work in familiar territory. This was a point well taken by Miles Davis when he decided on the simplicity of form in the groundbreaking material seen on *Kind of Blue*, and aptly demonstrates the truth of my opening quote from painter Terry Frost: 'If I use familiar shapes I can put any colour in the world in them.'

Discarding a melody as basic as 'I Got Rhythm' is very easy. It has some good points but, like 'C-Jam Blues', its rhythmic content is weak, even more so when compared to the rhythmic sophistication that jazz musicians are capable of when improvising. Thus, the melody has little or no appeal, but the form and the chord progression are attractive and many jazz tunes have been written using those elements.

In this regard, and as some will already have noticed, it was somewhat disingenuous of me to have said, as I did above, that 'I Got Rhythm' would be one of the common tunes heard at a mainstream jazz evening. Depending on who is playing, it might well be part of the repertoire. But it would be much more likely that one of the tunes which uses its chord progression will be played – a circumstance which serves to explain its absence from the top ten at *jazzstandards.com*. 'Rhythm changes' – the accepted name for the 'I Got Rhythm' chord sequence – can be heard in 'Cottontail' (Duke Ellington), 'Anthropology' and 'Ornithology' (Charlie Parker), 'Oleo' (Sonny Rollins) and many other tunes.

Melodies such as these may have been thought out in isolation, but some, at least, were undoubtedly the result of something developed while improvising on the original melody and chord sequence. This was then developed into a tune, perhaps, as in the original, using repetition and transposition as development techniques but with melodic ideas more in keeping with the improviser's own working language. Undoubtedly also, the cynic in me suggests, some of these tunes were written to gain access to the royalties that would otherwise have gone to the original composer and lyricist. If one accepts that the new composer has added a new melody to what is, although attractive, a fairly standard chord progression, then why not?

Echoing T. S. Eliot writing of the death of nineteenth century music-hall singer Marie Lloyd, art critic T. J. Clark said 'we are looking essentially for the ways such modest material might have been used, by the right performer, to do something as grand as "giving expression to the life of a class".' [2]

This could perhaps be seen as one definition of jazz, where the modest material used – the blues, the standard song form, repetitive melodies and so on – once provided a basis for 'giving expression to the life of a class'. But now the music – along with its social and geographical base – has widened, the modest material used links us to the past, while offering jazz musicians the opportunity to demonstrate the inherent infinite possibilities of the blues and standard song.

The deeper lesson, as we shall see later, is that less can be more. That modest material, or at times no material at all, can be sufficient to inspire brilliant jazz performances.

A MATTER OF CHOICE

There is an argument that audiences need to hear something they know, and that all jazz groups should include at least some standard material in their repertoire. Some would argue for the total primacy of standards in jazz. Pianist and educator Mark Levine doesn't go quite that far, but he does say that knowing the language is essential. 'The music of Cole Porter, Richard Rodgers and George Gershwin is as much a part of the language of jazz as is the music of Duke Ellington, Wayne Shorter and Joe Henderson. To ignore standards is like trying to compose classical music without studying Bach, Mozart and Debussy.'[3]

His point has relevance, at least historically, but my feeling is that today, although they may be useful in general jobbing terms, most standards have outstayed their welcome. Some musicians and composers find different ways of dealing with them, but how many more versions of the standard song 'How High the Moon', or of Kenny Dorham's jazz standard 'Blue Bossa' do we need to hear, before we store the tunes and all the myriad versions of them deep in the basement of the jazz museum, some of whose contents will be examined later in *WHY WOULD WE WANT TO REPEAT IT?*

In Paul Berliner's book *Thinking in Jazz* he reports a view that 'Blue Bossa' is so popular because it appears early in many fake books. These are collections of jazz tunes increasingly seen on music stands at jam sessions and casual gigs. But as the highly regarded bebop pianist and educator Barry Harris says 'This is terrible about these people playing from fake books, and then the fake book is wrong, there's no fake book that's worth shit. Even at jam sessions the people pull out a fake book, I can't believe it, they don't know anything.'[4]

§ *That comment came from an interview with Harris by Daniel Fedele and was extracted for the front page of a magazine I edited for some years, of which more later. One publisher – of fake books, admittedly good ones – withdrew his advertising because of this insult to fake books! Another (much bigger) used the extract prominently in one of his books without crediting our penurious magazine. With friends like these . . . . Well, with friends like these we eventually had to give up.*

Leaving 'Blue Bossa' aside – please – I can't agree that every jazz group needs to have some standards in its repertoire. Songs written by composers such as Porter, Rodgers and Gershwin, even Ellington, Shorter and Dorham, are, nowadays, outside the knowledge of all but the die-hard aficionado – which is to say outside the knowledge of almost all the potential audience for jazz.

Similarly, I don't necessarily agree that playing tunes from chart singers and groups, such as the currently popular choices by jazz musicians of tunes made familiar by such musicians as Björk or Radiohead, will, however good the tune may be, necessarily bring in new audiences. At least, not ones that stay. Although I must admit that an interesting point came up on an internet jazz discussion board: 'I found that Mehldau's [version of the Radiohead tune] 'Exit Music (for a Film)' provided an easy path into his music, those many years ago when I was a jazz novice. Even though I hadn't even heard the original, it spoke to me more immediately than the other tunes, be they standards or Mehldau originals.'[5]

And, staying with Mehldau for the moment, while writing this chapter I came across this riposte to an earlier discussion board posting. 'I think you are misunderstanding me here . . . I don't mean that [Paul Simon's song] 'Still Crazy After All These Years' *is* the most poignant ballad ever written – that would be insane . . . . I meant, that in Mehldau's hands the song achieves, in that moment, a beauty akin to being the best ballad ever.'[6]

It is my belief that what jazz has to do – and of course it won't be easy – is take its biggest asset, the actual performance, whether live or on record, and attempt to get that appreciated as something unique and life-affirming. The attraction of jazz, real jazz, is something that can be appreciated because of its immediacy. Its ability to communicate passion and excitement comes across whatever the material, and whether that material is known or not. If we don't accept that, then one might ask if nursery rhymes are the only material that is safe to play?

§ *Most jazz musicians will have stories of playing to the most unlikely audiences – mine were a shopping mall in Manila, and several small towns in the middle of Greece. In each place we played a programme of original music and received wild acclaim, because the audiences recognised the passion and commitment that was on show. (One could also cite wild acclaim being given, by what should be more knowledgeable audiences, to the most awful rubbish, but perhaps we shouldn't go there.)*

Leaving nursery rhymes aside, one can easily see that 'Stella by Starlight' is a good melody with an interesting chord progression, which accounts for its popularity with generations of jazz musicians. But not all the material jazz musicians are expected to play is as good.

To take one well-known example. Billie Holiday was undoubtedly given tunes to sing which were of questionable worth. But she was given them because publishers knew that she would be able to make something of them through her unique sound and interpretation. In a way one can apply that to any jazz tune. If the resulting performance including the soloing is great, what does it matter whether the tune they started with was something as banal as 'I Got Rhythm' or, as Ellington himself implied, as trite as 'C-Jam Blues'?

In a way it doesn't matter. Billie Holiday's singing 'What a Little Moonlight Can Do' still stands as a good performance despite the banality of the lyrics. But if – and this is sometimes a big if – jazz is about integrating the starting point with the improvisations built on it, if jazz composition is to mean anything more than a basic melody underpinned by a chord progression which has been in use for many decades, then it does matter. Which brings me to my other point mentioned above: the degree of elasticity, of flexibility, in the tune itself.

Billie Holiday *found* elasticity in the tunes – good or bad – that she sang, a skill she says she learnt from listening to Louis Armstrong and Lester Young. One can see that Miles Davis found the elasticity in his many different versions of 'Stella by Starlight', showing that such songs are capable of being interpreted in many different ways, even by the same musician. But what of tunes which, although written using familiar forms and chord progressions, have complex melodies and are generally played exactly as written? One could name such jazz warhorses as 'Cottontail', 'Ornithology' and 'Oleo', where the sole aim seems to be to outline the chord progression for the subsequent improvisations.

Undoubtedly this way of working is typical of much jazz practice, especially bebop and the styles derived from it, and one cannot deny that much good jazz has been created from it. But it raises an area of concern about the tune that has affected my thinking about jazz and jazz composition, and in some ways defines jazz for me. What I'm concerned with is how, not just the chord progression, but the tune, and the mood created by that tune, affect the improvisation, and the way that this translates into jazz composition.

As Ted Gioia said: 'the success of a jazz composition can be best determined by what the players do at that point in the performance when there are no black dots to play.'

CLASSIC JAZZ TUNE

'C-Jam Blues', recorded in January 1942 by the Duke Ellington Orchestra (available on The Blanton-Webster Band *RCA box set, an indispensable collection of Ellington's work from the early 1940s.)*

This performance of 'C-Jam Blues', which will be discussed further in THINKING OF A BETTER WAY, serves to introduce a series of 'classics', which will conclude each chapter. Not always my choice of the best example of what I have been discussing, but something that sums up the section and in some way acts as a pointer to the message of the book.

§ *Some years ago, while teaching at a music-camp workshop in Grosjnan in former Yugoslavia, I was approached by an American cello teacher who said 'We should collaborate.' As expected, the invitation for the jazz musicians to join his classes never materialised, but the twenty-five very young cellists he palmed off on me at odd times during the week did enjoy trying to make the simple melody of 'C-Jam Blues' swing. I even got them to improvise by 'thickening the melody', a textural improvising technique explained in* ROLLED STEEL INTO GOLD. *On the final night we appeared on local television, with the jazzers improvising above the earnestly sawing cellists!*

MORE ON REPERTOIRE

Mark Levine, in *The Jazz Theory Book*, discusses the blues and standard song form and the harmonies that are used.

American Popular Song, The Great Innovators, 1900–1950 , written by Alec Wilder, composer of such songs as 'I'll Be Around' and 'While We're Young', offers an exhaustive, musically aware, but somewhat idiosyncratic look at songs from composers such as Cole Porter, Jerome Kern and Richard Rodgers.

James Lincoln Collier's *The Making of Jazz* includes an interesting take on Billie Holiday's approach to popular song, pp 303–312.

2

JAZZ HAPPENS IN REAL TIME, ONCE

THE PERFORMANCE

dedicated to Miles Davis

Davis does not present his audiences with a product, polished and inviting admiration; we hear a dramatic process of creation from Davis as from few others.[1]

Each art had to determine, through its own operations and works, the effects exclusive to itself. By doing so it would, to be sure, narrow its area of competence, but at the same time it would make its possession of that area all the more certain.[2] (Emphasis added.)

What is exclusive about jazz is that what happens, happens in real time. There may well have been rehearsals; there may well be instructions on what to do; but, once on the stage the performance has to take over if real jazz is to be heard. The addition of a final word and a very important comma to the phrase which forms the title of this chapter is a mark of how key this concept has become to my thinking, strongly pointing towards a philosophy of what makes jazz different. The dedication of this chapter to Miles Davis is a mark of how he, though he may never have thought of that phrase, certainly lived it.

As a composer, for me the realisation that the *performance* is what matters, not what is on the paper, was an epiphany. Not that

I was classically trained and regarded the notes as sacred, far from it. But it was the realisation that jazz *needed* the performance, that, whatever you wrote, or borrowed, was incomplete until it was performed; that each performance should be – had to be – different; that was the revelation.

This approach is what jazz is about but, when I was told by a student involved in playing a piece of mine, 'The trouble with your pieces is that they only work in performance', I realised that not everybody sees it the same way. Many people have a mindset that is based on classical music, where a piece is rehearsed to iron out any problems, and the performance is the culmination of that process. In jazz, particularly of the kind I am interested in, although the difficult sections can be rehearsed, and a performance strategy developed, the problem is that the compositions *can't* happen until the actual performance. For me this is the beauty of jazz, and its very real strength. The performance is the crucial factor, not what's written or pre-planned. As Keith Jarrett said: 'Jazz is there and gone. It happens. You have to be present for it. That simple.'

MAGICAL PRACTICE

That the performance is the crucial factor is one of the explanations – and it's still a cause of great wonder to me – why one of the best moments of my listening life came in the main square of the small Andalucian town where I then lived. One of the occasional summer open-air concerts featured the Jerez guitarist Gerardo Nuñez with a bassist and *cajon* (box) drummer. The event was magical, the group moved between pure jazz, flamenco and a kind of punk thrash, changing direction by, as they say, turning on a dime. The magic of such a performance is what makes any art special.

Nuñez is a highly regarded Andalucian guitarist, known for mixing flamenco and jazz. His CD *Andando el Tiempo* (ACT) has the same bassist, Pablo Martin, and *cajon* player, 'Cepillo', I heard that night, plus, as guest stars, the Italian trumpeter Paolo Fresu and Spanish saxophonist Perico Sambeat. Unfortunately, as can often be the case, I don't think the CD is as good as the concert was. Records do have their place, as I have pointed out, but it cannot be denied that being there can make a difference, and that having an audience there can make a difference to the musicians. And, to be brutal about it, how the wishes of a producer or record company can alter a group's best intentions when they get inside a studio.

Naturally, we all wish that we could have been at many great performances: hearing the early Basie band creating a constant series of riffs as background behind the soloists; hearing the collective improvisations of the bands in New Orleans, each instrument with its defined role, but achieving an enviable interplay; seeing players such as Ben Webster and Stan Getz night after night in a club, weaving wonderful solos while demonstrating a very different palette of colourful and individual sounds; seeing Duke Ellington working *with* the sounds of his players to release his special magic; hearing Johnny Hodges with that ravishing tone . . . .

But how many times a year do we hear jazz that belies its name, performances where the routines are seemingly set in stone? A small group whose idea of jazz is a sloppy theme statement at beginning and end, sandwiching an interminable string of so-so solos; a big band whose performance includes dated swing ensemble playing, with the occasional solo added only for colour; a 'tribute' group playing the music of one of jazz's heroes, pandering to audiences but failing to capture what it was that made that group or player great in the first place. It may well be an exaggeration when applied to the cases I mention, but as Joseph Conrad wrote in his novel *Victory*: 'The Zangiacomo band was not making music; it was simply murdering silence with a vulgar, ferocious energy.'

There is another quote that, although somewhat cruel, could be applied to such music. Appropriately enough it was apparently said by an anonymous Indian about successful trash peddlers: 'I grow tired of watching my enemies eat.'

These approaches to jazz – the creative and the run of the mill – are widely divergent, but they represent the problems inherent in a performance-led art where, unlike say a play or an opera, the foundations can be very flimsy. It takes a good jazz group to make something of a scrap of a tune such as 'C-Jam Blues', or to breathe new life into something as mundane as the chords of 'I Got Rhythm'. When it does happen, though, one can see what it is about jazz that makes it special, and different from all other arts.

Searching for this creative essence – and finding it – is, or should be, the lifelong quest of jazz musicians. As I discuss in DEEPENING THE GAME, the crisis in jazz is that jazz as art has been forgotten, and the market has taken over. Not totally, of course, as there still is a great deal of good jazz being played, good jazz of all kinds from all over the world. And, to stick to the remit of this part of the book, many good jazz performances are still being created by groups of musicians getting together to play something from the jazz repertoire. And most of these performances will be in the tried and tested overall form of theme-solos-theme.

NORMAL PRACTICE

The theme-and-variations form is old and elemental. But it makes possible most of what we call jazz, for there is no other way to set up a comprehensible framework within which the musician can make his statement . . . throw it out, embrace 'free jazz,' and you abandon the lingua franca audiences can comprehend and thus lose financial support the artist must have to continue developing.[3]

There are, as the reader might imagine, a few places in which I would agree to differ with that comment by Gene Lees, a former editor of *Down Beat* magazine. He says that 'there is no other way to set up a comprehensible framework' and implies that the only alternative is 'to embrace "free jazz"'. Sensing some disdain in the inverted commas around free jazz, I would say that one only needs to listen to what many contemporary jazz musicians are doing, to realise that there *are* other ways and other alternatives. And, going back in time, we can easily hear that Ellington found a few, as did Mingus, as we saw with his 'Self-Portrait in Three Colors'.

Lees' implication that theme-solos-theme provides *in itself* the 'lingua franca [which] audiences can comprehend' is debatable, too. As I wrote in the first chapter, audiences can comprehend commitment and passion, whatever the musical form in which it is expressed.

Let's face it, theme-solos-theme can be restrictive. Fine when practised by players such as Charlie Parker and Dizzy Gillespie, who created wonderful music within that form. In such cases it may appear, as it seemingly does to Lees, that this is the only way to go. Listening to lesser musicians locked into that form because 'there is no other way' and, in the immortal words of Whitney Balliett, 'saying nothing at great length', one might, with reservations, agree with Wynton Marsalis' statement: 'But that kind of situation, where you have soloists that are just OK, that solo for a real long time, I don't think that was part of the plan.' (The temptation to ask *what* – or perhaps I should say *whose* – plan he's referring to, is almost irresistible.)

Leaving such reservations aside, there is no doubt that the theme and string of solos approach can be a straitjacket that is a stranglehold on jazz performance practice that could do with some loosening.

But there is another way of looking at theme-solos-theme, a way that has a connection with the subject of jazz form, which will be discussed later. As Charles O. Hartman says at the beginning of a fascinating discussion of a Lee Konitz version of 'All the Things You Are' in his book, *Jazz Text*: 'This string of solos can go on so long that it reduces the melody choruses at both ends almost to pro forma punctuation, making it clear that the performers feel less concern for structure than for continuation.

This is not a fault but an aesthetic, though not a modern European one.'[4]

That statement could be applied to many other great jazz performances. Listening to some of the many versions of Richard Carpenter's blues 'Walkin" that Miles Davis recorded between 1961 and 1967, one can hear Miles and the three different saxophonists he used during that period (Hank Mobley, George Coleman and Wayne Shorter) produce chorus after chorus of wonderful music. All created over the basic jazz form of a constantly repeating twelve bar blues progression.

One can also hear the variety of accompaniments provided by the different rhythm sections. The difference in approach between the earlier more straight-ahead group of Wynton Kelly, Paul Chambers and Jimmy Cobb, and the very free approach of the later players, Herbie Hancock, Ron Carter and Tony Williams, is a good illustration of how much jazz changed during the 1960s.[*]

§ *I once worked with Tony Williams. To be honest, while studying at Berklee, I was called late one Saturday afternoon to play bass on a gig in Cambridge, Massachusetts. It turned out to be a roast for me with almost every tempo being very fast. And all the while this very young kid on drums (he was then seventeen but looked thirteen or fourteen) regarded me in a very supercilious way – and played amazingly.*

Although I saw various concerts by different Miles groups in London in the mid- and late 1960s, I missed a club gig in America. While on the road in 1963 with the Jimmy Dorsey ghost band (well, I had to eat) we finished early one evening in St Louis. Nothing much seemed to be

---

[*] 'Walkin" appears on many Miles Davis recordings, the first being the classic 1954 Prestige recording for a septet, which has great solos from Lucky Thompson and J. J. Johnson. Later recordings for Miles' working quintets are much looser. The most notable are the two versions, recorded on successive nights, on *Miles Davis the Complete Live at the Plugged Nickel* 1965 (Columbia).

happening so we went to bed. Out for an early morning walk the next day I saw a poster for a Miles Davis Quintet club date the previous night! Some years later it was issued on record – but I was somewhat mollified to see by the reviews that, apparently, it hadn't been a good night for the band.

The later Miles Davis rhythm section was very adept at making subtle changes of texture and dynamics. But what also happens in the later performances of 'Walkin'' is that pianist Herbie Hancock stops playing completely at the start of each of Miles' solos, and again at varying points in the saxophone solos. This provides a definite change of texture but, in an interesting phenomenon, when Hancock finally does return, the rhythm section and the pianist's contributions seem much stronger than they would have if he'd played all the time. Other notable things happen in every performance. The theme *isn't* repeated, as is the norm in almost all blues theme statements. This could be seen as a manifestation of the jazz musician's common anxiety 'to get to the real thing', the soloing. Perhaps it is, but such changes subtly alter the expectations of the listener, setting up the feeling that something other than a routine performance is happening.

This feeling is enhanced when one considers how the melody is performed, particularly in the later recordings. Instead of being played in unison, exactly together, by the two front-line horns as we might expect, Miles and Wayne Shorter each play their individual versions of parts of the tune. Because of this the melody sounds different on each performance. This method of playing, what I have called 'shadowing', and musicologist and Mingus expert Andrew Homzy refers to as 'loose togetherness', was first heard in New Orleans music. Its use there may have been caused by a sloppiness of playing due to limited techniques, but, as Miles shows, it can be an effective musical device. It is one that was also used by Charles Mingus and, in his later work, by Gil Evans. My own use of the technique will be illustrated in ROLLED STEEL INTO GOLD.

Nowadays the fact that Hancock stops playing for a while, that the blues head is only played once, that the melody is not played in exact unison, may not seem so remarkable. Such ideas of loosening up the form and the performance have come into common usage since 'the revolutionary decade' and will be discussed in detail below.

One can also see great differences in the tempo and in how the melody is played in the various versions of 'So What'.* The original on *Kind of Blue* now seems somewhat sedate, but, in later versions, the tempo was faster and formality vanishes, with the melody being distorted and altered so much that it is scarcely recognisable. The first theme statement in the *Plugged Nickel* version has Miles adding some seemingly casual interjections to the tune, commenting on his own composition in a fascinating way.

The 'changes to the norm' made in such performances by Miles and others alter the music and change the traditional way of doing things. They can be pre-planned, or, as we can easily hear, they can happen during a performance. In a phrase, 'arranging without music', an area of jazz composing that is discussed later in WHO DOES WHAT WHEN.

READING PRACTICE

The music's mostly written down, because it saves time. It's written down if it's only a basis for a change. [5]

Listening to any great jazz player dealing with a known tune can be a revelation. Sidney Bechet's 'Summertime', for example, becomes just that – *his* 'Summertime', far removed from the original, almost operatic, way it is performed in *Porgy and Bess*. It's no exaggeration to say that the tune is made into a jazz composition

---

* For me the best versions of 'So What' after the original on *Kind of Blue* are the later ones, those on *The Complete Concert 1964* (Columbia Jazz Masterpieces), and *The Complete Live at the Plugged Nickel* box set of 1965 (Columbia/Legacy).

by the strength of Bechet's genius. And, as Charles Hartman says in his discussion of 'All the Things You Are' mentioned above, Lee Konitz is leading us 'far into the centre of the tune, yet always glancing outside and through it, he seems to act as a critic of the tune as he plays it.'[6]

Acting not so much a critic as a colourist, Ben Webster's unique slant on playing melodies was one of his great strengths. His versions of Billy Strayhorn's 'Chelsea Bridge',[*] first with the Ellington band and later with Gerry Mulligan, transform what's written, and the tune is never played exactly as it appears on the paper. Almost every note has different qualities of texture and, partially at least, demonstrate another of Ellington's maxims for jazz, that there should be 'some dirt in there, somewhere'.

Whether Webster knew that the tune was actually inspired by a painting of a different London bridge by the impressionist painter James McNeill Whistler is impossible to say. There have even been stories that Strayhorn made a mistake about the name of the bridge, but a close friend of his said that Strayhorn 'thought that Chelsea Bridge sounded better [as a title]: he did know the difference'. But what we can say is that what Webster plays resembles what is on the manuscript paper, in the same way that an impressionistic painting of a bridge resembles the bridge itself.

§ *My only encounter with Webster was when he, the star from the club downstairs, came to the upstairs part of Ronnie Scott's when my sextet was playing there in the late 1960s. More than a little drunk, he wandered around saying how great we were, and, mumbling 'get yourself a drink,' throwing dollar bills and pound notes on to the stage. Still playing, we watched in disbelief – at this, from one of jazz's master musicians, and at the sight of Pete King, co-owner of the club, gathering all the money up before shepherding Ben back downstairs.*

---

[*] *The Complete Gerry Mulligan meets Ben Webster* (Verve) has two alternate versions of 'Chelsea Bridge'. Each time Webster plays the melody it is noticeably different.

One of the problems associated with the 'jazz happens in real time, once' argument is that unless it was recorded, it's lost. We all know of gigs we've been to or participated in, where one feels that something happened that can never be heard again. Which is good if you were there, less good if you missed it. As Charles Hartman says: 'Why do people devote their lives to such an art? And how can we sit and listen to such an art being made and disappearing, without succumbing to overwhelming sadness? The answer, of course, is that music appears as continuously as it disappears . . . the sense remains that we are being allowed to participate in something irreplaceable . . . . The fundamental point, then, is not improvisation but presence.'[7]

In a word, the performance.

THE CLASSIC PERFORMANCE

Jøkleba! Live!, *a recording of a performance in Gothenburg, Sweden, July 7th 1994 (Curling Legs, 1996).*

Everyone will have her or his favourite classic performance. This could be something recorded in a studio, something as perfect (and unique) as *Kind of Blue*, or the recordings made by Louis Armstrong's Hot Five. Or it could be something heard live, or on a concert recording heard later. For me, perhaps Duke Ellington performing *In the Beginning God* in Coventry Cathedral, or, on record, the superb *Miles Davis the Complete Live at the Plugged Nickel 1965* (Columbia) which capture a brilliant band live, and at the top of its form.

Leaving these aside, though, I have chosen something that could well be considered as cheating – a full concert by a relatively unknown trio of Norwegian musicians, recorded on a CD that is nowadays difficult to find. But it's great, fantastic, wonderful and life-affirming at a time when one often despairs of what passes as jazz. That performance, the others listed above and many, many more, possess those qualities – the feeling that something unique happened, something that one is highly privileged to have heard.

To take one example from my classic performance. *Jøkleba! Live!* is almost all improvised from material supplied by the various members of the band, but there is also a version of Ellington's 'In a Sentimental Mood'. The melody creeps in about two-thirds of the way through the record; we recognise it, but can't quite believe that something that well-known is part of the performance – which until then had been very original and diverse. It fits, of course, but its very unexpectedness gives the reading of the melody and the subsequent performance an unworldly air, which is, I am sure, why they introduced it at that point.

Jøkleba is a trio of Norwegian musicians who, though they are known to some extent, deserve to be much more widely appreciated. As the group's pianist, Jon Balke states on his website, Jøkleba 'was founded in 1990 as a research into the possibilities of free improvisation. The music that developed was, however, a music that would dive into almost any style or form without hesitation, and with one purpose in mind: To continuously hunt for the core of inspiration, musical intensity and communication.'[8]

The band gets its name from the initial letters of its three players' surnames: Per Jørgensen, trumpet, vocals and percussion; Audun Kleive, drums and vocals; and Jon Balke, piano and keyboards. Balke is probably the best known through his large group recordings on ECM, although all three are highly regarded in the Norwegian jazz scene, one of the most vibrant and exploratory in the world at this time.

§ *I was turned on to the work of Kleive, who I consider to be one of a trio of great European drummers (alongside my long-time colleague John Marshall, and Jon Christensen, another Norwegian), when I learnt that Terje Evensen, a drummer and composer, then in his mid-twenties, had studied with him. I had heard Evensen at a concert, given by a group of young musicians totally unknown to me, one cold night in a small club in southern Norway. It was a pleasure from start to finish, more so for being totally unexpected. Jazz happened in real time once.*

MORE ON PERFORMANCE

Charles Hartman's *Jazz Text, Voice and Improvisation in Poetry, Jazz and Song* includes fascinating essays on Lee Konitz's version of 'All the Things You Are', and the work of Ornette Coleman, alongside discussions of Robert Creeley's poems and Joni Mitchell's lyrics.

Robert Walser's 'Out of Notes: Signification, Interpretation and.the Problem of Miles Davis' is a brilliant essay on Miles, discussing, with a complete transcription, his 1964 recording of 'My Funny Valentine'. It can be found in Krin Gabbard's *Jazz Among the Discourses.*

3

WELL MAN, WE JUST BLOW

IMPROVISING

dedicated to Harry Beckett

Improvisation, the seat of jazz, is a remorseless art that demands of the performer no less than this: that night after night he spontaneously invent original music by balancing, with the speed of light – emotion and intelligence, form and content and tone and attack, all of which must both charge and entertain the spirit of the listener.[1]

The one still insurmountable problem in jazz is the constant demand for freshness. Since the music hinges on improvisation, a soloist must continually produce new statements. This, in turn, makes demands that are so immediate and unflagging – more so than in any other art form – that the soloist is, often as not, forced to fall back on clichés by sheer creative exhaustion.[2]

These two quotes point to some of the problems in describing what happens in improvisation, something that has puzzled not just audiences but, I am sure, many musicians as well. One has to admit, however, that the title of this chapter, *well man, we just blow*, was a somewhat tongue-in-cheek answer from a musician in my band to the question 'How do you make such a little music last such a long time?'

§ *The question was asked by an audience member sitting on a banquette, immediately next to the trumpet section in* The Old Place, *a very small club in London's Soho. Club owner Ronnie Scott allowed us younger musicians to run the club for a year or so in the mid-1960s when he moved to larger premises in Frith Street. We took advantage of this by forming bands that otherwise might not have got an airing, and, because of this, the club is recognised as one of the breeding grounds for our generation of British musicians. The dedication to Barbadian trumpet player Harry Beckett, one of many musicians who developed their craft there, is a mark of respect to a long-time colleague, someone who has always improvised, always surprised, always delighted.*

THE HEART AND SOUL OF JAZZ

While one could argue that improvisation is not exclusive to jazz, there is no doubt that there is an *approach* to improvising that *is* exclusive to jazz. New Orleans music, swing, bebop, hard bop and free, may seem to have their separate improvising languages, but there are commonalities. These include inflections of the beat that add a rhythmic feel to the music, interpretations of melodies that add individuality to the phrases, and, contradicting the norm in classical music, an array of personal sounds by which a musician develops his own identity and puts his own stamp on a solo.

But soloing, as we now know it, was not always present in jazz. We now know that many solos previously thought to have been improvised were in fact written out. As Gunther Schuller points out 'if we could casually claim in the past that improvisation "is the heart and soul of jazz", then that is only technically accurate and true in recent decades . . . the full flowering of truly spontaneous jazz improvisation did not, *could* not, occur until the technical virtuosic abilities of the players had reached a certain level of total command.'[3]

Before one 'just blows' it is necessary to learn the language. Once the rudimentary techniques are learnt – by playing, or by practising from the books, play-alongs and DVDs now available –

musicians develop their own approaches. These are dependent on their historical place, but also affected by their own attitudes and circumstances. As Charlie Parker said, 'Music is your own experience, your thoughts, your wisdom. If you don't live it, it won't come out of your horn.'[4]

In more specific terms Cootie Williams said, 'Some people play on chord construction. I like to have a melody. I like to read the music down and see what the composer intended it to be,'[5] while Lee Konitz speaks of improvisation 'as coming in ten levels, each one more intense than the one before', going on to discuss his approach of moving through each of these levels.[6]

Although, as we saw above, Coleman Hawkins did not want to repeat his famous solo on 'Body and Soul', other musicians have a different approach. Stéphane Grappelli would 'pretty much play the same things on each tune. But it's because it's not conscious. This is the reason it sounds fresh and not stale . . . he gets up and every day is a completely new day. He's not consciously playing the same things: they're just sort of coming out. But it would always sound fresh, because for him it was honest, and that's the difference between creativity and non-creativity.'[7]

A jazz composer needs to learn about his soloists, how they want to do things, and to realise, that, after a certain stage, it's arguable whether a soloist should be told what to do at all. It's his solo and one should assume that he is there playing that solo because someone thought he could do a good job at that point. And that he could be trusted to do it. As Miles said in his inimitable way: 'I think the reason [John Coltrane and I] didn't get along at first was because 'Trane liked to ask all these motherfucking questions back then about what he should or shouldn't play. Man, fuck that shit; to me he was a professional musician and I have always wanted whoever played with me to find their own place in the music. So my silence and evil looks probably turned him off.'[8] Pianist Tommy Flanagan saw a kinder, more practical, side of Davis: 'He told me the kind of things he likes to hear and then showed them to me at the piano.'[9]

Ellington's approach was similar to that of Miles Davis. 'He would usually say something like "You'll find your way" or "Just do what feels right to you." It seems to have been a policy with him, possibly because he was afraid to spoil the instincts of the natural player.'[10]

The only general thing one can say about what the soloist does with his technique and background, is that he should be aware of the context, that he should relate, in an individual way, to the given elements. Playing notes that 'work', of course (however that requirement is interpreted), but acknowledging the surroundings, knowing where the solo fits into the composition, what it's coming out of, and what is coming up. In short, recognising that, even though they are both blues, soloing on a modal blues such as 'Freddie Freeloader' is different from soloing on a complex bebop blues such as 'Billie's Bounce'.*

The real role of the soloist in jazz should be to 'illuminate' the composition, shed some light on the given material in a way that perhaps no one else could. But many soloists simply want to play their own thing with no regard for their surroundings. As Roscoe Mitchell said, commenting on his own struggles as a composer with improvisers: 'Cat's playing and you don't know *what* he's playing! It may be a fine solo in terms of its own vocabulary but not relate at all to the piece you've written. To me, this is a sign of immaturity, both as a player and a human being. You can't even suppress your ego long enough to concentrate on the task that's placed before you.'[11]‡

---

* 'Freddie Freeloader' from Kind of Blue, is, basically, a two note resolving melody repeated and transposed several times over a bare bones blues progression. Charlie Parker's 'Billie's Bounce' has a typically complex bebop melodic line over an altered chord progression.

‡ I will return to Mitchell's comments towards the end of the book, as there are some points I wish to take issue with.

THREE KINDS OF IMPROVISING

The solo – when one person stands in front of the band and says his or her piece – is the obvious form of improvising. For many observers this *is* jazz, and the only kind of improvising that they recognise. But the realisation that there are two further ways of improvising has been of great importance in developing my thinking about jazz and jazz composition. There is nothing earth-shattering about the discovery, nothing I invented. These three ways of improvising have existed throughout the history of jazz, but articulating this allows a new way of looking at what *happens* in the music.

Distinct from the solo, there is a second, somewhat more hidden, approach to improvising, which we can call 'textural improvising'. This can be defined as 'using various degrees of improvisation to interpret the given material'. Put simply, what a singer does, what a rhythm section does.

When playing the melody of a standard song, a good singer, or a good jazz musician, does not simply present what's on the paper. As we saw with Ben Webster's impressions of impressions of 'Chelsea Bridge', they try to make the tune their own, changing the tone colour of some notes, delaying some, anticipating others, adding notes, taking some away, until what is heard, although obviously related, may bear little resemblance to what was originally written down.

Similar things happen when you hear what a rhythm section actually plays, compared with what they are given to work from, which is most often just some chord symbols (the C F and G7 of the 'C-Jam Blues' chord progression, for example). No bass notes, no piano voicings, no drum rhythms. Through their special magic (and a good rhythm section is, I believe, as close to a miracle as most of us are likely to get), they create an integrated whole, improvising textures from the given elements of pulse and harmonic basis, while accompanying the soloist. Supporting, interacting, and stimulating at the same time.

The effects produced by players such as Ben Webster, or those produced by a good rhythm section, remind us that, in addition to their improvising skills, the *textural* quality of sound and tone that jazz musicians create is highly developed and can be changed at will. This can open up what might seem, on the surface, to be the limited palette of colours in the conventional jazz group, a fact that Ellington, Mingus and others have incorporated into their composing and arranging.

The third kind of improvising, what we can call 'structural improvising', happens when the shape of a piece changes from performance to performance. In its simplest form, that of a small group in a jam session, the performance is shaped, not by a pre-set routine, but by what happens on stage, in real time. The order of the solos, and their length, changes because of the situation, because people feel different, because new elements, new musicians perhaps, are introduced into the equation. *The actual structure of the performance is changed, because of a different kind of improvisation.*

I stress that last sentence because, with music that is predominantly written down – almost all big bands, arranged small groups, classical music, and most if not all popular music – such structural improvisation cannot, by definition, happen. But the essence of jazz is not in a predominantly written or pre-planned music. Ideally it encourages improvisation – in the interpretation of the given material, in the solos, in the textural changes available to the rhythm section, and in the changes of form that can happen during a performance. These different ways of improvising underpin all jazz and we will return to them, tangentially, in *arranging without music* in the next chapter, and more deeply towards the end of the book.

LANGUAGE SKILLS

I have a small voice that asks very timidly "was Charlie Parker a good idea?" I watched Coleman Hawkins, Ben Webster and Roy Eldridge go out of business, literally, when Parker came in. [12]

As a swing-based songplayer, Ruby Braff would probably be appalled by the music of a free player like Charles Gayle, and Gayle's cult following probably considers players like Braff to be hopelessly old hat. What I admire about each of them amounts to the same thing: audible individuality, the conviction of each that his way is the only way for him. [13]

Listening to soloists as diverse as Barney Bigard, Coleman Hawkins, Charlie Parker, Miles Davis, Cecil Taylor, one can easily hear that there are different styles of improvising, different languages. In varying degrees these are all still in use today, as the Ruby Braff/Charles Gayle comparison by Francis Davis shows. But one style dominates, which raises some interesting and important questions. Why does bebop, whose historical period was more than half a century ago, or, to put it another way, should have been, by all historical precedents, over, finished, half a century ago, still play such a dominant role in the music? A dominant role that, in many ways, goes against the spirit of the music. As Gunter Hampel says: 'If you play bebop, everything is already worked out for you; the style dictates the way every instrument is played, the voicings, the phrasing. But in a free band, this must be made up between the people who come together to play, according to what will work for them.' [14]

The bebop language was forged in the 1940s in the clubs of New York by musicians such as Charlie Parker and Dizzy Gillespie. It was predicated on dealing with complicated melodies and complex chord progressions played at fast tempos. Almost all the contemporaries of Parker and Gillespie were eager to play in the same way, and with the same kind of sound. Which, and this is the problem, many people are still doing.

Undoubtedly the sheer technical demands of bebop fit well into the macho world that many people see jazz as inhabiting. It's an adrenaline rush to play fast, to play lots of notes, to impress the audience – and other musicians – with a testosterone fuelled display. Nothing wrong with that, except that in my view jazz needs to be recognisably individual and to *say* something. These values are in short supply in that kind of music, especially now, so long after its heyday. Although some musicians do acquire the technique and then use it in a different way, the overall result seems to be a staggering number of highly trained technical players working in that general style and showing no individuality while doing so.

Certainly, in listening to jazz today, we are constantly reminded of some cynical observers changing the Sondheim song title to 'Send in the Clones'. As the last line says (and whether it worries us or not) 'Don't bother, they're here'. The blame for this has to be laid at the door of a large part of the jazz education system. The hero worship of many teachers for the sheer technique exemplified in jazz by Parker and Gillespie is one reason. Another is that bebop, as a formulaic music, is relatively easy to teach. Put simply, 'each chord has a related scale, play some notes from that scale while the chord lasts, then the next chord arrives and you have another set of notes to choose from and so on.' Not that simple, of course, but the teaching of what is known as 'chord-scale' theory is rife across much of jazz education.

The crux of the argument is whether, as composer Pierre Schaeffer said about *musique concrète*, you look at music in terms of sound, not notes, harmonies, chords. If one thinks that jazz is just

---

* In April 2000 I presented a paper at the Leeds International Jazz Education Conference called 'Are Chord Scales the Answer?'. This was revised in November 2002 and is posted on *www.jazzcontinuum.com*

'notes, harmonies, chords' then chord-scales are fine, but if you think of it as 'sounds' then they may not be the answer.*

There is no doubt that for jazz musicians there is a language to be learnt, but it's not necessarily the same one for everybody. What needs to be learnt is the language that will enable the jazz musician to express himself or herself. If he or she wants to play fast bebop then they have to learn that language, and chord-scale theory is the answer. If you don't want to play fast bebop, then you don't need that particular language.

This will be seen as heresy by many jazz educationalists, and to soften the blow I would add that there is of course nothing wrong with learning to play in this way. But it's important to realise that my prejudice against this way of playing is not meant to be a negation of technique, only an argument against thinking that technique is all that is needed to be a jazz musician. Or thinking that one fifteen-year period of jazz's history – and its subsequent revival – says it all. It doesn't. Thankfully, there's a lot more to the music than that.*

§ *I have tried to address some of the problems involved in treating bebop as the language of choice in my educational work and in my writing. As well as setting up and running the degree programme at the Royal Academy of Music in London for ten years from 1989, I also wrote the degree programme for the jazz course at the Sibelius Academy in Helsinki, although all involved knew that what I had written would change once the course was put into operation, which is what transpired. Around these activities I have presented workshops, concerts and lectures throughout the world (although, surprisingly, not at Sibelius – I think the beboppers moved in the minute I left!)*

---

* In April 2000 I presented a paper at the Leeds International Jazz Education Conference called 'Are Chord Scales the Answer?'. This was revised in November 2002 and posted on *jazzcontinuum.com*

Speaking of musicians in the bebop period, Charles Mingus wrote: 'I wonder about the wealth of individuality and creativity we might have had and what they could have added to the evolution of jazz had they not been caught up in the Charlie Parker trend . . . . The followers who supposed Bird's greatness lay in his melodic patterns copied them without realizing that if Bird played [a diatonic scale] on his horn . . . he could play it millions of different ways with millions of different meanings.'[15]

Mingus went on to draw a parallel between Parker and another saxophonist: 'Recently a young man came to New York with a plastic horn who critics are saying will cause a new era in jazz . . . . George [Russell] said "I hope the critics won't do to him what they did to Bird" . . . . I said, "I know what you mean . . . . It would become an economic pressure on many who will think they have to play that way to make a living and the new camouflage for people who have no faith in their individuality."'[16]

The man with the plastic horn, Ornette Coleman, who will be discussed in more detail in INFINITE POSSIBILITIES, showed a different approach to the saxophone, a different approach to jazz, from that of Charlie Parker. His style was more abrasive, more discordant, with a much more angular approach to melody. Almost certainly because of this, he wasn't copied as much as Parker (wouldn't that have changed the world?), but he was, as we shall see later, one of the catalysts who brought individuality of voice and language back into jazz.

Such individual sounds are very much part of the contemporary jazz composer's palette and the language a jazz composer has to learn is writing for, and improvising with, such individual talents. This means understanding the characters of the musicians they are working with and deploying them to their best advantage in developing the music. As Duke said: 'You can't write music right, unless you know how the man that'll play it plays poker.'[17] Choosing the musicians in the first place is, as we will see in WHO DOES WHAT WHEN, an arranging decision that must be made before deciding what to do with them. Ellington, because of his chronological place in jazz history, only had two types to choose from – New Orleans players like Barney Bigard, and swing-era musicians such as Lawrence Brown.

Today, because of our chronological place in jazz history, and the wider diversity of musics now available, the choice of languages a jazz composer can work with is much wider. Even within what could be called the contemporary jazz language there are differences. Trumpet players such as Kenny Wheeler, Palle Mikkelborg, Dave Douglas and Tomasz Stańko may appear to come from the same general area of the music but their approaches to improvisation are so different, their sounds are so different, their experiences are so different. Jazz composers need to be aware of these differences in language and voice and, in Brian Priestley's apt phrase when discussing Mingus and Ellington, make music by cannibalising his musicians' very souls.

§ *In my experience good jazz musicians are usually highly intelligent people. What they do in 'spontaneously inventing original music' could be done by an idiot savant, but rarely has been. Most are widely read, have strong political views, can discuss the latest art, film and more. Some, God knows how, manage to combine music with a high-powered career outside of music. Saxophonist Art Themen, one of the musicians I use regularly and respect tremendously as an original voice, was for many years also a consultant orthopaedic surgeon. Another, Roger Dean, had a career in bio-chemistry, was later the Vice-Chancellor of the University of Canberra, and is now a research professor in music and sound. All this while continuing his career as a practising composer-improviser, in which he plays jazz keyboards in an avant-garde fashion, is at home in all areas of contemporary classical music, has played string bass in major London orchestras, and . . . . No, I can't go on. I find it hard enough just being a jazz composer.*

Their improvisation skills also mean that the conversation of jazz musicians can be a joy, sparkling and witty. Many comedians – Spike Milligan, Peter Sellers, Woody Allen – have come out of jazz. Many musicians are comedians too, or at least very fast with repartee. One brief example. When disturbed in the middle of a concert by a rogue taxi message picked up by the PA system, I remarked to the audience that such events sometimes give us trouble. Trumpeter Henry Lowther, added from the back row of the band, 'not half as much trouble as we must give them'.

CLASSIC IMPROVISATION

Sonny Rollins, 'Blue Seven' from Saxophone Colossus *(Prestige)*

Choosing this from the many classic improvisations is a reflection of its genius, and of the fact that Gunther Schuller's perceptive analysis of the solo is available in many anthologies. As Schuller says: 'with Rollins thematic and structural unity have at last achieved the importance in *pure* improvisation that elements such as swing, melodic conception and originality of expression have already enjoyed for many years.'[18]

Schuller's article was first published in *The Jazz Review*, November 1958. It has been anthologised in many places including *Musings*, and Robert Walser's *Keeping Time, Readings in Jazz History*. In his editorial introduction to the latter Walser comments that 'what is useful to historians need not be helpful to musicians: after coming across this article, Rollins resolved to stop reading reviews of his playing.'[19] There has also been dissent, somewhat exaggerated in this case I feel, concerning Schuller's canonisation of this particular method of improvising. 'In seeking to prove to classically oriented listeners that jazz improvisation is music of merit, [Schuller] deprecates jazz improvisers who may not share his aesthetic criteria.'[20]

MORE ON BLOWING

Paul Berliner, *Thinking in Jazz, The Infinite Art of Improvisation*. A well constructed musicological approach to the subject. Includes interviews with practising musicians and many musical examples.

Derek Bailey, *Improvisation: Its Nature and Practice in Music* nails its author's colours firmly to the mast of free music, of which he was an undoubted master. His take on jazz is dismissive, ten pages out of 140 including the comment 'but of young players seeking adventure there's little sign', a stance somewhat mollified by his quotes from Steve Lacy. He also covers other musics including Indian, flamenco and rock. He asks a baroque musician 'Could the performance ever be remarkable because of the performer's contribution, rather than the composer's music?' and gets the answer 'That would be an absolute artistic crime.'

Roger T. Dean, *New Structures in Jazz and Improvised Music since 1960*. This book is somewhat academic in tone, with plenty of musical examples, covers what it says in the title, including 'a composer-improviser dialogue' with this author, with whom Dean has worked with for many years.

Ingrid Monson, *Saying Something, Jazz Improvisation and Interaction*, is dry and academic in approach, but contains much of interest including interviews with musicians and some musical analysis.

4

WHO DOES WHAT WHEN

ARRANGING

dedicated to Don Redman

Don, who, having been a music major in college, recognised the beauty that could be obtained if music were organised harmonically. [He] set out to prove his point, over the objections of many musicians who felt that arranged music would take away from their creative ability.[1]

The history of jazz is based on musicians learning from each other in performance, and being able to learn from recordings. Because of this, and because a great deal is improvised, written music is not necessary, though few bandleaders would go so far as to say to a musician who asked about the music: 'When you hear two knocks, just start playing.'[2]

That was said to Lil Armstrong at the start of her career, when she was expected to know the style and have an idea of the tunes the band would play. This is not so far removed from the situation that was discussed in SOMETHING BORROWED, SOMETHING NEW. For some musicians at least, there are common styles and a common repertoire of tunes, and a group can improvise for a whole evening by using some of those tunes in the traditional theme-solos-theme form. This became the standard way of doing things in the bebop period, and is still common in much of today's jazz. Also common are two other bebop-based traditions: the small group instrumentation of trumpet, saxophone, piano, bass and drums, and, more often than not, the replication of that in the solo order.

Working within these traditions – familiar repertoire, set instrumentation, set roles, and theme-solos-theme form – is very much part of normal jazz practice. Everything is set. Everything, that is, except the interpretations of the tune and of the chord progression, and, most importantly, what develops *during* the performance. The very places where jazz happens.

ARRANGING WITHOUT MUSIC

Involvement in a performance within these parameters doesn't need, or usually get, much organising, or much arranging. If something more is needed it may well be simple enough to be worked out without being written down. Such changes are decided on during rehearsals, in pre-gig discussions, even, as Miles Davis demonstrated, during the performance itself. 'He's become a kind of roving conductor, walking from sideman to sideman, describing what he wants from them with a pump of his shoulders or a wiggle of his hips, blowing riffs into their faces and letting them pick it up from there.'[3]

These ways of organising a performance allow us to define arranger in somewhat different terms than may be the norm. A bandleader, indicating who should solo next, how long that solo should last and so on, is an arranger. Indeed, a bandleader deciding who is to be in his band in the first place is, in a very real sense, also an arranger, a point that will be examined further in the first of two chapters on Duke Ellington. A pianist who decides to drop out for a while at a point of his own choosing has also made a choice that affects the overall result, which is a kind of arranging. Indeed, the whole textural and dynamic flow improvised by a good rhythm section is arranging. As are any made-up backings that may develop behind a soloist.

This last example was a strong feature of swing-era big bands that, because of the greater numbers involved, needed more organising than the then prevalent small groups. Repeated rhythmic patterns – known as riffs – were made up to support and stimulate a soloist. They were often started by a single person, then taken up by the other members of that instrumental group. Other sections of the band would start something in support of, or in contrast to, the original riff until the arrangement was complete. Harmonies were either made up as they went along, or, as demonstrated by the Sy Oliver quote below, were given out by someone in the band during rehearsals.

These 'head arrangements' were made famous by the Count Basie band in the late 1930s. 'With most of our arrangements, one of the boys or I will get an idea for a tune . . . and at rehearsal we just sorta start it off and the others fall in. First thing you know, we've got it. We don't use paper on a lot of our standards. In that way, we all have more freedom for improvisations.' [4] Billie Holiday said of her time with Basie, 'Everything that happened, happened by ear. For the two years I was with the band we had a book of a hundred songs, and every one of us carried every last damn note of them in our heads.' [5] To make this work the underlying form and chord sequence has to be simple – hence the predominance of the blues and thirty-two bar standard song forms in the swing era, rather than the more complicated musical forms that were used at times by Jelly Roll Morton and Duke Ellington.

Trumpeter Harry 'Sweets' Edison gave this view of head arrangements when discussing his time with the Count Basie band: 'Our head arrangements sounded good, because we had them so well together, but as musicians were added to the band we had to have written music. We had to rehearse and learn it. Because you're looking at the music when you're playing, you don't have the freedom you had when everything was head.' [6]

But Sy Oliver, then a trumpeter, who developed into a very fine arranger for Jimmy Lunceford, Benny Goodman and Tommy Dorsey, had a slightly different view: 'I started writing just to avoid arguments. Smoke Richardson was musical director, and we used to make head arrangements, but they'd give out the harmony all ass-backwards, and it was hard to remember.'[7] The practice of musicians making things up within a given idea, arranging in the non-written sense, continues today, and has became a strong part of creative jazz arranging and composing as we shall see later.

WRITING IT DOWN

These head arrangements, seemingly produced in such a casual way, did, of course, often become formalised by the band playing the same riffs night after night. Also, musicians such as Sy Oliver soon realised that something different could be said, by organising who plays what when in a more formal way. However, as the quote above about Don Redman shows, this was not always a popular move. Arrangers also realised that, in some cases, their work could be published: reproduced in printed versions for use by other bands. Some music from that era is still being played today, but not enough, for reasons that will be discussed below.

§ *Sy Oliver's arrangement of* 'On the Sunny Side of the Street' *for Tommy Dorsey (available in many collections of Dorsey's greatest hits) is, for me, almost like Proust's madeleine cake, showing what the swing era must have been like. It has an infectious lilt to it which seems to take me back to the time – actually before I was born – when such music was played in dance halls across America. And when the close harmony vocal chorus comes in . . . . Get me a root beer and I'll shut up.*

To play these arrangements, early jazz musicians had, of course, to learn to read. Teaching a melody or harmony by rote is time consuming, and can lead to confusion as Sy Oliver's comment suggests. But it has been, and still is, a valid part of the music. Charles Mingus can be heard singing a line to be absorbed and then performed by his musicians in 'Meditations on Integration', and on 'Song with Orange' he is forced to sing one of the contrapuntal lines in what Brian Priestley called 'his wailing falsetto' when he realises he has more melodies than he has musicians to play them. Even when the musicians can read, and there are enough musicians around to play all the lines the composer wants, there is still a problem which jazz has to face up to. This is the inadequacy of the notation system, basically the same as that used in classical music. Although dependent on context and satisfactory up to a point, what has to be recognised is that the inflections, changes of timbre and attack, all the individual touches that a jazz musician is inspired to add, are impossible to notate accurately. Which partially explains why, when faced with a transcription of one of their own solos, the reaction of almost any jazz musician would be to say 'I can't play that'. And which also explains why, so often, classical musicians interpret jazz phrasing so badly.

Usually, but not always, an arranger works with a set group, writing either as leader or bandmember, or as a hired hand from outside the organisation. The size of the group, who the players are, and what instruments they play, is set, and which tune to arrange may also be a given.

But this still leaves many decisions to be made: whether to observe the accepted tempo and rhythmic feel of the given song, or change it for part or all of the arrangement; where to make any changes to the melody and where to add new rhythmic inflections; whether to stay with the given chord progression or alter it, subtly or drastically; whether to have an introduction, any interludes, an ending, and whether the material for these sections should come from within the piece or from outside; what instruments should be used to voice a passage and what style of voicings – the traditional, roughly parallel block voicings, or something different; how much improvising will there be, who will solo when and for how long; how will that soloist will be supported – by all or only some of the rhythm section, or by written backgrounds, designed to support or perhaps stimulate the improviser.

Faced with such a daunting list of decisions to be made, each one of which will affect subsequent decisions, it is not surprising that many arrangers fall back, in part at least, on proven techniques, drawn from the arranging methods which became established in big band writing as far back as the mid-1920s.

Early jazz, such as that heard in New Orleans and Chicago, was essentially a polyphonic (many-voiced) music, the individual lines of the frontline players weaving a collectively improvised counterpoint. But this approach had to change as the bands got bigger. 'By the mid- and late thirties, at the height of the Swing Era, when the fourteen-man big band had become a jazz institution, the music it played featured almost exclusively block chords, homophonic section writing [parts moving rhythmically together], and parallel voicings. This constituted a drastic swing of the pendulum and to this day it has never swung back fully to re-embrace polyphony [parts moving independently] in the large-ensemble context.'[8]

Schuller's point about the pendulum 'never swinging back fully' is a trifle pessimistic, as will be discussed in PART THREE, SKINNING THE CAT. But his comment also underlines one of the depressing facts about much of today's big band jazz. Put simply, it's dated – a view which will be dealt with below, and, in more detail, in chapter seven, WHY WOULD WE WANT TO REPEAT IT?

BIRTH OF THE GREY

The big band in jazz has an accepted instrumentation of trumpets, trombones and saxophones with a rhythm section of piano, bass and drums, and possibly a guitar. Through history the number of players in each section has varied in small ways, and certain doubling instruments may be in vogue – most notably clarinets in the early days, but the big band section grouping is one of the basic pillars of standard jazz writing practice.

Generally speaking, big band arrangements have a fairly set formula, using functional harmonies, often within the common blues or standard song forms, and they are in a constant tempo throughout, with the main melody coming at the beginning and being repeated, possibly with some variation, at the end. The rhythm section play all or almost all the time and solos, usually not very long and customarily with some kind of background accompaniment, are interspersed within the written passages.

The written passages, if not in unison, use a standardised voicing technique (known to generations of Berklee students as 'four way close'). Using all or some of the four basic chord tones – root, third, fifth and seventh – the instruments are voiced as closely as possible. Depending on the era and the interests of the arranger, altered notes and higher chord extensions such as the ninth, eleventh and thirteenth, may be used in addition or as replacements. The chosen notes are allocated, in the appropriate range, to members of a distinct section, such as trumpets, trombones or saxophones, or groupings such as the whole brass section, or the full ensemble. Cross-section voicings, using a mixture of instruments from each of the disparate sections, are relatively rare.

These traditions – set instrumentation, standard material and block voicings – have provided much good jazz. They have been expanded on and developed since, as we shall see below. But the traditional methods of big band writing have also been used to supply and, in some ways, create a homogenised big band market that feeds the seemingly insatiable needs of what, for want of a better phrase, we will have to call 'jazz education'. It's not much of an exaggeration to say that most arrangers in jazz today have decided to satisfy the needs of that market. This will be discussed further in *WHY WOULD WE WANT TO REPEAT IT?*, which takes a look at the good and bad aspects of tradition in jazz.

One side effect of the market taking over, and feeding what is seen as the 'needs' of jazz education, has been that the work of such writers as Don Redman, the dedicatee of this chapter, and Fletcher Henderson, its classic arranger, have largely been ignored. The three other arrangers I focus on below, Neal Hefti, Thad Jones and Sammy Nestico, all owing a debt to Redman for originating this type of arranging, are still widely played. Whether

or not, particularly in the latter two cases, this is a good thing, I
will discuss below.

Don Redman (1900–64), a musically well-educated saxophone
and clarinet player, started to write when he joined the Fletcher
Henderson band, 'a Dixielandish outfit, like most groups of
the time', in 1923. Redman wanted to change this because, as was
said in the opening quote, 'he recognised the beauty that could be
obtained if music were organised harmonically'. As Gunther
Schuller points out: 'Ironically, the very skills required to master
collective improvisation and simple "head arrangements" spelled
the doom of the pure New Orleans style. The virtuosity, soloistic
prowess, and sheer individuality of a Louis Armstrong or a Sidney
Bechet prophetically carried the seeds of a new direction in jazz:
the solo concept, and with it the need to arrange or compose a
framework in which the soloist(s) could operate.'[9]

Even though the Henderson band, like all the others of the
time, essentially played for dancing, Redman wasn't afraid to
experiment with new ideas. He integrated the soloist *into* his
arrangements as well as writing what are now called 'arranger's
choruses', writing out an extended solo-like passage for the complete saxophone or brass section. Additionally, he took the old
work-song tradition of call and response and updated it, making it
what Gunther Schuller calls 'the single most influential ensemble
idea in the entire Swing Era'.[10] This big band device still exists,
but Redman's striking trademark voicing of a trio of clarinets,
taken from Paul Whiteman and later used by Ellington, is little
used today. Which is part of the problem. Redman's arrangements
were colourful, still seem colourful, especially so when one compares them with the grey music (a term I'll return to) that one
hears in so much in current big band writing.

Stylistically, they may be dated – although there's nothing
wrong with that of course – but they still have life and validity.

Undoubtedly, the arrival of Louis Armstrong in Henderson's
band a year after he joined was crucial to Redman's development
'finding a confident voice of his own, and gradually allowing his

compositional instincts to dictate what he did . . . . It was [the] potent combination of distinctive individual voices within an increasingly coherent and consistent framework that became the Henderson band's lasting contribution to big-band jazz.'[11]

As for the Henderson band's 'lasting contribution to big-band jazz' and its use of 'distinctive individual voices within an increasingly coherent and consistent framework', I would only add, once again, that this is a lesson that has not been learnt by many of Redman's successors.

One who did learn from Redman was, perhaps ironically, his first employer Fletcher Henderson (1897–1952). He contributed many arrangements to the Benny Goodman band-book from the mid-1930s, one of which, his version of 'King Porter Stomp' (available in many collections of Goodman material), is credited with starting the swing era. As always, the best view is that of the musicians involved, and trombonist Dicky Wells said 'Fletcher had a way of writing so that the notes just seemed to float along casually. You just had to play the notes and the arrangement was swinging . . . his music used to make you feel bright inside.'[12]

Neal Hefti (1922–2008) came to prominence as trumpet player and arranger with the Woody Herman band in the mid-1940s. 'The Good Earth', his composition for Herman in 1945, written when he was only twenty-three, shows great compositional and arranging skill. He also contributed to 'Apple Honey', which Woody Herman, quoted in the liner notes, called 'one of the band's many heads. Everybody would contribute . . . Neal especially. This one is based on the chords of 'I Got Rhythm', one of the better B-flat tunes.' (*Woody Herman, The Thundering Herds 1945–1947*, CBS, contains the two tracks mentioned as well as other good material from his bands.)

Later in his career Hefti scored a number of films and – fanfare, please – wrote the theme music for the television series *Batman*. Apart from his work with Herman, his overwhelming claim to jazz fame is a set of arrangements he wrote for *The Atomic Mr. Basie* album (Blue Note Records) in 1957. These include such tunes

as 'Li'l Darlin'', 'Whirly-Bird' and 'Splanky', arrangements seemingly in constant use by big bands around the world, although few
play 'Li'l Darlin'' at the correct, very slow, and therefore difficult
to play, tempo. These scores also serve as models for student
arrangers. (Mine was a version of Hoagy Carmichael's 'Rocking
Chair' in the 'Li'l Darlin'' mode, but that was during my time
at Berklee, and I now have more than a few doubts as to
whether such charts should be presented as 'originals' by grown-
up writers.)

One of the aspects of jazz writing that is worth exploring is
why the 'Basie style' has become so popular with jazz arrangers,
yet some of the better ideas seen in the band's work have largely
been left by the wayside. Head arrangements still have their place
in some areas of the music, but many big band leaders seemingly
have no interest in making any changes, however minor, to a
bought-in arrangement in order to make it fit their particular
band better. Not even by adding an extra chorus for a good
soloist, or encouraging part of the band to make up some backings behind a soloist to loosen up the chart.

§ *One of the people I interviewed for the Churchill Report,* [*] *John Rapson,
now director of jazz studies at the University of Iowa, said: 'I have
actually had experience as a judge at jazz competitions where the directors
showed incredulity at suggestions that something different than what was
in the score (especially drum parts) ought to be played.' One observer has
called such competitions 'an extension of the school's athletic programme'.
They are a depressing part of much American school and college jazz
education. At the time I was writing the report I watched a college group
rehearse for such a competition. During a break I asked the students if they*

---

* The Churchill Report was the end result of a Churchill Fellowship to
look at jazz education in America awarded to me in 1992 when I was at
the Royal Academy of Music in London. The report was published in full
in Volume One, Number One, Spring 1994 of *Jazz Changes* magazine.

would wait around to hear the other groups. They looked surprised, as if that had never occurred to them.

Hefti's music for *The Atomic Mr. Basie* has its detractors but for me it represents, in the main, some of the best of Basie's later work. The style is, as one might expect, essentially as outlined earlier. Common jazz forms played in theme-solos-theme style, with a fair amount of block voicings and shortish solos. But there is air in Hefti's pieces, some space around the solos, some lightness in the writing, which could be why these pieces have become jazz classics. 'Duet', for example, a feature for two muted trumpets, is a joy throughout, with its many subtle voicings, while 'After Supper' and 'Li'l Darlin'' are masterpieces of mood.

Referring to these as 'arrangements' follows the wording on the cover – 'E = MC2 = Count Basie Orchestra + Neal Hefti arrangements' – but Hefti actually composed all the tunes as well. Given that, and the somewhat formulaic nature of the arrangements, possibly the best phrase would be 'composed and arranged by . . . .' This is a matter of nomenclature that can be confusing.

The role of the arranger, or commonly 'orchestrator', is clear cut in musicals, and with most singers, where arranging is a very specific skill. Nelson Riddle's writing for Frank Sinatra comes to mind, as does Jonathan Tunick's for Stephen Sondheim's musicals. In jazz, as we have seen, there have also been excellent arrangers, orchestrators, of their own and other people's material. As a broad definition one could say that if there is obviously a tune followed by band variations and improvised solos, this could be said to be an arrangement. When the tune is written by the same person then one could say it was 'composed and arranged'.

So far, so simple, but if one looks at classical composers, there is usually no separation of roles. The composer has written all the notes and usually made the 'who plays what when' decisions while writing those notes, or soon afterwards. There is no doubt that this calls for a 'composed by' tag, as one can sense a form, hear recurring ideas, sense an overall control. It's the work of one person, played by a group of others.

In this regard, one must add that contemporary composers such as Thomas Ades, Magnus Lindberg and many others have a control over the orchestral palette that is awesome and, sadly, points up the inadequacy of many in jazz who dress up their scores in orchestral ways. This reinforces my view that jazz must find its own strengths, but doesn't negate the necessity for good colourful scoring, when appropriate, as Ellington, Strayhorn and Gil Evans knew well.

Although the dividing line may still be blurred at times, I think one can separate a jazz composition from a jazz arrangement in the same way. When the compositional aspects become more important, more involved, more integrated with what the soloist(s) are doing, then it becomes a jazz composition. When this is not apparent, it is an arrangement.

The 'Basie style' which has become so dominant in jazz big band writing is typified by Sammy Nestico (born in 1924), who, almost certainly, has a few of his published arrangements (six hundred or so and still counting) in almost every big band library in the world. He is described in *Inside the Score*, an analytical book on jazz scoring, as 'probably one of the most gifted writers ever to hit the jazz band scene', which is as far from the truth as one is ever likely to be. His writing is the opposite of Hefti's, relying very strongly on full ensembles, all voiced to move up and down together, using solos just as colour, rather than for any real musical reason.

Some of these criticisms apply to the third of my chosen arrangers, although I may well be pilloried for saying it. His reputation is high, much higher than Nestico's among musicians and, seemingly, he is revered much more than Neal Hefti, who is, to my ears, a much better writer.

Thad Jones (1923–86), older brother of drummer Elvin, was, like Hefti, a trumpeter, and a very good one. Charles Mingus, who he worked with for a time, called him 'the greatest trumpet player I've heard in this life'. He wrote and played for Count Basie from 1954 to 1963 and is in the trumpet section on *The Atomic Mr. Basie* album. He also led a 'ghost' version of the Count Basie band for a period in the mid-1980 and in 1965 he co-formed the Thad Jones–Mel Lewis Orchestra.

Jones' style was somewhat more adventurous than Hefti's, being more harmonically and rhythmically aware, but still very much rooted in the stylistic ideas laid out by Redman and others in the twenties and thirties. Block section sounds abound, all generally played at one steady tempo, although double time passages do occur. There is more solo space in his writing, but it lacks lightness and air when compared with, say, Gil Evans and Gerry Mulligan, or Neal Hefti's writing for the Woody Herman band. There's a tired air about it all, although, like Nestico, he's very popular among college bands and many other big bands. Why this is, I'm not sure. Perhaps it's the good time big band feeling, although, in Jones more than most, this is completely lost on me. Its aim always seems to be to show off the technical prowess of the band itself, not to write jazz, not to think of the soloists except in general non-specific terms. But . . . that's probably the nub of the disagreement!

This is a point I will return to in *WHY WOULD WE WANT TO REPEAT IT?* where I make the claim that the Thad Jones–Mel Lewis Orchestra, now known as The Vanguard Jazz Orchestra, aided by Nestico's work with Count Basie from 1970 to 1984, was the starting point for much of today's generally dull big band writing.

CLASSIC ARRANGEMENT

Fletcher Henderson's arrangement of Jelly Roll Morton's 'King Porter Stomp' *for Benny Goodman.*

More will be said about Morton in *THINKING OF A BETTER WAY*, where he is considered as Duke Ellington's only competitor, but suffice it to say for now that 'King Porter Stomp', composed as early as 1906, is one of the great jazz compositions and has been arranged by composers as diverse as Henderson (1935), Gil Evans (1958 and 1975) and Bob Brookmeyer (1994).

Anecdotally, Henderson's arrangement is said to have changed jazz: 'the first realization that something was afoot came at a ballroom in Oakland [northern California], when huge advertisements for a forthcoming appearance by Guy Lombardo initially convinced Goodman that he had turned up on the wrong night. He recalled, "It was impossible to believe that so many people had come to hear us. I called for *King Porter Stomp*, one of Fletcher's real killers. Before [trumpeter Bunny Berigan] had played four bars, there was such a yelling and stomping and carrying on in that hall I thought a riot had broken out."'[13]

The reason, as Gunther Schuller points out, was that due to the different time zones across America, the band's *Let's Dance* programmes, recorded as late night events on the east coast, were heard in prime time in California. This meant that the 'young dancing crowd had been listening to Goodman's exciting Henderson arrangements for months and were fully ready to meet and greet their new musical hero'. Here was a happy and rare coincidence: a large segment of the public seemed to prefer the best and most advanced arrangements the band had to offer; not, for once, the worst. Incredibly jazz – at least one kind of jazz – had reached a potentially huge audience.'[14]

MORE ON ARRANGING

Paul Berliner, *Thinking in Jazz*, Part Three, 'Collective Aspects of Improvisation', looks at some of the practical issues of how musicians learn to arrange, with and without music.

Gunther Schuller's *Early Jazz* and *The Swing Era* both carry good descriptions, with musical examples, of how big band arranging styles developed.

Rayburn Wright, *Inside the Score, a detailed analysis of eight classic jazz ensemble charts*, is an analytical look – useful as far as it goes – at arrangements, all available on record, by Sammy Nestico, Thad Jones and Bob Brookmeyer. My reservations about the work of the first two are expressed above. Brookmeyer's turn comes later.

Fred Sturm, *Changes Over Time, the Evolution of Jazz Arranging*, looks at various arrangements of 'King Porter Stomp', 'Chant of the Weed', 'Take the 'A' Train' and 'All of Me' by Don Redman and Fletcher Henderson, among others. The book also has relevance in connection with my look at advanced arranging in DON'T BE AFRAID . . . , where it is also recommended.

The section on head arrangements in Barry Kernfeld's *What to Listen for in Jazz* has many musical examples from early Basie, particularly his classic 'Jumpin' at the Woodside'.

PART TWO

SHOWING THE WAY

5

ONE PLUS ONE MAKES THREE

DUKE THE COMPILER

dedicated to Ellington's musicians, without whom . . .

Ellington plays the piano but his real instrument is his band. Each member of his band is to him a distinctive tone colour and set of emotions, which he mixes with others equally distinctive to produce a third thing, which I like to call 'The Ellington effect'.[1]

Jazz depends on its musicians to make it work. More so than any tune, as the free improvisers show us, more so than any arrangement, as they, and the beboppers, also show us. More so, even, than any composition. Which may seem a strange comment to make inside a book called *the jazz composer*. But the devil is in the detail, in this case the word 'jazz'.

Although they operated in very different areas of music, the careers of Duke Ellington (1899–1974) and Dimitri Shostakovich (1906–75) were roughly contemporary. Shostakovich was working within a discipline with a centuries-old tradition, with access to a long history of ideas and a language that was well established. He wrote six operas and some brilliant string quartets, but his main forte was lengthy orchestral symphonies for large resources. He may have had occasional collaborators, but in the main he was the very picture of a classical composer working alone, in receipt of state subsidy and support (at least some of the time), presenting his work to an audience via a conductor and an orchestra, and having it preserved, even to this day, by a publisher.

Ellington's life was somewhat different. He was working in a discipline that was just becoming established. In the early days of his career, the New Orleans style, with its collective improvising and strongly identifiable musicians, was dying out. Coming in were the big bands of the swing era with their dependence on a uniformity of sound and approach. Ellington took a path between these two styles, choosing musicians from both camps and absorbing ideas from both sides of the divide.

As a result he produced music unlike either. Music that, because it was different, had to be worked out 'in real time' with the active involvement of the musicians concerned. He was, to a much larger extent than any classical composer, involved in almost all of the performances of his music (excepting, of course, other people's performances of his popular songs). His manuscripts were not preserved by a publisher for posterity and further performances but, as we shall see later, were often mishandled and sometimes lost. Like most jazz musicians of the time he operated in a commercial world, and, for most of his career, subsidised his band with the royalties from his popular songs (an opportunity *not* available to most jazz composers). This was Ellington's way of working, and the contrast with Shostakovich points up some very real practical differences between classical and jazz composing.

The commercial pressures – and opportunities – undoubtedly shaped Ellington's thinking. But, crucially, his attitudes were also affected by his chronological time. His best work happened in his, and the century's, early forties. As such it absorbed New Orleans music and swing, but preceded bebop and, most importantly, it preceded the radical changes that happened in the late 1950s. Ellington was aware of those developments of course and, in some important ways, anticipated them, as we shall see in INFINITE POS-SIBILITIES. The full potential of jazz – *as it was then* – was achieved by him. But it is my contention that the changes of the late 1950s opened up jazz composition to such an extent that only after that time were the full possibilities of the art form able to be seen and acted upon.

I realise that in saying this I am in danger of being persecuted by the Ellington police (who will come into our story, and possibly my studio, later) but even they should be aware that no artist can do everything, and that every artist is bound by the period he lives in. 'Even the most original talent cannot proceed beyond certain limits which are fixed for it by the date of its birth. Not everything is possible at all times, and certain thoughts can only be thought at certain stages of the development.'[2]

What we need to be concerned with is not mindlessly supporting the 'Duke is God' argument (see below for more on this), but realising what he *did* with what he had to work with. And, whisper it on an untapped phone line, where he failed. And, absolutely no argument here, where he showed the way for those able to see. In his music he showed what jazz was capable of, and saw a potential for jazz that no one else did. A huge claim that can be proved by listening to his music, and by bearing in mind a simple comment made to Ellington by Lawrence Brown, one of his trombonists: 'I don't consider you a composer. You are a compiler.'[3]

Ellington is reported to have been angered by that remark, but I think that, had he thought about it more, he would have realised that it was a compliment to what was part of his identity as a true jazz composer. Someone who, *of necessity*, compiles his music using the talents of the musicians around him. Sometimes, as we saw with 'C-Jam Blues', he even used the tunes written by his musicians and he often used ideas suggested by his musicians during rehearsals. In a very real sense we can see that Ellington took the idea of *something borrowed, something new*, the phrase I used in the first chapter to describe the jazz musicians' repertoire, and applied it in a way that took jazz in new directions.

What he got from his musicians, what he got from everything else around him, was grist to his mill as composer and showed a totally different set of musical influences and imperatives from those of Shostakovich. He was influential in a different way, too.

Shostakovich's symphonic tradition, writing a lot of music to be played by a lot of musicians, was a strong one, but past its heyday. Ellington's approach, allowing the individual sounds and soloing skills of his chosen musicians to play a big part in his compositions, was new and sums up a way of composing that is unique to jazz.

BORROWING THE TUNE

There seems little doubt that those compositions that bear Bubber's name along with Ellington's were primarily created by Miley. These include the three most important works of the period – recorded in late 1926 and early 1927 – 'East St. Louis Toodle-Oo', 'Black and Tan Fantasy' and 'Creole Love Call'.[4]

Undoubtedly, Duke Ellington wrote many great compositions. But there is no doubt that, in the early days, he took material written by others in the band and, sometimes without crediting them, called it his own. Some were aggrieved enough to complain about it or even, at times, go to law. Others didn't care, or possibly felt that complaining was fairly pointless. At the time bands were more co-operative and copyrights less likely to be an issue, although there is a story of Johnny Hodges sitting on the bandstand counting imaginary money whenever one of his disputed songs was played.

In connection with this, Barney Bigard's possible claim to composing credits for 'C-Jam Blues' is put in an interesting light by a comment he made when he joined the band as a replacement for Rudy Jackson. Jackson it seems had brought 'Creole Love Call' to Duke, claiming it was his tune – although he had in fact stolen it from King Oliver! Bigard said 'I guess I couldn't blame [Duke] for getting rid of a guy that brought on so much trouble to his band. I mean, nobody needs law suits.'[5] However, Bigard himself sued Ellington some years later over his claim to have written 'Mood Indigo'. He won, which meant his name was on the music and he was able to collect royalties. 'I missed the boat for twenty-eight years on royalties. I didn't get a dime.'[6]

As the opening quote to this section shows, many of Ellington's best-known compositions are said to have been strongly influenced by, indeed wholly written by, his musicians, and this also applies to his more popular songs. 'Sophisticated Lady' is said to have been written by Lawrence Brown and Toby Hardwicke, and 'Caravan' by Juan Tizol. Tizol allegedly sold 'Caravan' outright to Irving Mills, then Ellington's manager and purported 'co-composer', for twenty-five dollars, but he did get some royalties from Mills later. 'Mood Indigo', as we saw above, was taken back by Barney Bigard, but only partially, as Ellington – and Irving Mills – are also listed as composers.

Two tunes, 'Take the 'A' Train' and 'Chelsea Bridge', are credited solely to Billy Strayhorn, and are generally acknowledged to have been written by him, but in a sign of the matter's incestuousness, there is some discussion as to whether, and to what extent, Ellington had a hand in them. Strayhorn commented that 'who wrote what' was a 'whodunit game indulged in by the band (which always puzzles me, because I think my playing and writing style is totally different from Ellington's).'[7]

Duke's borrowing of tunes and parts of tunes from musicians, and then taking some or all of the credit, has been proven in some cases and rumoured in many others. But as Strayhorn pointed out, there is more to it than that: 'something like a solo, perhaps only a few notes, is hardly a composition. It may be the inspiration, but what do they say about ten percent inspiration and ninety percent perspiration? Composing is work. So this guy says you and he wrote it, but he thinks he wrote it. He thinks you just put it down on paper. But what you did was put it down on paper, harmonized it, straightened out the bad phrases, and added things to it, so you could hear the finished product. Now, really, who wrote it? . . . . But the proof is that these people don't go somewhere else and write beautiful music. You don't hear anything else from them. You do from Ellington.'[8]

BORROWING THE MUSICIANS' IDEAS

The band was motivated around him and everything depended on his being in it, not only because of his solo role, but because of the phrases he knew and because of what his knowledge contributed in the background.[9]

A very heavy influence in that early band was trumpeter Bubber Miley (1903–32), the 'him' of Mercer Ellington's quote above. As Ellington said, 'Our band changed its character when Bubber came in. He used to growl all night long, playing gutbucket on his horn. That was when we decided to forget all about the sweet music.'[10] One critic observed that 'the performance [of Ellington's music] is a kind of collective creation, restoring, within the narrow confines of a single band, the social character of New Orleans music.'[11] This could well be put down to the influence of Miley and other New Orleans style musicians who were in the Ellington band at that time.

Discussing an effect in one of the three compositions that Miley is said to have written with Ellington, 'East St. Louis Toodle-Oo', Gunther Schuller says: 'Here we find a dramatic example of what has been called the "Ellington effect". It is evident . . . that Miley deserves much credit for this quality, at least in its early manifestations . . . . It is a mark of [Ellington's] talent and vision as a leader that in these early days of his band, when he was learning to use the materials he had in hand, he let his musicians lead the way in forming the band's style.'[12]

Although his control of the band became stronger over time, Ellington continued to acknowledge the help he got from his musicians. Speaking in 1944 he said, 'There's no set system. Most times I write it and arrange it. Sometimes I write it and the band and I collaborate on the arrangement. Sometimes Billy Strayhorn, my staff arranger, does the arrangement. When we're all working together, a guy may have an idea and he plays it on his horn. Another guy may add to it and make something out of it. Someone may play a riff and ask, "How do you like this?"

The trumpets may try something together and say, "Listen to this" . . . . '[13]

When outsiders wanted to photograph primitive people they were sometimes refused permission because, it was claimed, of the fear that the camera would capture the souls of those being photographed. In a not dissimilar vein New Orleans trumpeter Freddie Keppard (1890–1933) is said to have been so afraid of others stealing his ideas that he played with a handkerchief over the valves of his trumpet. Ellington, with the connivance of his musicians, was far more open about 'stealing their souls'. He realised that he *needed* his musicians and it was necessary for him to become so familiar with them – even knowing 'how they play poker' – that he was able to use them as his personal colours. 'I know what sounds well on a trombone and I know what sounds well on a trumpet and they are not the same. I know what Tricky Sam can play on a trombone and I know what Lawrence Brown can play on a trombone and they are not the same, either.'[14]

Ellington recognised that the difference between musicians, between the individual *approaches* of musicians, is important. This is a mark of his special talent – and his luck in having a regular band available to him. The intimate knowledge of how his soloists played was hard-won in the early days through constant performances and many hours of rehearsals. 'If there is any secret to the Ellington method, it is this: for every hour of actual performance there are at least two hours of intensive rehearsal.'[15]

Trumpeter Rex Stewart, who was with the band from 1934 to 1945, saw it like this: 'He would produce some frayed scraps of manuscript paper with, say, a few notes scribbled down for the reeds, then produce something similarly cryptic for the trumpet and trombone sections.'[16] This way of working – or, to be more accurate, a way of starting to work – reminds me of a story I was told some years ago. When Gil Evans was picked up at Heathrow airport before a prestigious London gig, he was asked by the road manager if he had the commissioned piece with him. 'I've got it here somewhere,' he said, before fishing a small, crumpled piece of paper from his back pocket! (Gil Evans' late work, to which this anecdote refers, is discussed in *TAKING A CHANCE*.)

Such working methods inevitably lead to problems with preserving the music, but at times Ellington had a back-up plan. Journalist H. A. Overstreet, an observer of the band's first European tour in 1933, made the point that while Ellington was working out an arrangement with the band, trombonist Juan Tizol was engaged in making a written score. This would be taken away and possibly revised by Ellington before the next rehearsal, but would also be available if a score was needed for publication. However, when there was written music, things weren't that simple.

As trumpeter Benny Bailey said, there would be 'all those different versions of his pieces floating around the band. All the cats had five or six arrangements of the same piece. And when you joined the band, no one would tell you which one was the current one. They'd let you find out too late that you were playing the wrong one, and you'd scramble for another. Ellington was always rewriting the parts.'[17]

Probably the best description of how Ellington worked was given in an oft-quoted statement by Billy Strayhorn which introduces this chapter and which gave rise to the phrase 'the Ellington effect': 'Ellington plays the piano, but his real instrument is his band. Each member of his band is to him a distinctive tone colour and set of emotions, which he mixes with others equally distinctive to produce a third thing, which I like to call "The Ellington effect".

'Sometimes this mixing happens on paper and frequently right on the bandstand. I have often seen him exchange parts in the middle of a piece because the man and the part weren't the same character.

'Ellington's concern is with the individual musicians, and what happens when they put their musical characters together. Watching him on the bandstand, the listener might think that his movements are stock ones, used by everyone in front of a band. However, the extremely observant may well detect the flick of a finger that may draw the sound he wants from a musician.

'By letting his men play naturally and relaxed, Ellington is able to probe the intimate recesses of their minds *and find things that not even the musicians thought were there.*'[18] (Italics added)

Strayhorn's observations show how Ellington worked not only with the written notes that were presented to the musicians, but with the musicians themselves. Such methods would seem very alien to classically trained musicians who, by and large, expect everything given to them to be very specific. But, by his way of doing things, Ellington showed that he was working in a different way, was still experimenting and wasn't afraid to change his ideas. And that things in jazz aren't written in stone.

Ellington was able to use his musicians in such interesting instrumental combinations that it is sometimes difficult to tell how a particular chord is voiced. As André Previn observed, 'Stan Kenton can stand in front of a thousand fiddles and a thousand brass and make a dramatic gesture and every studio arranger can nod his head and say, "Oh, yes, that's done like this." But Duke merely lifts his finger, three horns make a sound, and I don't know what it is!'[19]

Ellington said, 'We write from the same perspective as before. We write to fit the tonal personalities of the individual instrumentalists who have the responsibility of interpreting our works.'[20] But to Ellington this meant something more than knowing how they play their instruments, which amplifies a point I made in my chapter on improvising, above, that it is the whole person who is involved in playing, not just the musician. As well as knowing 'how they play poker', Ellington said, 'As a group of musicians we understand each other very well. We have identical feelings and beliefs in music. Our inspiration is derived from our lives, and the lives of those about us, and those that went before us.'[21]

In basing his work so firmly on the talents of his musicians, Ellington developed the very important but little discussed point that the role of a jazz composer is often not only to write the tune, but to be involved in the performance as a musician, as well as having an important contribution to make as bandleader. And, as we saw in *WHO DOES WHAT WHEN,* this includes choosing the musicians. In a phrase relevant to this chapter, the bandleader is *compiling a band.* But compiling a band from a perspective different from that of most bandleaders.

As trumpeter Fred Stone, who was in the band for six months in 1970, said, 'The Ellington Orchestra is the only musical outfit I know where the members are hired solely on the basis of their strength and individuality. It is the only orchestra I know where you are not required to become an exact percentage of the section you're playing with; where you are not required to match the sound of the previous member.'[22] This thinking was taken to extremes at times, with the band carrying two bassists or two drummers, because Ellington had found someone else whose playing he liked and asked them to join the band, regardless of the fact that there was already a bassist or a drummer on his payroll. There is a connection here with some free groups today who use two drummers, two bassists, indeed any instrumentation, as a matter of course, recognising that the specific instruments used are of far less importance than the people playing them.

To state the obvious, the sounds and soloists available to a composer are chosen from the musicians available at the time. But how do they get there in the first place? Again, to state the obvious, they are asked to be in the band. Good bandleaders have the knack of choosing the right people – Duke, Miles Davis, Art Blakey, are all excellent examples of this – and I can immodestly record that I was once told I had 'the knack of turning raw youngsters into hardened professionals'.

Once in the band, musicians are selected for a particular solo because of their specific skills. Once again Ellington is a prime example. He allocated a solo not to a specific chair, such as second or third trumpet, but to a specific person, such as Ray Nance or Rex Stewart.

Ellington was a lax disciplinarian, allowing the band members to wander on to the bandstand late, and sometimes drunk. He thought it was too much trouble to reprimand them, preferring the light touch. As one of his sidemen said: 'If someone's acting up, he'll say, "I hired you because you were the best on your instrument and because I assumed you were an adult. I am going to continue on that assumption." And that's usually it.'[23]

Speaking of arguments over money Ellington has said, 'I won't let these goddam musicians upset me! Why should I knock myself out in an argument about fifteen dollars when in the same time I can probably write a fifteen-hundred-dollar song.'[24] However, Clark Terry's view is that 'For all the seeming looseness of direction, Duke really runs things and, it seems to me, that his main goal as a leader is to mold a man so fully into the Ellington way of playing that he finds it hard to pull away.'[25]

Musicians did leave, of course, an occurrence that was often greeted with dismay by Ellington fans, and composer Raymond Scott wrote 'When Cootie Left the Duke' to mark the departure of trumpeter Cootie Williams. But as Billy Strayhorn said, 'Lately, personnel changes have prompted the comment that what I call the "Ellington effect" has been replaced by something different. This, I believe, comes about from listening with the eyes instead of the ears. The same thing has happened every time there has been a change during my stay, and, even before my time, the advent into the band of the very people who have left brought forth the same remarks.'[26]

Leaving was not always a good move for the musician concerned. Very few did anything of real significance afterwards because, as composer William Russo pointed out in a record review in *Down Beat* magazine, the soloists in Ellington's band, by subordinating themselves to the whole, have, 'ironically achieved so much more originality than they might have if they had proceeded along more standard lines.'

Ellington's choice of musicians and his 'manipulating' of them inside his compositions is far more important than what notes he gave them to play. His willingness to voice across sections, and to use instruments on their own, or in pairs, instead of the conventional four-part block voicings, all came from his desire to use his musicians as *individuals* rather than just instruments. The notes and voicings Ellington used can be studied from the records, and the various scores and books now available, and it may seem perverse not to go into them further in a book on jazz composition. But, while not wishing in any way to restrict the study and performance of Ellington's scores, the bigger prize comes from realising that while these notes and voicings can be studied, they can't be recreated in any precise and meaningful way, *because the people who made them are not there to play them.*

That fact needs to be at the heart of any discussion about the jazz composer. It is an explanation of why the jazz composer, unlike his tune-writing and arranging counterparts, doesn't have the choice of staying in the old ways. Tunes and arrangements written today may or may not reflect the changes that have happened. But if a musician wants to be a jazz composer – at least in my definition of the term, which implies being a creative artist – he has to absorb Ellington's philosophy. He has to take account of the developments of the late 1950s *and* follow Duke Ellington by being creative for himself, while choosing and using – and developing – the talents of the musicians around him.

'It is true that Duke drew a great deal from Williams, Miley, Bigard, Hodges, and the rest; but it is equally true that none of these men had important careers in jazz apart from Ellington . . . He brought out the best in them. By choosing when and what they would play, he paraded their strengths . . . . We thus have to see Duke Ellington as we see a master chef. The chef does not chop all the vegetables himself or make the sauce with his own hands. But he plans the menus, trains the assistants, supervises them, tastes everything, adjusts the spices . . . . And in the end we credit him with the result.'[27]

CLASSIC ELLINGTON COMPILATION

'East St. Louis Toodle-Oo', Duke Ellington and his Cotton Club Orchestra. There are various recordings but the best, the one analysed by Schuller in Early Jazz, is the one recorded for Victor on December 19th, 1927.

The tune is credited to Ellington and Miley, but Gunther Schuller asserts that it was 'primarily created by Miley'. Certainly Miley is prominent, playing, in his unique growling way, the main thirty-two bar theme as a solo. Apart from the melody (which, adding more fuel to the borrowing scenario, 'may well be pure folk song') the main interest is in the form. Unusually, the last section is a recapitulation of the first eight bars of the theme only. 'The importance of this ending lies not so much in the fact that a felicitous choice was made, but that such a choice was *possible*. It was possible because 'East St. Louis Toodle-Oo' was not a collection of thirty-two- [or] twelve-bar "take your turn" solos, nor was it a totally improvised ensemble piece, but in its faltering way a *composition.*'[28] And a composition *compiled* by Ellington, Miley and the other two soloists, quite probably helped by the others in the band as well. It was part of the beginning of something new in jazz.

MORE ON ELLINGTON

Duke Ellington, *Music is My Mistress*, his autobiography, is somewhat scrappily organised, but an interesting read nonetheless.

Mark Tucker ed., *The Duke Ellington Reader*, an exhaustive indispensable historical anthology of most of the writings about Ellington, including some of his own words.

James Lincoln Collier, *Duke Ellington*, is somewhat controversial and criticised by the Ellington police, but contains much of interest.

As my extensive use of them shows, Gunther Schuller's *Early Jazz* and *The Swing Era* are invaluable sources of material on Ellington and his music.

Duke Ellington: The Blanton–Webster Band (RCA), a three disc set, contains much excellent music from what is generally acknowledged to be Ellington's best period.

6

THINKING OF A BETTER WAY

DUKE THE COMPOSER

dedicated to Duke Ellington and Billy Strayhorn

*Duke simply thought of a better way of doing the same thing after he
wrote the music, so he changed it.* [1]

Duke Ellington's methods reflect the phrase *something borrowed,
something new* in that his genius was to assimilate the talents of his
musicians into his own way of working. That combination produced hundreds of jazz compositions, ranging from tunes like
'Sophisticated Lady', to band compositions such as 'Ko-Ko', to
longer works, some for the band alone such as *Black, Brown and
Beige* and some, like his musical *Jump for Joy,* for other resources.
All this activity has produced a body of work unlike that of anyone else in jazz, and confirms Duke Ellington's position as the
number one composer in jazz.

I doubt that anyone would want to argue with that, although
there has been an area of dissent with regard to his longer works.
Usually those who do criticise are very quickly put in their
place by the Ellington police, who, 'only doing our job, guv',
have rushed to pour scorn on those particular brush fires.
Inevitably, some of that dissent will again crop up here because,
much as those who try to protect Ellington's reputation might
prefer things to be, it can't just be wished away. But, as I show

below, there may be other, less contentious ways of looking at the longer works.

THE POPULAR SONGS

In SOMETHING BORROWED, SOMETHING NEW I spoke of tunes to improvise *from* (where the chord progression is more important to the jazz musician than the melody), and tunes to improvise *with* (where the melody is more interesting, and open to different interpretations). Duke Ellington's songs, including such masterpieces as 'Sophisticated Lady', 'Prelude to a Kiss', 'In a Sentimental Mood' and many more, were almost always tunes to improvise with. Indeed, most of them were originally written to feature specific instrumentalists in the band.

Inevitably the tunes did attract lyrics – usually, not very good ones – in an attempt to make them more commercial, but their provenance as instrumental features means that the melodies are far more difficult to sing than those of Duke's song-writing contemporaries such as George Gershwin or Irving Berlin. 'Prelude to a Kiss' for example, has a very complex bridge, while the first two bars of 'Sophisticated Lady' are difficult to get around because of the unusual connections between the notes. As Gunther Schuller has pointed out Ellington's finest songs are much more in the realm of art song than pop tune.

Given the history we examined in the last chapter, it is not surprising that there is some dissent as to who was involved in writing what song. 'Satin Doll', royalties from which are said to have helped finance the orchestra for years, has been variously credited to Ellington, Strayhorn, and to them both. The list of compositions in *Music is My Mistress* gives Ellington sole composer credit, but has Strayhorn as *co-lyricist* alongside Johnny Mercer (a lyricist of some note, with 'Skylark', 'Blues in the Night' and 'Moon River' to his credit). Strayhorn's biographer David Hajdu says, 'Strayhorn fleshed out an Ellington riff sketch with harmony and lyrics – an ode to Strayhorn's mother, spun around Strayhorn's pet name for her' and that Johnny Mercer was brought in 'to replace Strayhorn's oedipal lyrics with ones evoking more commercial male–female love.'[2]

Irving Mills was Ellington's manager – and publisher – from 1926 to 1939. His view that he made Ellington's 'importance as an artist the primary consideration'[3] has a great deal of truth in it, and Ellington himself praised Mills' contributions to his success. However, he is also credited as 'co-writer' of some of Ellington's compositions, a claim that has led to much criticism over the years. The usual charge is that he was a white manager ripping off the black entertainer, and given the history of such managers – Joe Glaser with Louis Armstrong, for one – there may well be some truth in that.

Mills said, 'I wrote 'Sophisticated Lady' with him, and 'Mood Indigo', 'Solitude', 'In a Sentimental Mood' . . . ' He also said that Ellington 'followed instructions. He did what I wanted.'[4] Although one might bristle at the master–servant tone, Mills may well have contributed to the tunes in some way. He was active as a singer, and perhaps this link could justify his claim to be credited with some of the lyrics. As a publisher he would have been entitled, perhaps even encouraged, to make some suggestions about the songs, but that was part of his job. There is no proof that I know of that he really did contribute anything to the actual music, and my ever-present cynicism comes into play when he is credited as co-composer of some of Ellington's greatest hits.

Seemingly Ellington was happy with the arrangement – the management arrangement lasted thirteen years after all, and the publishing deal probably still has a few years to run (with, as far as I know, no law suits hovering as with some of today's young-songwriter/older-manager agreements). Mills looked after the business, and the royalties that Ellington received were enough, as we have seen, to keep the band going for most of his career. And they were substantial. He tells of going to borrow $500 from his agent in 1943 and, while waiting, being given his mail which included a cheque for $22,500 from RCA Victor, an enormous sum at the time.[5]

THE MINIATURES

Whether other people were involved in writing Duke's popular songs or not, one can't dispute their merits. But they have always needed a performance to make them into jazz compositions. I think of the imaginative interpolation of 'In a Sentimental Mood' into a set of almost all original material on *Jøkleba! Live!* Or of Andy Bey's wonderful readings of 'Prelude to a Kiss' and 'Satin Doll' on *American Song* (Savoy Jazz). Or of . . . well, the list is almost endless, and deservedly so.

However, some of Ellington's material, far less popular with other artists for understandable reasons, are jazz compositions in themselves – although of course they still need 'moving off the paper'. It's on these that his reputation as a jazz composer was built, and why it lasts. Compositions such as 'Ko Ko', 'Main Stem', and 'Cotton Tail', are part of the vast storehouse of masterpieces that make Ellington's place as *the* jazz composer impossible to dispute. Known, at times somewhat disparagingly, as miniatures, these are fully realised compositions lasting between three and four minutes. Actually, it is possible to make the case that these pieces are *performances* rather than compositions, especially as we now only know them from recordings. Composition and perform-ance meld into one, so much so that one can't imagine them being played by any other band, a point I will return to in *WHY WOULD WE WANT TO REPEAT IT?* Ellington was a master of this genre, writ-ing compositions which included more variety of content than anyone would have thought possible, and saying what they had to say in the time frame of a single side of an early record.

Even within the seemingly restrictive parameters of a simple twelve-bar blues played in theme-solos-theme form, we can see that Ellington was up to something new. The first big band recording of 'C-Jam Blues' (1942) starts with the simple tune played in single notes on the piano, 'a minimal rendering of a minimal tune, showing that he not only understood the virtue of simplicity but also was not afraid of it'.[6] After the theme statement, each of the five soloists takes a four bar unaccompanied break before their solo. These four-bar breaks are, contrary to usual practice, *outside* the twelve-bar blues form. It is only behind the last solo, that of the alleged composer Barney Bigard, that the band comes in. This leads to an exuberant final ensemble chorus, with Bigard still wailing over the band's contrapuntal lines. That last chorus, the minimal theme statement, and the changes to the norm in the solo chorus, are enough to make this a little gem of jazz composition.

To take another simple example. Ellington's 1930 arrangement of 'Mood Indigo' achieves something remarkable by going back in time. It uses the classic New Orleans front line of clarinet, trumpet and trombone, but in a totally fresh way. The style in New Orleans music is to have the clarinet playing freely above the trumpet melody, while the trombone decorates the bass line below. Ellington still has the trumpet (muted here) on the lead, which in 'Mood Indigo' is in the instrument's easy middle register, but just below it is the trombone, also muted, with the second voice. The notes are high for the instrument and exposed in the voicing, making them difficult to play well and balance correctly. The third voice is an octave and a sixth below, an unusually wide separation when voicing chords, and is given to the clarinet in its very low, 'chalumeau' register. The result uses old ingredients to produce a totally new sound, one with three very distinctive timbres: the trumpet's pastel-shaded melody, the trombone's slightly aggressive added colour and, a long way beneath, the clarinet's mysterious low notes. After solos from the trumpet and clarinet, and an Ellington piano interlude, the main theme returns. 'That is all there is to it. But, like most great music, it leaves us with a sense of completion, a finality, a feeling that everything needed has been said. Duke Ellington played 'Mood Indigo' countless thousands of times over his life and recorded it again and again, but never did he top these first versions made with three horns and a rhythm section. If ever less was more, it was here.'[7]

'Cotton Tail' (recorded in 1940) looks forward to bebop, both in its melodic line and in its adventurous scoring. Based on the chords of Gershwin's 'I Got Rhythm', and making bows to the original both in the writing and in Ben Webster's solo, it features many aspects worth mentioning. Gunther Schuller discusses it over four pages in *The Swing Era* ('it would not be difficult to devote the better part of an entire chapter to [it]') and points out that 'The jazz avant-garde of the mid-forties all drew upon the ideas in this seminal record.' The form, ostensibly AABA over thirty-two bars, as in the Gershwin original, is quickly subverted by Ellington writing a new theme, only *four* bars long, for the last section of the first chorus. This serves to introduce a stunning two-chorus solo – long for its time – from Ben Webster.

Indeed there is subversion right from the start of 'Cotton Tail'; there is no introduction, as was customary, and the melody, very unusually, starts on the ninth of the first, tonic, chord. The bridge, a series of resolving dominant seventh chords, is voiced in a different way each time using voicings that, as Schuller reminds us, 'would become a bop convention some years later'. Then there is a saxophone soli chorus that, although not a new idea, is one of the best examples of a device which in later years became something of a cliché in big band writing. Like Schuller, I could write more but . . . it's a masterpiece; listen and wonder!

There are other masterpieces – many of them – but the three I have chosen to discuss show some of the factors that contributed to them all. First, as we have discussed, Ellington's control over his musicians, his ability to blend their individual timbres until 'only the closest listening will reveal what combinations of what instruments with what mutes are playing what, to produce this shifting sonority'.[8] Then, using his knowledge of 'how they played poker' and everything else at his disposal, his enviable ability in placing each soloist into just the right solo spot. And, finally, for that solo spot to be a meaningful part of the composition.

However, before this type of collaborative magic could happen, something had to be organised, either on paper or in rehearsal. Exactly what was organised was very fluid. Even in something as familiar as the blues or a thirty-two bar standard song, there were changes to the form such as the four-bar solo breaks *outside* the chorus of 'C-Jam Blues', and the new four-bar melody in the first chorus of 'Cotton Tail'. Also, in a field where theme-solos-theme on the original source was usually enough, there would often be more than one theme, more than one set of chords, as well as new melodies on the original chords. Behind the soloists, and setting them off to wonderful effect, there would be interesting counterpoints and backings.

Backing a soloist with something more than just the rhythm section, with something other than the band playing minimal riffs or sustained chords, was somewhat rare in jazz, and in some instances still is. This was part of Jelly Roll Morton's talent too, which will be discussed below. These touches provide different levels of interest, what has been called 'the technique of divided attention', a subject we will return to below.

These new ideas came into Ellington's music while, for much of the time, he was writing music for people to dance to. This needed a steady pulse, which was usually made very obvious by his swing-band contemporaries. With Ellington 'there is a high degree of subtlety in treating the inexorable fundamental dance beat. It is never disguised, indeed often stressed, but it is combined with the flowing bass so adroitly that it provides the sturdy substructure on which Ellington rears his luxuriant structure of moving parts, forgotten except that it provides the measure by which to appreciate the boldly declamatory freedom of the upper voices.'[9] Those comments may seem a trifle flowery when read today, but, according to Mark Tucker in *The Duke Ellington Reader*, the essay from which it comes, *Black Beauty* by R. D. Darrell written in 1932, was 'the first major critical statement on Duke Ellington's music. Provocative, insightful, in many ways prophetic, it remains one of the most important articles ever written about Ellington.'[10]

All these ideas contributed to making the pieces I have named, and many others, into *jazz* compositions, into performances that we still marvel at all these years later. My personal favourites are 'Cotton Tail', 'Ko-Ko', 'Main Stem', 'Jack the Bear' and 'Harlem Air Shaft'. I could go on but listening to any or all of the ones I have listed will give a flavour of what Ellington and his band were up to. Not everything that Ellington did was as great, and some compositions were not even great at all. (*Is that someone banging on the door?*) But, enough of it was great for the rest of us to want to follow Miles Davis' suggestion: 'I think all the musicians in jazz should get together on one certain day and get down on their knees to thank Duke.'[11]

One question that remains is how Ellington came across these ideas and compiled them into such masterpieces – and, understandably, this is something of a mystery. Most composers don't really know how composing happens, and, after it has happened, remember so little of the creative process that they will ask in bewilderment, 'did I write that?' Reading about Ellington one gets the impression that he was so busy travelling that he didn't even have time to think that far. But what he did have was a band to use as his personal 'scratchpad'. He recorded a huge amount of material at his own expense, some of which was issued as *The Private Collection* (Saja Records), a set of ten CDs containing much interesting material.

'Duke was on the right track because he wasn't afraid to experiment.' That comment from Jelly Roll Morton sums up Ellington's attitude, and why I continue to harp on his identity as a compiler. Although, and this is to put the Ellington police off the scent for a while, a compiler who *became* a composer. He became a composer by learning how to use the individual timbres and soloing styles his musicians made available to him, and by constantly experimenting with the melodic, harmonic and formal aspects of his compositions.

Having a band available to experiment with gave him ideas. But mainly he was experimenting because, as a self-taught musician, he knew no other way. And to be honest, there was no other way. No schools, no method books, no way of learning how, except by listening and trying things out.

Trying things out is something Ellington continued to do throughout his life. Irving Townsend, his producer at Columbia in the late fifties and early sixties, says of a television scoring assignment, 'He arrived with a box of music at noon. At midnight he left the studio having recorded half of what he brought with him and half of what he put together in the studio. I don't think one segment was finally used just as it was written before the session, but all could have been. *Duke simply thought of a better way of doing the same thing after he wrote the music, so he changed it.*'[12] (Italics added.)

The depth of meaning behind that last sentence is breathtaking in its implications. It adds another dimension to the portrait of the jazz composer that is now emerging.

THE LONGER WORKS

Ellington's lack of musical education has been blamed for his failure in writing successful long works. Given the income from his popular songs, and the acclaim he got for them and for his miniatures, one might wonder why he wanted to write longer works in the first place. One can't forget, either, that the bulk of his work was always going to be in dance halls and jazz clubs, and that, for a sizeable part of his composing life, there was a de facto time limit for recordings of three to four minutes. In addition to this, there were increasing signs of dissent within the band. The musicians felt that learning new material for the sake of one or two 'grand' performances was too much of a chore when, instead, they could happily continue playing the known material. As Max Harrison points out: 'His bandsmen have been lavishly praised for a number of good reasons, but securing adequate interpretations of his more ambitious pieces was to remain a problem for Ellington.'[13]

Interestingly, Billy Strayhorn said he had very little to do with any of the longer works, 'other than maybe discussing them with him. That's because the larger works are such a personal expression of him. He knows what he wants. It wouldn't make any sense for me to be involved there.'[14] This is somewhat at odds with what one reads of some collaborations that did happen, but both Strayhorn and Ellington were masters of the art of obfuscation when talking about their work. In the early sixties I, and other people from Berklee, prodded Strayhorn for some clue, any clue, about his music after he'd 'chatted' in a talk to some fans in New York, but he was giving nothing away. Freddie Keppard lives!

Ellington was an ambitious man, and recognised that one way out of the dance halls and into the concert halls was to do something different, to write long compositions, and for them to have some programmatic subject. (This is a trend common even today, when writing a long composition, especially one with a 'programmatic theme', promises access to funding and venues usually unavailable to 'normal' jazz.) The best known of Ellington's longer works is probably *Black, Brown and Beige*, premiered at Carnegie Hall in 1943, but, as we will see below, Ellington subsequently only played extracts from this work, which brings us to one of the main criticisms of him as a composer.

Most of Ellington's longer works are best categorised as 'suites', collections of short pieces which, though they need a connecting titular theme, need not have any musical linkage. Ellington's many works of this kind, including *Such Sweet Thunder,* commissioned by the Stratford, Ontario, Shakespeare Festival in 1957, and *The Far East Suite,* written in 1966 after the band's tours of the Middle East and Japan, contain some wonderful material. Looking only at the two I've named, and adding *Black, Brown and Beige* to the mix, one discovers such ravishing melodies as 'Come Sunday', 'Star-Crossed Lovers' and 'Isfahan', to name only some of the ballads. Heart-wrenching stuff, especially when performed by Johnny

Hodges, as all three were. (In that regard, I remember hearing, in the market square of a small French town in the midst of all the usual Christmas music, another version of 'Come Sunday' – this time a recording of Mahalia Jackson's. It was a very apt choice for the season and its purity made nonsense of everything else that the town hall chose to play us that day.)

But ballads such as these are, like almost every other section of every long work by Ellington, *separate* pieces, which bear little or no relation to the other movements that surround them. In a way, there's nothing wrong with that. In fact, it could be said that Ellington was writing *his* kind of long work, not the long works expected of him by others, or those created using classical writing forms.

But first, to examine one of my three ballads more closely. 'Star-Crossed Lovers', one of the Shakespearian vignettes presented by Ellington in *Such Sweet Thunder*, is a beautiful melody in a sensuous arrangement. It features Johnny Hodges and Paul Gonsalves, and is very successful in portraying the star-crossed lovers from *Romeo and Juliet*. However, there is, as they say, a backstory. When preparing an Ellington tribute record while I was at Berklee, we were sent various lead sheets from Tempo Music, Ellington's publishing house. One of these was for 'Star-Crossed Lovers', which I subsequently arranged for the record. But there were annotations on the lead sheet which showed that "Pretty Girl', words and music by Billy Strayhorn', had at some time been altered to become 'Star-Crossed Lovers', composed by Duke Ellington and Billy Strayhorn'. No music was changed, just the credits.

§ *The record* A Tribute to Duke Ellington, Jazz in the Classroom, Volume VIII *was one of a Berklee series of jazz records of student originals or 'tribute' arrangements. That tradition is now discontinued (but check out recordings from the California Institute of the Arts if you want to hear fresh student work). The Berklee Ellington album was well reviewed in* Down Beat, *where, I'm happy to report, critic Bill Mathieu said of my arrangement, 'Jazz is not being written better than this.'*

David Hajdu says that while they were working on *Such Sweet Thunder* Ellington called Strayhorn at home and suggested that Strayhorn 'save time and simply steal the music – albeit from himself'.[15] 'Pretty Girl' had been previously recorded by Johnny Hodges on *Creamy* two years earlier, and also by the Ellington band five months before the *Such Sweet Thunder* sessions. One could see that Ellington was still borrowing tunes, still compiling his material, but, as always, the proof is in the pudding. With the title attached, it works.

As hinted above, there is a different way of looking at Ellington's longer works. Gunther Schuller defends *Black, Brown and Beige* saying that 'by 1940s' jazz standards, especially in respect to tempo considerations and intricacy of form, the performance was almost miraculous. The critics unanimously failed to realise that in a work like *BBB* – a work rooted in jazz tradition – the essence of *performance* was a much more important factor than some of the technical aspects of composition.'[16] (*Performance* italicised in the original.)

Schuller's defence of the piece points sharply to the decade when *Black, Brown and Beige* was first performed; puts the stress in the phrase 'jazz composition' on the first word; and draws attention to the way that performance is of the essence in jazz. These are all important factors in the arguments of this book.

Ellington is said to have been so stung by the contemporary critical reaction to *Black, Brown and Beige* that he subsequently only played extracts from it, and never recorded the full piece. The entire composition was reconstructed and recorded in 1972 by two British musicians, Brian Priestley (also a critic and author of *Mingus, a Critical Biography*) and Alan Cohen. They analyse and largely defend the work in a series of articles, concluding, 'As to the developmental techniques which were new to Ellington at the time, their use remains rare in his work . . . . What must be borne in mind is the cheerfully unacademic nature of his whole approach to the large-scale work: just as his harmonies are perennially unorthodox, and his counterpoint no more classical than his touch at the piano, so the form of each movement seems to have been created spontaneously. Unlike certain other jazz "composers", Ellington was pre-eminently a composer who was also a "jazzman".'[17] The last sentence, like Schuller's comments above, fits perfectly into the overriding view of this book.

Following the train of thought expressed in some of the criticisms of Ellington's longer works, we may arrive at the view which says that jazz is a minor art, incapable of sustaining long compositions. Critic Dan Morgenstern has commented that 'jazz is an immensely concentrated music. Western – late western – assumptions about the superior value of large, complex and time-consuming structures in music gave jazz an inferiority complex. But no jazz composer – including Ellington himself – has yet created a "large" work of merit and stature comparable to the three-minute masterpieces of classic jazz.'[18] I would agree about the inferiority complex but, as Morgenstern's 'yet' implies, and I suggest below, there is a chronological reason for jazz's failure to create long works at that time.

There is another possibility: that Duke was incapable of writing 'a large work of merit and stature comparable to the three-minute masterpieces of classic jazz'. (*Be quiet. I'll let you in soon.*) While writing favourably on 'Reminiscing in Tempo', writer Max Harrison, an acute critical observer of jazz, has grave doubts about some of the later works. 'All too often when unable to extend a structure any further [Ellington] would simply invent something else. The new idea might be excellent, but it would be quite unconnected with what had gone before, and the results of this procedure might be called *not compositions but compilations*.'[19] (Italics added.)

This train of thought led Harrison to contemplate what might have happened if Ellington had given up his band. After citing works from Ornette Coleman, Charles Mingus and George Russell, he ends his essay thus: 'It is sadly ironic that, despite the ambition which drove him to bring forth such an enormous quantity of music, these peaks were scaled in locations remote from

the Ellington camp. Perhaps those who come after us will be able
to decide whether this was a judgement on one who might have
become one of our century's greatest composers but who instead
persisted in leading a band.'[20]

Like others before him, Harrison seems to equate long works
with compositional greatness. I would argue that regardless of his
longer works Ellington had already proved himself 'one of our
century's greatest composers'. Harrison also wishes that Ellington
had taken himself off to an ivory tower, rather than consistently
leading a band. Which rather misses the point of jazz. Jazz composers need their bands, need the band's performances of their
music. Not that we can do it as often as Duke did – if only – but
it's where we differ from other composers.

In connection with this, the British critic Ron Atkins raised
an interesting point when he said, 'The jazz ensemble as a kind of
family extension once seemed an admirable concept, though one
wonders whether it helps artistically in the end: the advantages of
friendship or personal commitment weighed against the need for
new blood to inspire new ideas. As the composer who uniquely
exploited individualism, Ellington should have been given the
chance to write for, say, Roland Kirk or Eric Dolphy.'[21] Wishful
thinking in the case of Ellington, but this is an aspect of jazz composing where contemporary composers can excel. Rarely having
access to a full-time band, they have the opportunity – if they care
to take it – to tailor their compositions to suit each specific group
of musicians they are working with.

There are undoubtedly reservations about Ellington's later
work, which, if we are talking about longer works in the accepted
sense, I would agree with. But before I open the door to the
Ellington police, who have been out there for some time trying
to break it down, I would propose that there are two other alternatives. The first is to say that jazz *at that time* was incapable of
creating long works in the accepted sense of the term. As critic
Kenneth Dommett, writing in *Music & Musicians* in 1967 said, 'Jazz
has not yet evolved a form capable of utilising its special qualities

coherently over an extended time scale. Until it does, ideas of 'the order of those which gave rise to *In the Beginning God* must inevitably come stunted to birth.'

'Utilising (jazz's) special qualities coherently over an extended time scale' is something that contemporary jazz composers have been concerned with for many years. This is something that, after short discussions on Ellington's competition and his co-composer, will be the main focus of the remainder of this book. But first I owe it to the Ellington police – *come in and make yourself comfortable* – to propose the second alternative. And to put Ellington into perspective.

The second alternative, as the quotes from Schuller and Priestley/Cohen show, is that one can think of the longer works in a different way. They are the work of a *jazz* composer, one who had unacademic views on everything and who, helped immeasurably by his musicians, was concerned, not with what was on the paper, but with how it turned out in *performance*. Schuller warns about taking Johnny Hodges' contribution for granted, and Priestley and Cohen make the point that 'the form of each movement seems to have been created spontaneously'. One could argue that the form of an overall Ellington suite, with pieces borrowed from elsewhere, things radically changed in rehearsal, pieces discarded, other sections added later, was also 'created spontaneously'. As I will propose below, this is one, very 'jazz' way of looking at longer works. Remember the comment from above: 'Duke simply thought of a better way of doing the same thing after he wrote the music, so he changed it.'

Having made that effort to mollify the Ellington police I now intend to undo most of that with some other observations. Ellington wasn't God. He wasn't perfect. Everything he wrote was not of the same high standard as his best work. To pretend otherwise does him a disservice. (I remember a student commenting, after a lecture that elaborated on some of these points, that it was good to hear someone who wasn't afraid of criticising Ellington. The lecture had been given by James Lincoln Collier, a friend and near namesake but no relation, who has been harassed by the Ellington police more times than most of us have played 'Satin Doll'. The Marsalis police have him in their sights, too, as we shall see in DEEPENING THE GAME.)

Like all of us, Ellington was caught in his time. Which was a time before *Kind of Blue*, before Ornette Coleman, before the jazz language changed. He was, of course, around when these changes happened, but was too old perhaps, too set in his ways perhaps, to really absorb them, even though, as we shall see in *INFINITE POSSIBILITIES*, he foresaw many of them. He was, in compositions such as 'Cotton Tail', way ahead of the pack in showing where the big band was going. In much of his work he achieved heights, in sheer variety of texture and effective use of his soloists, which have still rarely been surpassed. And he started to show some developmental ideas for longer *jazz* works that were to become of great importance.

Certainly, he wanted to do more. But he wanted to do things before jazz was capable of doing them. In a nutshell, and *please leave now, you know where the door is*, he saw more than anyone – except Jelly Roll Morton perhaps – what the real potential of jazz was.

THE COMPETITION

Ferdinand Joseph 'Jelly Roll' Morton (1890–1941) was the self proclaimed 'inventor of jazz' and the first real jazz composer. He wrote some of the best known early jazz tunes, among them 'King Porter Stomp', 'Milenburg Joys' and 'Wild Man Blues'. He also had views on the music that were ahead of their time, some of which have yet to be assimilated. 'Not until 1926 did they get a faint idea of real jazz, when I decided to live in New York . . . . New York's idea of jazz was taken from the dictionary's definition – loud, blary, noise, discordant tones, et cetera, which really doesn't spell jazz music.'[22]

Morton also drew an interesting distinction between ragtime, then very current, and jazz, which was just emerging. 'Ragtime is a certain type of syncopation and only certain tunes can be played in that idea. But jazz is a style which can be applied to any type of tune.'[23] That 'jazz is a style which can be applied to any type of tune' is a sentiment with which I fully agree – as long as we don't specify 'style' too closely. It sums up one of the messages of this book: that a jazz composition can be made out of anything.

Interestingly, what jazz compositions are rarely made out of today are structures as complex as Morton's were all that time ago. Showing their debt to ragtime they were, like 'King Porter Stomp', my *classic arrangement* in WHO DOES WHAT WHEN, 'multi-thematic structures which embodied . . . a definite detailed compositional conception, which had to be retained in performance to a much greater extent than is usually required in jazz.'[24]

As critic Martin Williams said in relation to 'King Porter Stomp', 'we can see a direct and clearly identifiable influence of Morton's work on jazz. In the variations on the trio, we hear figures which are typical of Morton, which Henderson's arrangement used and passed to Goodman – a kind of scoring for brass . . . which set a pattern used by everyone during the "swing" period (even Ellington: hear 'Bojangles' for the clearest instance). And one can hear it still in the arrangements of Ernie Wilkins, Quincy Jones – and everyone who writes big-band jazz scores.'[25]

Morton's orchestral style owed much to New Orleans collectivism, but his compositions and ideas were the opposite of the polyphonic style of that period. The improvised sections in his compositions were well planned, not solely improvisations over a chord progression as became the norm. As Schuller says they 'provided a whole new sense of continuity, and a formal conception . . . with several strains combining into larger complete ideas . . . . It was, moreover, an innovation only a composer, thinking in larger structural terms, would make.'[26]

Given all this, it is perhaps surprising that Duke Ellington was not one of Morton's supporters, but it seems that there was a history of antagonism between the two men. With talk of lawsuits from Morton – about Duke's penchant for 'borrowing', of all things! – and denigrating remarks from Ellington about Morton's prowess on the piano, one can see that there was a problem. Additionally, Morton was, of course, well established when Duke's career started, and they were both, perhaps, too much engaged in trying to find solutions to some of the same problems, to fully appreciate each other's work. (I have felt this about some of my worthier contemporaries. For some of the less worthy I usually snarl something along the lines of 'I've thrown away better ideas than that' and put some Ellington in the CD tray.)

Whether Ellington liked Jelly Roll or not is immaterial. Morton made his mark, and although his work is not as much appreciated as it should be, his reputation is established. As Martin Williams says, 'the real challenge that Morton's work represents is not a result of Morton the composer, the orchestrator, the theorist, the formalist; it is the fact that in him jazz, by the mid-1920s, had produced an artist.'[27]

THE CO-COMPOSER

Ellington called Strayhorn 'Swee' Pea' (for his resemblance to Popeye's baby) and offered a characteristic response to those who called him his alter ego: 'Let's not go overboard. Pea is only my right arm, left foot, eyes, stomach, ears, and soul, not my ego.' [28]

The collaborative way that Ellington and Billy Strayhorn (1915–67) worked together is the subject of many stories and anecdotes of late night discussions, themes played down telephone lines, similar ideas being thought up a continent apart and so on. This has led to much confusion although Strayhorn himself said that he could not understand why: 'my playing and writing style is totally different'.

There are differences, of course, but the confusion continues to linger. Much has been cleared up in Dutch jazz researcher Walter van de Leur's excellent, very analytical, highly musical book on Strayhorn's work, in which he looks at original manuscript in both composers' hands to address the issue. He sums up the situation thus: 'The Ellington–Strayhorn team consisted of two different composers, who not so much co-wrote music but rather functioned as each other's sound-board and source of inspiration . . . the distinctions between their oeuvres can be found in a number of characteristics, such as in the musical "fingerprints". The most distinctive facet is the two composers' individual approach to musical form.'[29]

The confusion surrounding who wrote what has been somewhat exacerbated by some of their working methods. The annotations on the lead sheet of 'Pretty Girl'/'Star-Crossed Lovers' were mentioned above. As was the instruction by Duke that, to save time, Strayhorn should 'steal from himself'. There is another story that when he and Ellington needed a theme for a commission from Orson Welles, Strayhorn went up to his hotel room, rummaged in a drawer and came down brandishing some manuscript paper saying, 'Will this do?' And it probably did, because like 'Star-Crossed Lovers', it could be made to fit by a title change, and by the special magic that Strayhorn and Ellington possessed.

That magic produced a lot of good music, some of which has been covered above. What we should be concerned with here are Strayhorn's strengths as a composer in his own right, and they are considerable. He did after all write 'Take the 'A' Train' one of the most popular melodies in jazz, as well as other great tunes such as 'Chelsea Bridge', 'Something to Live For' (Ella Fitzgerald's favourite song, apparently), and the amazing 'Lush Life', the tune and lyrics for which he wrote when he was only twenty-one. His last composition, 'Blood Count', one of the most beautiful tunes I have ever heard, is my *classic Ellington performance* below.

Part of Strayhorn's role with Ellington was as staff arranger. He arranged many of Ellington's own tunes, standard songs and several of his own for different versions of the band, different singers, different occasions. He contributed to many of

Ellington's miniatures as an arranger, and wrote many of his own, 'Rain Check', 'After All' and 'Daydream' among them. One of my personal favourites is the aptly titled 'The Intimacy of the Blues', one of his last compositions. Very simple, very 'Ellington'. The leader is said by van de Leur to have added three sections to Strayhorn's score, then deleted them, leaving the piece in its original, perfect, form. Like Ellington's, Strayhorn's miniatures are small masterpieces showing an immense variety of textural colour, harmony and melody.

Ellington was, unsurprisingly, strongly affected by Strayhorn's death at the age of fifty-one, and a few months later he recorded a tribute album, *And His Mother Called Him Bill*. Fittingly, all the tunes were Strayhorn's music and it is, to my ears, one of the better late Ellington albums. (*Oh, hello. Are you still here?*)

There was a charming story in the original liner notes of how Ellington, bereft, sat at the piano as the band were packing up after the session, playing a solo version of Strayhorn's beautiful 'Lotus Blossom'. The tape was still running and, as Ellington played, the band stopped talking and gathered round to listen. My high regard for both men was touched by this, until my cynicism (a jazz musician's prerogative, remember) stepped in and asked how many times I had been in a studio where the engineers left the tape running after a session was over. The gaff was well and truly blown when, on the CD reissue of the album, an *alternate take* of 'Lotus Blossom' appeared (played by Harry Carney, accompanied by bass and piano instead of Duke alone). The story has gone down in legend. It is reported with a straight face by Strayhorn's biographer, David Hajdu, and one writer even complains of the changed running order of the CD spoiling the moment! Undoubtedly it was a publicist – 'never letting the truth stand in the way of a good story', as a musician colleague used to say – stepping in to dress up something that didn't need any dressing up. But no matter. The performance – and that of 'Blood Count' from the same album – is still moving enough to make me, as Ellington said about Bubber Miley's playing, weep 'great, big ole tears'.

THE CLASSIC ELLINGTON PERFORMANCE

'Blood Count' from And His Mother Called Him Bill (RCA Bluebird).

Not written by Ellington, not, as far as I know, arranged by Ellington, but a wonderful example of jazz composition at its best. Which means showing Ellington's influence in one way or another.

'Blood Count' was written in hospital by Strayhorn when he was dying, which accounts for the black humour of the title. In essence, the arrangement, probably at least suggested by Strayhorn, is another of his gorgeous ballads featuring Johnny Hodges, but this time instead of his usual languorous approach, we hear pain and aggression. The way the band play the piece is perfect – the background chords at one point seem to stalk the melody in a very macabre way. The whole is a fitting tribute to Strayhorn and the genius of Ellington and of his band. As Gary Giddins points out, 'Jazz is no less collaborative than cinema, and credit for the perfection of 'Blood Count' can be passed around to the writer (Strayhorn), the director (Ellington), and the star (Hodges).'[30] The band and Hodges never played the piece again, but there are great recordings by Mark Murphy – with some moving lyrics added by M.B. Stillman – on Kerouac, Then and Now (Muse), and by Stan Getz on Anniversary! (Emarcy/Verve).

MORE ON STRAYHORN

Walter van de Leur Something to Live For, The Music of Billy Strayhorn, a highly musical and analytical look at Strayhorn's work. An indispensable supplement to any study of Ellington's music.

David Hajdu *Lush Life, a biography of Billy Strayhorn*, a well written, generally non-analytical, look at Strayhorn's life.

MORE ON JELLY ROLL

Jelly Roll Morton: *The Complete Library of Congress Recordings*, (Rounder Records, 2005). A seven CD set of the famous 1938 recordings, including Alan Lomax's biography, *Mister Jelly Roll*, plus a new eighty-page book with many rare photographs.

Two essays on Morton worth reading are Martin Williams' in *Jazz*, edited by Hentoff and McCarthy, and Gunther Schuller's 'The First Great Jazz Composer' in *Early Jazz*.

FOR MORE ON ELLINGTON see the recommendations at the end of the previous chapter.

PART THREE

REDISCOVERING

THE POTENTIAL

7

WHY WOULD WE WANT TO REPEAT IT?

THE JAZZ MUSEUM

dedicated to Keith Nichols

If there is one musician who proves that there is no such thing as a limiting, straightjacketed jazz tradition, it is Ellington, which makes it so ironic that he is such a hero to the neoclassicists.[1]

According to Marsalis, jazz went crazy in the 1960s for the same reason the rest of the world did: no one was tough enough, dedicated enough, man enough, to live up to responsibilities. Although it's difficult to fault Marsalis as a trumpeter or bandleader, I sometimes wonder what it says about this era in jazz that so resolutely conservative a young musician has become its cynosure.[2]

Tradition is the handing on of fire and not the worship of ashes.[3]

Those quotes go some way to summing up the problem of the jazz museum. Musicians, fans and critics do want to repeat the past, and Wynton Marsalis came along at the right time to help them do it. But in doing so they demonstrate the aptness of this delicious phrase from author Eric Nisenson: 'Playing music that has been thoroughly explored decades in the past is like rediscovering New Jersey.'[4] They also forget what jazz is about, for which there is little excuse. As we saw in the last two chapters, Ellington was there to show us the way. To quote Nisenson again '[Ellington] understood *the nature of the music* better than anyone, until, arguably, Miles Davis.'[5] (Italics added*)*

As Ellington and Miles knew, the nature of the music is in the way it allows individuals to express themselves. But in much of jazz this has been forgotten, and there's no doubt that for many years we have been surrounded by music masquerading as jazz. Music that attempts to recreate, relive, the past in various ways.

PRESERVING THE SOUNDS

Music is preserved in various ways. In the mind of course – my memories of seeing Duke Ellington, Charles Mingus and Miles Davis in concert are still very strong, even though the events were many years ago.

Music is also preserved in recordings, which can be said to give a permanent feel to something that, by my definition, was only meant to happen in real time once. But would we want to be without our recordings of Louis Armstrong, Duke Ellington, Miles Davis? In fact, as I argued earlier, there is a case to be made that the performances on jazz recordings such as Armstrong's 'West End Blues', Ellington's 'Ko-Ko', Miles' and Gil Evans' 'Summertime', have produced exemplary jazz *compositions*. Jazz compositions that blend what's written with what's improvised, and which, because of the individual identities involved in the performance, cannot be played in the same way by anyone else.

This stance could be said to dismiss the efforts of most repertory bands and tribute performances. This is something that, with only a few exceptions, I am happy to do. One only has to think of the Lincoln Center Jazz Orchestra's 'recreation' of John Coltrane's *A Love Supreme* to see how absurd some of these 'tributes' are. The original was a collection of fairly minimal themes by Coltrane, transformed into an amazing *performance* by the improvisations and interactions of Coltrane and his quartet. To even think that this could be translated into another genre – that of the big band, which is almost always guaranteed to lack any of the jazz capabilities of Coltrane's original group and concept – shows a degree of condescension and a devastating lack of awareness which, I am afraid, typifies Marsalis. As the critic Kenny Mathieson said: 'It just seems a pointless exercise . . . to paraphrase another of Wynton's heroes, for me this is not only a case of well you needn't, but no you shouldn't.'[6]

If there needs to be a jazz canon, a list of master works comparable perhaps to those of Bach, Beethoven and Brahms, then it has to exist, can only exist, in its performances. Of which Coltrane's *A Love Supreme* would be one. For those of us not lucky enough to have heard the piece at its only live performance, at a French jazz festival in July 1965, we have to rely on the recording.

In other words, preserving the jazz canon, stocking the jazz museum, means remembering that a composition such as *A Love Supreme* is complete in itself. Any subsequent performance has to start, not from the premise of a canonic piece that needs to be reverently preserved – it already has been, on record – but from the premise that something new can be made from it. Something that, while paying tribute to the original, changes it in some meaningful way. One could suggest the Fletcher Henderson reworking of Jelly Roll Morton's 'King Porter Stomp' for Benny Goodman, and Gil Evans' later reworking of the same tune, included in the aptly titled album *New Bottle Old Wine*.

But what if a band *does* want to repeat it? To play either of those versions of King Porter Stomp, the Evans/Davis 'Summertime', Duke's 'Ko-Ko', or Louis' 'West End Blues'? The first problem might be to get hold of the written music, the second – well, I'll come to that later.

Critic Bill Mathieu once wrote in *Down Beat* that the Gil Evans arrangements for *Sketches of Spain* 'should be preserved under glass in a Florentine museum', and one could say the same for the all the music I've mentioned. Unfortunately, in many cases preserving jazz scores in a Florentine museum, or even just a library, could well be wishful thinking. As we have seen, Ellington's way of working, especially in his earlier days, meant that notes were allocated and possibly changed again and again in rehearsal; the Basie band's head arrangements were made up on the bandstand and memorised; Gil Evans' starting point for a long composition late in his career was, as we have seen, a scrap of paper produced from his back pocket. These examples reflect the different approach a jazz composer has to his music manuscript, compared to that of a classical composer.

Even when jazz does start from predominantly written music, a lot may be left to the performance itself. Allied to this, a full score may never have been written, a change in personnel may have meant some radical alterations, parts may have been memorised, the original may well have been lost or damaged while the band was on tour. All this in contrast to the classical world where scores, and the parts for each player, are usually meticulously prepared, and then preserved by orchestral librarians and publishers.

However, help in preserving the written music has been at hand throughout jazz's history. Collections of music by Ellington, Strayhorn, Mingus, and other composers have been published or have become available for study and research. Some of these scores have been recreated from the original parts with an expert ear transcribing those that were unclear or missing. Others will have been built up from scratch – often scratchy old records. But, as Walter van de Leur says in his book on Billy Strayhorn, 'the challenges in transcribing big band jazz are daunting . . . attempts to transcribe Ellington's and Strayhorn's music, full of unorthodox voicings and unexpected instrumental combinations, all too often do not accurately render what was actually played, as some examples of published transcriptions over the past years have shown.'[7]

Some musicians, like my dedicatee Keith Nichols, and others such as Andrew Homzy and David Berger, have spent a large part of their lives making classic jazz music, accurately transcribed, available in a written form for performance and publication. But this raises the question – why would they want to spend their time 'rediscovering New Jersey' by playing and transcribing old music? Why, as good jazz musicians themselves, would they not subscribe to the Miles Davis philosophy: 'Why do you want me to do that again? Didn't I do it good the first time?'[8]

Respect and love for a particular style of music would seem to be a good enough reason. But it brings up the problem of why jazz should be preserved in this way. If jazz is accepted as something creative, something that exists as an expression of the individualism of the musicians concerned, then, apart from our memories and the recordings, why would we want to preserve it in a replicable form? The obvious reasons would be that people want to study it and play it. But this again begs the question why.

Jazz does not have the historical background of classical music where the availability of scores from Beethoven to Bartók and beyond is taken as a given. Orchestras need the written music for performance (although, for some pieces, one could ask 'why so often?'). Performers can, while listening to recordings, study the scores to learn about form, orchestration, voicings, and how the composition is interpreted differently by various musicians. This is good preparation for a career spent honing interpretations of somebody else's music. But the demands of jazz are different.

One could argue that jazz practice needs to include some experience of playing music such as the various versions of 'King Porter Stomp', or of trying to get as near perfect a copy of New Orleans music as can be managed. I would agree with this to some extent, and indeed strongly support it in terms of jazz education. Indeed, the almost total exclusion of early jazz is one of the disturbing factors of the current jazz education culture, which concentrates on swing era big bands, and the bebop style and language. I made an attempt to point this out in the Churchill Report on jazz education in America and my book *Interaction, Opening up the Jazz Ensemble* was an attempt to do something about it. A review in the IAJE's *Jazz Education Journal* said that the book 'holds the promise of liberating the music and our classrooms like nothing I have encountered in print'.

If the situation has changed in recent years, I'm not aware of it, nor am I intending to take credit for it – well, perhaps just a little. But I doubt it has changed. The attitudes of many jazz educators are irreversibly locked into the bebop box. (Far too many if one stops to think about the real meaning of their job title.)*

Critic Clement Greenberg, speaking of painting, made the following comment which has a great relevance to matters of preservation and jazz education. '[This] state of affairs has usually resolved itself into . . . an academicism in which the really important issues are left untouched because they involve controversy, and in which creative activity dwindles to virtuosity in the small details of form, all larger questions being decided by the precedent of the old masters.'[9]

Although one can see that knowledge of all forms of jazz will be useful to a musician, what is disturbing today is that pressure from the market, pressure from the need to 'woo' audiences, has led to an ever increasing number of repertory and tribute bands. As *New York Times* critic Ben Ratliff said, 'When I talk to nonjazz friends about what I'm going to see and hear, they don't quite get the emphasis on tributes and reworkings of. They feel rightly suspicious that a purportedly living art form should have so much abiding interest in its glorious past.'[10] What Ratliff doesn't get around to mentioning is the associated problem of musicians taking a limited snapshot of what went before and passing it off as their own. This traduces the word jazz even more, and is something that is dealt with below in *preserving the style*.

---

* I should add that one of the few places where I would praise Wynton Marsalis and his Lincoln Center organisation, is in their efforts to make Ellington scores, accurately transcribed by David Berger, available to school bands around the world. This makes accessible, at the level it is most needed, music that the students would not otherwise be exposed to, and there can be no argument with that. However, if I had my way, I would add these words of Eric Nisenson to all the parts on a cautionary sticker: 'If there is one musician who proves that there is no such thing as a limiting, straightjacketed jazz tradition, it is Ellington.'

The main argument against repertory bands, an almost overriding one, is that the music they play existed at a particular time and place, played by a particular set of musicians, using a particular set of instruments. Although there are exceptions that parallel the urge of early classical music groups to use only authentic period instruments, repertory bands are often happy to use, for example, contemporary drum sets and high-powered amplification when playing music written many years before these came into use.

In contrast to this, there are some repertory bands which insist that, as well as the original music, the original solos be recreated. Although this avoids the problem of solos being out of context, it raises two more areas of concern. As we have seen, notating what a jazz soloist does is almost impossible, although an approximation can be made, with the new soloist learning the nuances from the recording. But this still leaves the unavoidable problem – that this is a different person, playing the music at a different time. Not surprisingly, Duke Ellington's music is a favourite with repertory bands but, as we have stressed above, his music was written for a particular set of musicians in a way that few other writers have been able to emulate. How can that be repeatable?

The feeling that there is a canon of jazz music that should be played constantly has come from the need, in some people's eyes, for jazz to be considered in the same way as classical music. Discussing repertory groups, one jazz critic was in favour of 'groups that strictly recreate the old *as if it were Mozart and Haydn*, which is indeed a worthwhile pursuit'.[11] (Italics added.)

Resisting the temptation to scream 'but it's not Mozart or Haydn, it's jazz' into the afternoon quiet, one must admit that the practice of establishing such a canon is now expanding at a considerable rate. Bands – and at times orchestras – now give concerts recreating Basie, Ellington, Paul Whiteman, as well as such one-off masterpieces as the Gil Evans re-compositions of the music from *Porgy and Bess*. Virtually every notable jazz group through history seems to have been given this kind of 'tribute'. Sometimes it works but, as the Lincoln Center Jazz Orchestra's *A Love*

Supreme shows, there are problems in developing a museum culture in a music that exists in its specific performances.

I am not, of course, suggesting that Coltrane's music should not be played, or that other musicians should not do try to do something different with it. But there's the rub. Something has to be done with it, as Gil Evans and Miles did with the music from *Porgy and Bess*. Something that makes the piece live for the players involved. Not just exist as a pale reflection of an event that was once luminescent.

Critic Max Harrison raised another angle on jazz's past, saying 'jazz has been in too much of a hurry, rushing through its resources, failing properly to explore avenues of potential major growth'.[12] One could cite the stark explorations of standards, taken up and then dropped by Miles Davis in the mid-1960s; the attempts to bring the music of Herbie Nichols into focus and so on. All laudable and, as long as something is done to make them live for today, I can see no possible objection. What I do object to is the slavish attempt to recreate something that's gone.

Some would argue that works such as the Gil Evans version of *Porgy and Bess* deserve to be preserved and recreated, that they are the equivalent of a Beethoven symphony. I wouldn't disagree, except to say that, unlike a Beethoven symphony, *Porgy and Bess* has had its definitive performance. Which was the one that featured the man it was written for, Miles Davis, conducted and supervised by the man who arranged it, Gil Evans. There may well be things that could have been improved (and certainly are in the recording), but in jazz it's the performance that matters, and in jazz it's the performance that is unique. To return to the title of this chapter – but remembering my caveat about jazz education – 'why would we want to repeat it?'

Perhaps I'm being too hard. Perhaps some jazz needs to be performed in the same way to a possibly new audience. I say 'possibly new' because, in many cases, such recreations are aimed at the nostalgia crowd, who, if they do leave their record players' performances of what they know well, want to hear a more-or-less exact present day recreation of it. They then think they are hearing jazz. Or perhaps just being entertained, which is not always the same thing.

I have, of course, no objections to audiences *per se* – or being entertained – and can recognise the argument that such tributes may, in the words of one writer, provide an epiphany for someone new to the music. But I have difficulty in accepting the increasing number of repertory bands and tribute bands that are beginning to dominate today's jazz scene.

What *could* be done with repertory bands was succinctly expressed when critic Francis Davis suggested that the American Jazz Orchestra, formed in 1986 as a repertory band by critic Gary Giddins, with John Lewis as its musical director, should put 'an emphasis on composition that would make the goal a workable one of *reinterpreting* (for example) Duke Ellington's written scores, not the hopeless one of replicating his orchestra and soloists'.[13] (Italics added.) Davis cited a performance of Ellington's 'Harlem', which guest conductor Maurice Peress 'brought back to life in a manner that sidestepped comparisons to the original'. He continued 'Think of such masterpieces and near misses as Ellington's 'Reminiscing in Tempo' and 'The Three Black Kings', Mingus' 'Half Mast Inhibition' and 'Don't be Afraid, the Clown's Afraid Too' . . . . Then you have an inkling of what this repertory orchestra's proper repertory should be.'[14]

Davis' suggestion was made in 1986 and still hasn't been taken up by any band I know of. What we do have are more and more trips down memory lane. One recent festival I attended had tributes to so many past musicians that I despaired of hearing anything new. 'The idea is that reevaluating old minds should stimulate new minds. But I don't see it happening nearly as much as it should. What I do see, for sure, is the use of old, familiar names selling tickets and propping up an ailing jazz business.'[15]

Ailing the jazz business may be, though, as we will see below, there is much good music still being created by musicians who see jazz as a living art, as a music that should be appreciated for what is happening now. This is a view that I share, and one that has, without doubt, affected my income. It has also affected my stance on the next section *preserving the style.*

§ *Early in the 1990s I was asked to take part in a festival at the Barbican in London celebrating British jazz of the sixties. The organisers wanted me to play my old arrangements with as many of my old musicians as I could gather together. Apart from the fact that I've changed, my music has changed, and that I am not interested in recreating the past, the musicians have changed also. One has even become a millionaire by making symphonic suites out of the many advertising jingles he has written. Good luck to him, but I wouldn't ask him to be in a present day band of mine, let alone be part of a recreation exercise. A good time was had by those who did take the shilling, but I was glad to be out of it.*

I should add that this stance has not stopped me relishing the fact that records I made thirty or forty years ago are now being reissued and have, once more, been well received. These are records of performances – *live and in the studio – at that time, and as such are part of my development.*

However, as Miles said, 'I don't want you to like me because of Kind of Blue. *Like me for what we're doing now'.*[16] *As my long-time drummer John Marshall commented, these reissues 'are all very well. But we're still making music, and one hopes we've got better at it. Why aren't people interested in that?'*

To which my ever-present cynicism responded 'They'll catch up. We just have to wait another thirty or forty years . . . .'

PRESERVING THE STYLE

If there are arguments against preserving older jazz by means of tributes and repertoire bands, then the same arguments undoubtedly apply when discussing preservation of the style. I have written elsewhere about the stranglehold the bebop language has on much of today's jazz and, in that the compositions and arrangements are as derivative as the soloing language, this aspect of preserving the style has been dealt with. What concerns me here are the musicians who 'take a limited snapshot of what went before and pass it off as their own'.

Although this does happen in small groups, in terms of jazz composition the main offenders by far are those who continue to write and perform big band music in the style which, as we saw in WHO DOES WHAT WHEN, was first developed in the 1930s by writers such as Don Redman and Sy Oliver. That source, as we also saw, has been absorbed and modernised, and the focus of attention – and imitation – is now on two 'newer' styles: the Count Basie band of the 1950s and 1960s, and the long-lived Thad Jones–Mel Lewis band, now metamorphosed into the Vanguard Jazz Orchestra, the Monday night house band at the Village Vanguard.

I have nothing against these original sources – well, perhaps I get bored too easily by the Thad Jones–Mel Lewis band – but a lot of ink has passed across jazz writers' manuscripts since those days, most of it directed at preserving, and only mildly updating, the style pioneered by Redman. Among the changes are that the arrangements usually last longer – certainly seem to – because more time is available on records than there was in the past. Most often, the additional time is filled with more, or longer, solos, and more padding in the written parts, rather than with meaningful development. The tempos may well be faster, a move away from the swing-era dance bands, but this has easily led to a macho-fuelled louder, higher, faster, ethos where subtlety is lost.

Such arrangers are working within a very tight period of time and stylistic effect. What one hears in the arrangements and the soloing, is drawn from the swing era plus some additions from the bebop, and hard bop periods. A time-span of thirty years at most – and one which ended more than forty years ago. These writers seem most interested in homogeneity of sound, of approach, and of language, rather than mining the individuality of the musicians as Ellington did, finding new tonal palettes as Gil Evans did, exploring new avenues of composition as Charles Mingus did.

Some parts of the language *have* changed. Certainly harmonies and voicings are more complex, some different instruments are used, and cross-section voicings, following Ellington's example, are sometimes present. Even in these cases, though, the language is restrictive. Pleasant enough at times but still rooted in a group of musicians moving around together. One has only to compare these arrangements with what writers such as Gil Evans and Gerry Mulligan have done, let alone classical composers, to realise just how limited the orchestral and harmonic range usually is. These are matters we will come back to in DON'T BE AFRAID . . . .

Admittedly, some traces of newer possibilities do pop up at times but, generally, seem to be put there in an attempt to be trendy. Some scores even have sections of collective improvising, but tellingly they are usually very short, perhaps only three or four bars. I remember seeing one instruction that said 'Everybody play a solo in any key', a request which is not only illiterate, it's impossible. To make matters worse, it's gone before it can have any effect and, crucially, is usually played with such a lack of conviction and integration, that it only serves to show how pointless the idea was in the first place.

Many of the arrangements written in this style are written for publication. By definition, for anonymous bands. The personal connection between writer and musician is lost, and one gets the sense that the arrangers are not trying to use individual talents – how could they when they are unknown to the writer? – but are more concerned with impressing the musicians, who, in their turn, are trying to get a 'perfect performance' of an often complex piece.

The concept of striving for a perfect performance fits strangely with my idea of jazz. For me, the music's strength is that risks are taken, new things are tried. How can one expect this to result in perfection? A great performance perhaps, but rarely, if ever, perfection. But, of course, the idea of perfection is bound up with achieving as exact a rendition as possible of something that is written down. Which comes from the ethos of classical music rather than jazz.

Again, maybe I am being too black and white, but I am reminded of a comment made to me by one of the older foot soldiers (the non-improvising players) in a radio band. 'With X [a well known conductor] we have to concentrate on getting every note played exactly right, in intonation, in inflexion, in everything. With you, we have to remember instructions and play the notes freely, not as they are written . . . and that can be difficult.' The riposte from the band's pianist, a younger player, was perhaps cruel, but certainly apt: 'Your trouble is that normally you don't have to think.'

Following this line of thought further, it's interesting that most of the books about jazz composing are concerned with arranging, and, more specifically, with the minutiae of harmony and voicings. They are, in the main, based on practices that preserve the style I have been discussing, rather than suggesting that something different can be done with it. More crucially, they fail to address the issue of improvising, and how it fits into the arrangement or composition. There is an unwillingness to address the very issue that makes the music what it is.

It seems that there is a specific genre called big band music, which has been taken over by what we could call 'style preservation'. Contemporary big band records are highly praised, with few if any noticing that what they are hearing has been done many times before. Dave Holland's big band is the flavour of the month as I write (that is if we ignore Maria Schneider's, of which more later). Only one critic that I've seen drew attention to the resemblance between Holland's music and that of other bands such as Quincy Jones, Don Ellis and Buddy Rich. Everyone else seems to behave as if the very fact of having a big band is enough. Perhaps it is, but we should not be living in a time warp. We should remember the past, not repeat it.

The result of all this is the continuing plethora of music that could have been written any time in the last fifty or so years. What, to borrow Gil Evans' phrase about dance bands, we could call 'formaldehyde bands', playing music which I have variously called grey music or yard music. Grey because there is little life or colour to it, yard music because there are usually yards and yards of it going nowhere. In a phrase, a stale outdated style which lacks depth.

But there's no denying it is popular. Audiences like it because it's not challenging, it is based on something familiar, and has a surface excitement. Big band musicians like it because it raises the adrenaline with its technical challenges. Critics like it because they have a benchmark of familiarity against which it can be measured. And there is a market for such music in college big bands and elsewhere. Statistics gathered some years ago show that arrangements of TV theme tunes far outsold some of the better grey music available, and that they in turn far outsold transcribed material from such as Ellington. In jazz as art terms this is a serious matter. The potential of jazz – and its heritage – is being neglected to feed a seemingly insatiable market, but a market where there is more than enough material already available. Does the world need another pseudo classic jazz chart? In my world no, but others may wish to differ.

All this is part of the museum culture which is present in far too much of today's jazz scene. But what grates, is the perception that this kind of music, and those involved in it, are at the cutting edge. The introductory quote from the *Jazz Education Journal* referred to Toshiko Akiyoshi, Sammy Nestico, Bob Florence, Maria Schneider and Jim McNeeley as 'those who (within the last twenty-five or so years) have extended the idiom of big band composition'. These musicians are the very visible core of a group of big band writers who supply music for publishers to sell to college and high school bands. The purchase of such material is undoubtedly driven by director approval and audience acclaim, even, though one hates to admit it, by the needs of the players to express themselves by playing louder, higher, faster. One could well argue that this *is* the way in which 'the idiom of big band composition has been extended within the last twenty-five years'. If that's true, then heaven help us.

The fact that the writers cited are, in the main, using a style of writing that had its genesis so many years ago is a sign of, shall we say, narrowness of vision (although it may well lead to broadness of bank account). It is also a pale copy of, and undermines, the work of the classic big band writers such as Don Redman and Sy Oliver. Their charts are worth preserving and playing, but they need to be played alongside arrangements that show as much originality, as much imagination.

These words, from an anonymous speaker from the floor at an IAJE panel in the 1990s on big band writing, underline the problem. 'I'm depressed about the music that's being played . . . it all sounds the same . . . . There's no dramatic development in these mediocre charts, no "unique character". Students aren't dumb. Good repertoire needs to be promoted by somebody who is excited by it.'

There is, of course, imagination and originality in some of the writers named. Schneider and Akiyoshi are more interested in form, and both use more colour in their choice of instrumental voicings. This could be a reflection of the fact that they are women. But I would prefer to regard them as *aware musicians* – who could be of any sex – reacting against the unnecessarily macho-fuelled aspects of much big band jazz.

It could be said that I am exaggerating the importance of that one quote about 'those who have extended the idiom of big band composition', but the distressing fact is that it is typical of the high praise given to the arrangers named. Rather than 'extending the idiom of big band composition' one can make the case that those mentioned (and I would add Bob Mintzer to the list) have so skewed the genre that they are responsible, separately and together, for the sheer *dullness* of most big bands today. There is overwriting in all senses. There are lots and lots of notes, with little or no space around them; the section voicings are generally undiluted, and the sounds are brassy in the cheapest sense of the word; backings for the soloists are very full, and usually ignored, possibly because the soloist can't do anything else with them. There's no life to the arrangements, they're arid and cold and very mannered. It's all superficial, there's no depth, nothing that says there are real people playing. In other words, the very antithesis of jazz.

There is one curious omission from the composers mentioned in that list, Bob Brookmeyer. He is usually talked of in the same breath as McNeeley and Schneider, and it may be that his omission is the exception that proves the rule. He has been more imaginative in his concepts, much more so than any of the others except, possibly, for some of Maria Schneider's work, and he has moved away from the traditional route in many of his arrangements.

However, Brookmeyer's work is, for me, somewhat clinical. As a composer friend of mine said 'his music has no smell to it', and we both find it lacking in what Duke called 'a little dirt'. Some of this would seem to be down to the mindset of a classical composer manqué, as expressed in this comment, very strange coming from a jazz composer, which will be discussed further below: 'You don't write in a solo until you've completely exhausted what you have to say.'[17]

The writers discussed are successful, for sure, but part of the message of this book is to ask whether that kind of market-led success is important unless there is some art attached. If one compares, for example, the three pieces I mentioned earlier – Armstrong's 'West End Blues', Ellington's 'Ko-Ko', Miles' and Gil's 'Summertime' – with any of the work of those named above, one sees a difference in musical quality so vast as to be seemingly insurmountable. And let's not bring in comparison with, say, Charles Ives' *The Unanswered Question.* (Which, to forestall comment, I would put any of the three pieces I mentioned up against. All four are interesting compositions, with life, with originality, with humanity.)

But there are jazz writers who could stand this comparison, who do realise the importance of their soloists, and whose music has that necessary dirt. Their music, while still very accessible is, I would warrant, unknown to most if not all big band musicians and directors. I am speaking of bands such as Mark Harvey's Aardvark Orchestra in Cambridge, Massachusetts, The Paul Cram Orchestra in Halifax, Nova Scotia, Roberto Bonati's ParmaFrontiere Orchestra and Geir Lysne's Listening Band in Oslo. Their music demonstrates a different language, a much more contemporary language, a much more *individual* language, than that used by Schneider, Brookmeyer or McNeeley, whose music is so firmly rooted in the past.

Those who I've named above, and many others, still retain elements of the style we have been discussing, and recognise the importance of Ellington, and of *The Atomic Mr. Basie*. But they also recognise that something very important happened fifty or so years ago, and in their music one hears new ideas and sounds, and a recognition that the avant-garde exists. All facets that serve to make their compositions fresh and exciting. In a word – interesting. Like Duke.

PRESERVING THE WORD

Jazz is Negro music. It has a tempo that's been handed down for a generation. It's easy and it rocks. There's no need to blow hard. Relax. Close your eyes and improvise melodies of beauty.[18]

Jazz is a terrible word. In fact, I'm not even sure what's meant by the word. We are now beyond jazz; as the original masters pass on, all we're left with is copies of the original.[19]

I'm not sure if anyone has ever defined it and that's because it doesn't exist unless it's happening.[20]

As these examples show, there have been countless attempts to define jazz, and some effort has been made to find new ways of naming it. Rahsaan Roland Kirk called it 'Black Classical Music', The Art Ensemble of Chicago called what they did 'Great Black Music: Ancient to the Future', and we are told that Duke Ellington 'mistrusted the word "jazz", his definition of it was "freedom of expression".' Ellington's view was, 'There are simply two kinds of music, good music and the other kind,' adding, 'And let's not worry about whether the result is jazz or this or that type of performance. Let's just say that what we're all trying to create, in one way or another, is music.'[21]

I would also add that the phrase *the sound of surprise,* once used as a book title by Whitney Balliett, goes some way to telling us what jazz *should* be.

However, there are those inside jazz who think they can define it, or at the least feel able to discuss it in absolute terms. Big bands playing in the tradition represent one pole, bebop represents another. Another can be seen in the marketing of jazz and in the adoption of the word to apply to bland music as seen in 'smooth jazz', 'the latest jazz vocal sensation' and so on. Most of us might object to that but, depending on one's viewpoint, there could also be objections to free jazz, 'because it doesn't swing', dixieland jazz, 'because it's derivative', composed jazz, 'because there's too much written down' and so on and on. Should we not accept that jazz is a broad church, and that trying to define it, to pin it down, is a mug's game?

Perhaps we should listen to the music. As critic Abbé Niles said in 1929 about listening to Ellington: 'the strangeness, the bitter, salty wit and humor, and the flashes of defiant, unwilling beauty which characterize good jazz; examples, in short, by hearing which anyone who will take the trouble may learn whether he likes jazz or not.'[22]

That quote still stands, but only up to a point. Many people who like certain areas of the music today may never have bothered to listen to Ellington. And, if they did, they might well find it so far removed from the packaged products they listen to, that they can't see any connection. Similarly, the person who has been listening to Ellington all his life, may fail to see the connection when they are exposed to avant-garde jazz. The salty humour and unwilling beauty may be apparent, but if their ears are closed to the sounds that they are hearing, then they will say: 'That isn't jazz.' And, to them, it isn't. It doesn't conform to the sound-palette and, let's face it, 'comfort area' of what many know as jazz.

Certainly none of us will like it all. I can enjoy listening to Louis Armstrong, Charlie Parker, Miles Davis, John Surman, Albert Mangelsdorff and many, many more, but have a blind spot when it comes to certain players. Pat Metheny and Dave Liebman come to mind. Both are contemporary musicians, but they are very different, reflecting in their styles two of the many diverse paths that came into jazz after what happened in the revolutionary decade. Undoubtedly they fit one general definition of jazz – 'individual expression through improvising', but then comes the very important matter of whether one likes it or not. If pressed about these two, I would say that there are too many notes flying around, and in both cases, this is allied to tone qualities I dislike. They have their fans – certainly more than I do – and, like Voltaire, I would defend their right to do what they do. But, I don't have to like them. Nor, and I'm in good company here, do I have to like the main exhibit in the jazz museum, banished to the basement in a room marked 'is this the way to New Jersey?' But before we take a look, a few markers as to the philosophy of the jazz museum as I would like to see it.

PRESERVING THE SOUL

Why can I play it over and over again? As many times as a Beethoven quartet, save that I'm not going to compare the two, since jazz isn't music perhaps so much as a form of expressionism, maybe actually more analogous to literature or poetry, than music? But where the heck, in what passage or movement of prose can I find the selection, the discipline, unselfishness, spontaneity, freedom, and final concision, and form of this darn thing? As well as the chaos, mournfulness, despair? These qualities ought to be in prose, this rhythm ought to be manifest in any interpretation of the modern world: but it simply isn't. [23]

While acknowledging the past, the best contemporary jazz composers, including those mentioned above, recognise that there are elements of jazz that define it. Elements that should be preserved, not slavishly, but as an *essence*, as something that can be used as inspiration, as memory, as un-slavish tribute. Elements we could call its soul. Elements that, perhaps not surprisingly, are at the core of this book.

Improvisation – or the appearance of improvisation – is essential to jazz. There have been exceptions, but these are few and far between.

The sanctity of the jazz performance is a result of improvisation, and leads, inevitably, to the truism that jazz happens in real time, once.

Anything – or nothing – can be the basis of that performance. Written music can be useful – 'to save time and as a basis for change' – but is not essential, and too much of it may well inhibit a good jazz performance.

Though not essential to jazz, the presence of a constant pulse, the recognisable jazz language of swing eighths, the energy and raw power of a big band, have all had a very strong role in making jazz what it is, and can still be useful. As can the basic blues and standard song forms, and straightforward functional harmony.

What matters is not what's written down, or what's presented as the starting point. What matters is what the musicians do with it.

Preserving the soul of jazz is not a matter of notes, but of philosophy.

THE CLASSIC MUSEUM PIECE

Wynton Marsalis – taking care of business, or a long vacation?

The established cats who should have been setting an example were bull-shittin', wearing dresses and trying to act like rock stars. So when people heard me, they knew it was time to start takin' care of business again.[24]

Back in the 70s [Wynton] showed up at my house by surprise . . . . He wanted to listen to a little bit of the Davis Plugged Nickel *album and he said he wanted to watch me while he was listening to it. That means, to me, that he recognised at that time he was in a position to grasp the profundity of what was going on at those* Plugged Nickel *dates. Somewhere after that, between when he left my house and now, that grasping process is on vacation – quite a long vacation.*[25]

It will be no surprise that, in the tradition of the British television programme *Room 101*, where a celebrity guest is asked to nominate things and people to be banished to the feared room of George Orwell's *1984*, I would wish to banish Wynton Marsalis to the basement of the jazz museum.

I have no objection to him doing what he does, and cannot deny that he has helped jazz considerably in terms of support and publicity. However, although he does seem to have calmed down somewhat lately, the problem I, and many musicians, have with him, is his arrogance. The feeling that he is preaching, telling all jazz musicians, in the special way which strongly reminds me of born again fundamentalists, that he knows right, and until everybody agrees with him they are damned, condemned to a lifetime of listening to bad jazz-rock and execrable free jazz. Well, few of us would want that fate either, but what he hasn't realised is that there is good jazz rock, good free jazz, and very much more besides. And that the future of the music lies in a very different place than he thinks it does.

It took fellow-trumpeter Lester Bowie to point out that
Wynton Marsalis 'is using a partial concept of the tradition . . .
what about the tradition of innovation, creativity, moving forward, being contemporary. Is that not part of the tradition of jazz?
What about the tradition of having and maintaining *an individual
voice*. Tradition has to be taking the music as a whole.'[26]

Miles Davis' typically acerbic comment was '"Preserve this"
and "preserve that" – the way they're going we'll have blacks back
on the plantation. I mean, it already *is* preserved. Isn't that what
records are all about?'[27] Amen to that. The lasting legacy of Miles,
Lester Bowie, and all the other great jazz musicians who have
gone before, will not be slavish recreations, but original works
using the real traditions of the music.

We might even rediscover some of the better parts of New
Jersey in the process. And learn to look at them in a different way.

MORE ON THE JAZZ MUSEUM

Alyn Shipton's *A New History of Jazz* is a good place to find out
how the museum was built, with some myths explored, others
exploded.

The New Grove Dictionary of Jazz, edited by Barry Kernfeld, now
available on-line, is an invaluable resource for jazz history.

The Penguin Guide to Jazz on CD, edited by Richard Cook and Brian
Morton, published in 1992 and regularly updated, has been criticised for bias, but is nevertheless an indispensable guide to what
is available.

Robert Walser's *Keeping Time, Readings in Jazz History* and *Hear Me
Talkin' to Ya*, edited by Nat Shapiro, are among the better collections of articles and comments adding much of interest to the
background of jazz history.

8

INFINITE POSSIBILITIES

THE REVOLUTIONARY DECADE

dedicated to Miles, Ornette, and Mingus, who, with a little help from their friends, changed jazz forever

Jazz can be defined, but only in terms of a flexible, growing art which changes as the conditions under which it is performed change, and because thinking individuals arise, who, responding to fresh needs, add something new to something old.[1]

The turning point was the seminal Kind of Blue, *that gorgeous, introspective collection of first takes so smoothly executed that hardly anyone recognised it for the insurrection it was.*[2]

Before the late 1950s there was one main way of doing things. The New Orleans style, predominant up until the late twenties, was superseded by swing, which dominated in the thirties. In turn, swing was succeeded by bebop in the mid-forties, which merged into hard bop in the early fifties. Although there were off-shoots of these different styles, and some interesting tributaries emerged, the majority of musicians played in the prevailing style.

Since the late 1950s this one right path approach has changed, and the language available to improvisers and composers has been greatly extended. Earlier styles still exist, and continue to be popular, but there has been a revolution in jazz thinking that has had a profound effect on the music. Musicians can now develop their own language instead of following one particular path. As Miles Davis said, 'I think a movement in jazz is beginning away from the conventional string of chords, and a return to emphasis on melodic rather than harmonic variations. There will be fewer chords but infinite possibilities as to what to do with them.'[3]

Those circumstances, the 'infinite possibilities' spoken of by Miles Davis, have been responsible for the widening of the main stream of jazz from one specific tributary to a very broad river. A river that encompasses jazz from all over the world, in a diversity of styles that would have been unimaginable fifty years ago.

This revolution has passed many people by. As we saw in *WHY WOULD WE WANT TO REPEAT IT?*, there are those who prefer their jazz to be from the past, to be safe and comfortable. Why is this? Why is it that a sizeable majority of jazz fans – and musicians – cannot recognise that jazz changed irrevocably in the late 1950s? Not just because of Miles and *Kind of Blue*, but because of others like Ornette Coleman, Cecil Taylor and Charles Mingus. Why, in a nutshell, isn't everything in a music that's meant to be creative, creative?

Some of the possible answers have been suggested above. Chiefly, that the bebop language maintains such a stranglehold on jazz, that its supporters wear blinkers, preventing them from appreciating what else is available, and from realising the real possibilities inherent in the music. This state of mind is, partially at least, responsible for the rise of the market, and the failure of much jazz to reach its true potential, a potential that was clearly shown on *Kind of Blue* (Columbia/Legacy).[*]

Recorded in 1959, the album represents a single concrete example of what was possible in the new circumstances. It contains a series of brilliant jazz performances, built from simple material

---

[*] Not surprisingly, there have been various editions of the record produced over the years. Some of them were discussed in *Jazz Changes* Volume Seven, Number Two.

that, while being firmly rooted in the past, have an entirely new dimension to them. As Gary Giddins said, few have recognised the insurrection it represents. The fact that the album has had such a revolutionary impact, while seemingly remaining everyone's favourite jazz record, is astounding.

KIND OF BLUE *IN PERSPECTIVE*

The compositions on *Kind of Blue* were almost all written by Miles Davis (1926–91), who 'wanted the music this new group would play to be freer, more modal, more African or Eastern and less Western.'[4] But, as Jimmy Cobb, the drummer on the sessions, noted, 'a lot . . . was composed in conjunction with Bill Evans. The ideas and music were mostly where Bill was coming from.'[5] (I will look further into Bill Evans' input, and more closely at the five tunes on the album, in *NO MORE BLUES?*.)

South African trumpeter Hugh Masekela said of the record, 'It was the simplest jazz – it had a lot of African overtones. Miles juxtaposed the modern, fantastically, against something very primitive . . . . It had very deep Congolese overtones for me.'[6] Bassist Ron Carter, who joined the Miles Davis band a few years later and was a member of the amazing mid-sixties rhythm section, recalled a concert he heard in the early sixties where Miles 'played this tune that had a different kind of order to it – the changes were not what we would call at the time normal changes. I couldn't figure out what was going on. I could *feel* the chords but I didn't know what they were doing . . . . It took me a while to begin to understand that . . . they were playing a form of scales.'[7]

The 'form of scales' that Carter heard are known as modes. 'So What' – probably the tune that Carter is referring to – is built on the Dorian mode, the C major scale, starting on its second note. (Or, we could say, the white notes of the piano starting on D.) This gives a different distribution of intervals – semitones and tones, or half-steps and whole-steps – than those of the normal major scale. Starting on the major scale's third note, fourth note and so on, will produce different modes, because the intervals are distributed differently.

'So What' uses the Dorian mode for the whole of the thirty-two bar AABA tune. The only change is that the B section uses the same mode, but one that starts on E-flat (a half-step up from D, and thus the Dorian mode in the key of D-flat). More important than the notes involved was the idea that the harmonic movement had slowed down so much it was almost non-existent. Such simplicity was in direct contrast to the mores of bebop, a music predicated on improvisers dealing with complex melodic lines and harmonies within generally fast tempos. The new approach fitted in with Miles' aesthetic of melodicism and his feeling that there should be space in his soloing, and that it was not necessary to fill every bar with lots of notes.

Davis had been developing his ideas on modes since the mid-1950s. He showed this clearly in the music he improvised for Louis Malle's *Lift to the Scaffold* in 1957, and with his tune 'Milestones' recorded the following year, (both of which will be discussed in *NO MORE BLUES?*).

He had seen what could be done with scales by listening to Khachaturian – 'the thing that intrigues me are all those different scales he uses . . . they're different from the usual western scales.'[8] He had also been using scales in his recordings with Gil Evans. 'When Gil wrote the arrangement of 'I Loves You, Porgy', he only wrote a scale for me to play. No chords . . . . And in 'Summertime', there is a long space where we don't change the chord at all.'[9]

Miles' sense of space is seen to wonderful effect in his solo on 'So What'. He is very lyrical, working from *within* the scale, playing around the available notes, There is a great deal of openness in the solo, which, though incredibly simple, is highly melodic. So much so that George Russell later orchestrated the solo and regularly used it in his band's performances. The contrast with John Coltrane's improvisation on the same tune is immense. Coltrane, much more complex rhythmically and melodically, is working *from* the scale, working inside his aptly named 'sheets of sound' approach, seemingly wanting to get all the notes into every chord.

In the contrast between these two solos we see the genius behind the idea of simplifying the starting material. Each soloist – and the other front line soloist Cannonball Adderley fits snugly between the styles of Davis and Coltrane – is allowed to be an individual. Each can present his own view of the material without being forced by fast tempos and constantly changing chords into a specific way of playing. Each soloist in turn can show some of the 'infinite possibilities' implicit in such simple music.

IN THE AIR

Kind of Blue was not created in a vacuum. Nor was its release solely responsible for the changes we are discussing. Many of the ideas that helped shape jazz from the late 1950s had started to emerge during the previous decade. Even though bebop was still the dominant language, and Charlie Parker still the man to idolise and follow, there were many who felt the need for change. The involvement of Charles Mingus and Ornette Coleman will be discussed below, but undoubtedly some of that change came about because of the musicians involved with, and the music performed by, a nine-piece band led by Miles Davis. The group played for only a few weeks in a New York club during 1948, but the music they subsequently recorded, on an album that became known as *The Birth of the Cool*, connects us sideways to Duke Ellington and Billy Strayhorn, and forward to what André Hodeir, discussing *Miles Ahead*, called 'a rebirth of the Ellington spirit'.

The link between Miles Davis and Ellington was the Canadian composer and arranger Gil Evans (1912–88). He first made his mark with Claude Thornhill, whose dance band of the 1940s had its own distinctive sound, but showed the influence of Ellington and Strayhorn. 'From the moment I first heard 'Chelsea Bridge', I set out to try to do that. That's all I did – that's all I ever did – try to do what Billy Strayhorn did.'[10]

Also involved in *The Birth of the Cool* was Gerry Mulligan. His quartet with Chet Baker was very popular in the early and mid-1950s, and his Concert Jazz Band, again strongly influenced by Ellington's ideas, emerged in 1960. 'Mulligan was a neo-classicist in the best sense of the word; his music always reflected earlier jazz styles while always remaining personal and often forward-looking and innovative . . . his classic pianoless quartet . . . seemed to resonate echoes that were eerily but unmistakably reminiscent of early New Orleans ensemble jazz.'[11]

Another writer in the *Birth of the Cool* band, pianist John Lewis, was behind the formation of the Modern Jazz Quartet in 1952, the same year that Mulligan started his quartet. The MJQ's music, though much more formal than Mulligan's, did swing at times and some notable music was produced. But the main thrust of the group was towards classical structures reflecting Lewis' 'fascination with polyphony and European music [which] began very early . . . . My most wonderful discovery from that time was when I first heard Bach.'[12]

Not directly involved in *The Birth of the Cool*, but around at the time, was composer George Russell, whose book *Lydian Chromatic Concept of Tonal Organisation,* first published in 1953, has been credited with laying some of the theoretical ground for the use of modes. Though the book may have had some influence, my feeling is that the ideas of changing what jazz *was* into something that worked from a simpler basis, were 'in the air' and many musicians were experimenting with new ideas. Modes, new harmonies, piano-less quartets, classical influences, lydian concepts and much, much more – all helped shape the way jazz changed irrevocably in what I have called the revolutionary decade. In among all this activity were two musicians whose efforts were crucial.

ORNETTE AND MINGUS

Charles Mingus' fear that Ornette Coleman (born in 1930) would get swallowed up by hype, when he burst on the scene in the same year that *Kind of Blue* was recorded, was well justified. The press, as always looking for a sensation, found Coleman irresistible with his long hair, eccentric dress, plastic saxophone, and a style of music that was very different from the prevailing bop and hard bop scenes. In 1960 *Newsweek* wrote about Coleman's 'frazzled horn' and 'snarling, snorting blats', deciding that 'Yes, modern jazz is controversial. But . . . jazz has never been more alive. And it still has something new to say.'[13]

In his playing of the alto saxophone – and, later, trumpet and violin – Ornette was very individual. Whereas a player like Johnny Hodges would distort a note in order to slide into the correct one, Coleman would deliberately change the sound of notes to give his playing additional colour, and he has spoken of the same note having to *sound* different when played in two different tunes.

The spirit of the blues-based but angular melodies of Ornette Coleman – to be discussed further in *NO MORE BLUES?* – was carried through into his solos, and those of his regular partner, trumpeter Don Cherry. Forsaking harmony, the group's solos aimed to 'forget about the changes in key and just play within the range of the idea'. Coleman's idea, revolutionary then and only partially accepted now, was that the soloists could start with a melodic statement and develop the ideas of that melody, and its mood, throughout their improvising. Such an idea was not new (see Sonny Rollins' 'Blue Seven', my classic improvisation in *WELL MAN, WE JUST BLOW*), but what was new was the concentration on motif-ic development, and the absence of any harmony to base the solo on. Like Mulligan some years before, he didn't want a piano or guitar to state the chords, although, unlike Mulligan, there were, deliberately, usually no chords to state. Coleman's credo was 'let's play the music and not the background'.

This development meant that, because there was no chorus length and repetition of a set chord progression, solos could be as long as the soloist chose to make them – which, it must be said, is not always welcome. A side effect of Coleman's approach was that, even if there was a constant pulse, the need for it to spell out the same number of beats to every bar was rendered unnecessary. The pulse became a constant flow, used to assist the soloist rather than stating or stressing a predetermined time signature.

Miles Davis, for fairly obvious reasons – he was, after all, ploughing the same furrow – was never much of a fan of Coleman. He is said by pianist Paul Bley to have been at Coleman's opening night in New York where he 'stood talking to the bartender with his back to the stage, as though he was thirsty and just happened to stop in for a drink.'[14] Mingus was somewhat acerbic, but more generous on the effect he saw Coleman as having. 'Now aside from the fact that I doubt he can even play a C scale in tune, the fact remains that his notes and lines are so fresh. So when [disc jockey] Symphony Sid played his record, it made everything else he was playing, even my own record that he played, sound terrible. I'm not saying that everybody's going to have to play like Coleman. But they're going to have to stop playing Bird.'[15]

Coleman's place in jazz history is as assured as that of Miles and Mingus. Critic Francis Davis said: 'With Ornette Coleman, jazz established its permanent avant-garde, its "new" that would always remain new – comparable to the ongoing attack on tonality in classical music, on narrative in post-First World War fiction, and on representation in twentieth-century art.'[16]

Meanwhile, back in what was seen as the normal jazz scene, the arrival of *Kind of Blue* in the record stores coincided with the release of *Blues & Roots*, one of Charles Mingus' best albums, and Duke Ellington's soundtrack record, *Anatomy of a Murder*. Mingus (1922–79) was the direct descendant of Ellington, using his musicians and their strengths and weaknesses to create, sometimes with the help of the musicians themselves, a library of unique jazz compositions.

Although I used part of this comment from Mingus' biographer, Brian Priestley, when talking about Ellington, it is worth repeating in full for what it says about Mingus: 'Duke Ellington in his best work had set such an impossibly high standard of cannibalizing his musicians' very souls, as if by some beneficent form of osmosis, that only a handful of bandleaders have ever tried to emulate him (as opposed to copying his stylistic features). No one, until Mingus, had taken what Ellington achieved with New Orleans and swing-style musicians and tried to apply it to the more rigid and complex language of bebop, and to the more insistent virtuosity of its players. That Mingus often made it work should not blind us to the enormity of his self-imposed task.'[17]

Because Mingus was working in a later time period than Ellington, he was able to take advantage not only of the bebop language, but crucially of the 'new' thing – in fact, he was part of the group of people who *created* the new thing. But this was always done with a remembrance of the past, particularly the work of Ellington. Much of Mingus' music was composed, but he was always aware that space needed to be left for the musicians, in their soloing as well as, interestingly, in the 'written' parts. As trombonist Jimmy Knepper said: 'He sang them to us, or played them on the piano . . . . It was a very time consuming process to learn his tunes,' adding later, 'He didn't want anyone to write out his parts. He wanted you to play like you just thought of it yourself, even if it wasn't exactly what he wrote.'[18]

There is a connection here to the comment that 'Duke simply thought of a better way'; but Mingus went further, allowing the musicians to think for themselves, to add their individuality to what he had written. He was willing to trust the musicians, and accept the consequences. For more on this approach, and more on Mingus, see TAKING A CHANCE.

Sadly, Mingus was unable – because of the changed economic situation, lack of subsidies and, one must admit, his own temperament – to have a band full-time as Ellington did. If he had, things might have been different and one can only regret what jazz lost because of this, including ideas for large-scale works that would never be realised. Since his death, his compositions continue to be performed by musicians around the world, most noticeably by a regular big band of New York musicians managed by his widow, Sue Mingus. She says that he is now being recognised as a great composer rather than 'just' a bandleader and bassist. But, regrettably, one can feel that the magic, and the genius, is somewhat dissipated by his absence from the bandstand.

One should add that Mingus' influences were seen in much more than jazz. While visiting London in 1960 to work on the film *All Night Long,* he met the late and much lamented musician Alexis Korner, whose Blues Incorporated band 'was formed out of his admiration for Muddy Waters and Mingus in equal proportions . . . . By dint of sparking off the whole "British rhythm-and-blues" movement which begat the Rolling Stones, among others, the band had an incalculable indirect influence on American pop and rock music of the next two decades.'[19] (It was on that visit that Mingus, after turning down the musicians on offer from the film company, went around the clubs looking for musicians he could work with, and discovered trumpeter Harry Beckett, my dedicatee in WELL MAN, WE JUST BLOW.)

THE LEGACY

I have made the claim that the developments of the revolutionary decade changed jazz forever. A bold claim, and one that can only be justified by leaving aside what many are happy to call jazz. Which, flourishing a banner with 'jazz happens in real time, once' emblazoned on it, I am more than happy to do.

To demonstrate this in a somewhat crude way, I will present a before and after scenario on the main aspects of the music. 'Before' is a look at what was happening in bop and the swing-derived big bands prior to the late 1950s, and, of course, much of this is still happening. 'After' shows some of the possibilities that arose because of the changes brought about by Miles, Ornette,

Mingus and others. And, to demonstrate his pervading influence on jazz writing, I have added a note as to how Duke Ellington anticipated some of these changes.

Before: The classic small group instrumentation was the bebop quintet of trumpet, saxophone, piano, bass and drums. Big bands were sixteen or seventeen strong: four trumpets, four trombones, five saxophones, piano, bass, drums and possibly guitar, and used section or ensemble voicings almost exclusively.

After: In small groups anything goes, from solo recitals to the pianoless groups of Gerry Mulligan and Ornette Coleman, and to groups of only saxophones or trombones, or, perhaps, even tubas. Larger groups may well not respect section groupings, and also use more unusual instruments, such as bass clarinet, tuba, bass saxophone and string instruments, individually or as a group.

Duke: Used flute, bass clarinet and violin as colours and solo instruments, as well as sections of three clarinets. His trademark cross-section voicings, producing sounds difficult to analyse, were taken up by many writers after the late 1950s.

Before: The sounds and solo style produced by improvisers were based on following specific people. In the bebop period most instrumentalists tried to emulate Charlie Parker, or trumpeter Dizzy Gillespie.

After: Individuality of sound came back – returning us to what happened before bebop, and reminding us of Bob Brookmeyer's cri de coeur as to whether Charlie Parker was a good thing.

Duke: Took many of his ideas from New Orleans music, not least the stress on the individuality of his musicians. (In this respect, while listening to Sidney Bechet's 'Muskrat Ramble', I noted that it always strikes me, when I listen to this kind of music, how interesting it is compared to bebop: colourful, flowing, not afraid of individual sounds, with short, melodic solos, collectivism, solo breaks, and stop choruses.)

Before: Solos were by single instruments accompanied by the rhythm section all playing together, and using a regular pulse.

After: Individual solos still exist, but are often mixed in with what else is happening, resulting in more interplay between the front line players, and between them and the rhythm section. Two or more soloists can play together, a link back to the collective improvising seen in New Orleans music. A regular pulse need not be present, and, if it is, could be in a time signature different from the standard 4/4, and is likely to be broken up by the interaction between the rhythm section players.

Duke: Often had soloists playing a counterline to another player, or the band playing the melody while the soloist commented on it. He used the rhythm section flexibly and colourfully and at times used two bassists or two drummers.

Before: Themes were played at the beginning and end, were most often twelve- or thirty-two bars long, and were separate from the soloing, creating the theme-solos-theme form. Melodies were drawn from elsewhere, or built on a borrowed chord progression. They relied heavily on repetition and transposition. Small groups usually played the faster tunes in unison as written, while the slower ones were arranged for the group, or interpreted by one of the soloists. Big bands used block voicings for most of the theme statements.

After: Regular forms still exist but new forms are common. Melodies are still in use, but are often freshly written. Sometimes they are only a simple sketch, making their point by implication rather than direct statement, as with 'Flamenco Sketches' or 'Freddie Freeloader'. Tunes may be more angular, and rely much less on the common developmental ideas of repetition and transposition.

Duke: Often broke away from the concentration on twelve- and thirty-two bar forms. His melodies were simply stated, often played in eight bar segments by different musicians, or, if by the band, in constantly changing textures. The melodies were usually well constructed and, often, highly original.

Before: Soloing was on the form, and on the underlying functional harmony chord progression that repeated over and over. The improvising language could be New Orleans style, swing era or bebop, with the latter style – most often a string of eighth notes with little or no space – dominating.

After: Solos are often integrated with the melody statements. They can use all or just part of the chord progression, which is not usually based on strict functional harmony. Soloing, which may go on for much longer, can be on modes, the alternation of two chords, or, as Ornette Coleman showed, spun off from the melodic line as a development of the mood of the piece. The improvising language uses a more individual sound and approach, and is often more spacious.

Duke: His soloists were chosen for their individuality and for the way that they would react to the given situation. They used a more melodic improvising language, and were not afraid of leaving space in their solos. Solo length was, usually, only eight or sixteen bars, with Ben Webster's two chorus solo on 'Cotton Tail' being unusually long. At times, soloists simply acted as observers, commenting on what was going on around them.

Before: Compositions were played as separate items, and were usually short, rarely more than a few minutes long.

After: Jazz compositions can last anything from three minutes, less at times, to over an hour. Pieces are often played without a break, or possibly even mixed together, to form continuous sets. Longer works can be suites made up of shorter pieces, or constructed in a way that allows the composer to develop his ideas over a longer time scale.

Duke: Wrote many suites, which became continuous sets, or parts of sets. His longer works showed a different approach, one that, as we have seen and as we will explore later, has great importance for jazz composing today.

What all this proves, apart from the fact that Duke was ahead of his time, is that jazz has changed. Whether that's a good thing or not will depend on where you're standing. And what your view is on progress in the arts.

DOES JAZZ NEED TO PROGRESS?

The history of art and art's condition at any time are pretty messy. They should stay that way. One can think about them as much as one likes, but they won't become neater; neatness isn't even a good reason for thinking about them. [20]

As we have seen, Coleman Hawkins declined to play 'Body and Soul' in the same way as he had on his hit record. Lester Young, too, said about the possibility of repeating his Basie band days, 'I don't play that way anymore. I play different; I live different. This is later. That was then. We change, we move on.' [21] And, as we have seen, Miles said 'Why do you want me to do that again? Didn't I do it good the first time?'

But there are people, fans and musicians, who think that everything that came after, say, Sidney Bechet is not jazz. Or after Charlie Parker. Or after . . . well anybody they idolise. There is often a devil to be afraid of as well. With many it was Ornette Coleman, although his early music seems, to some of us at least, remarkably normal at this remove. Echoing what has been said about certain jazz trends and musicians, one somewhat over-the-top article I saw about classical music, dismissed Beethoven as 'a narcissistic hooligan . . . almost everything that went wrong with music in the nineteenth and twentieth centuries is ultimately Beethoven's fault. Poor old Schoenberg was simply taking Beethoven's original mistake to its ultimate monstrous logical conclusion,'[22]

I prefer the following approach, from a jazz critic, which is inclusive, not exclusive, and shows us what the music is about, and how it *needs* to change. Part was used as the opening quote to this chapter, but, for its message, it is worth repeating in full. 'Jazz can be defined, but only in terms of a flexible, growing art which changes as the conditions under which it is performed change, and because thinking individuals arise, who, responding to fresh needs, add something new to something old. The "something new" is to be judged . . . by whether it is a genuine addition to the music, to its human content, technique and expressive breadth. When it is, the result is "real jazz" precisely because it is different, and because experiment and change are in the essence of jazz.'[23]

First published in 1948, that extract, from Sidney Finkelstein's *Jazz: a People's Music* contains propositions that, as Max Harrison commented when reviewing the book's reissue in 1964, are 'as relevant now as on first publication and will remain so'.

To return to my mantra. Jazz is something that 'happens in real time, once' and that real time, for jazz composers today, is very different from the way it was for Ellington, Miles or Mingus. We must be true to our time – in truth, we can't avoid being true to our time. But it is my belief, verging on an obsession, that the changes that have happened because of the 'revolutionary decade' opened jazz up in such a way that the jazz composer, indeed the jazz fan, the jazz critic, cannot avoid them. Indeed it could be argued that there is more chance of someone not into jazz finding their way into the music through one of the many different paths that have been opened to them by this revolution, than if they were given only one choice of 'what the music sounds like'.

It is also vital that we do not forget the past. As Clement Greenberg has pointed out the record 'shows no case of significant innovation where the innovating artist didn't possess and grasp the convention or conventions that he changed or abandoned . . . . Nor did he have to cast around for new conventions to replace those he had shed; his new conventions would emerge from the old ones simply by dint of his struggle with the old ones . . . [which] would somehow keep being there, like ghosts, and give ghostly guidance.'[24]

CLASSIC MOMENT SHOWING JAZZ'S INFINITE POSSIBILITIES

In 1998, hearing Børre Mølstad, who was then eighteen and completely alone in a school theatre at the southernmost tip of Norway, not playing 'Ornithology' or 'Stella by Starlight', but Ornette Coleman's 'Lonely Woman' *on a tuba,* I realised, not for the first time, that times – and tunes – were changing.

I later came across this comment on other Norwegian musicians by critic Mike Zwerin: 'When the trio segued surprisingly but effortlessly into Ornette Coleman's haunting 'Lonely Woman', the inevitability of the odd connection between Coleman and this isolated Nordic village at the end of the road was revealing. The accordionist Eivin One Pedersen explained that the song used the same harmonic scheme as Norwegian folk songs. It was more evidence of how jazz is turning out to be the true 'world music'.'[25]

MORE ON JAZZ'S INFINITE POSSIBILITIES

Ekkehard Jost's *Free Jazz,* although now somewhat out of date, is a good overview of the musicians who created what we now call free jazz.

Ashley Kahn, *Kind of Blue, the making of the Miles Davis masterpiece,* contains fascinating coverage of events before, during and after the recording sessions that produced Miles' masterpiece.

Ian Carr, *Miles Davis: The Definitive Biography* is a good introduction to the work of Miles Davis.

Brian Priestley, *Mingus: a Critical Biography*, is a detailed and sometimes analytical look at Mingus' life and music. (For other books on Mingus see chapter 13, *I HEAR A SYMPHONY*.)

Will Friedwald, *et al*, *The Future of Jazz*. An email 'conversation' between a group of jazz critics on where the music is coming from and where it's going. Though somewhat woolly at times there are some provocative points.

Howard Mandel's new book *Miles, Ornette, Cecil*, subtitled *jazz, beyond jazz* contains much interesting material on the three musicians and their place in the development of 'the revolutionary decade'.

Arthur C. Danto, *After the End of Art, Contemporary Art and the Pale of History* is a thought-provoking book on what is happening in the art world, which has some interesting parallels to today's jazz scene.

9

DEEPENING THE GAME AMID THE BACKGROUND HUM

JAZZ AS ART

dedicated to all those who see no other way of doing it

What is fascinating now is that it's going to be much more difficult for the artist, because he must really deepen the game to be any good at all.[1]

The stuff I'm complaining about is cheap. It's not doing anything . . . . When I read the first page of [Walter Abish's novel] How German Is It I said, wait a minute, this is doing something. Here's a house that is lived in![2]

Looking at what is happening in jazz today, one sees something interesting, if at times distressing, going on. There is a lot of activity in all areas of the music, and, deservedly so in most cases, more attention being paid to jazz from outside America. But to be brutal about it, there is an awful lot of rubbish being presented under the name of jazz in every country. As critic Bill Shoemaker said, 'the argument/discussion is not so much America versus Europe as real jazz versus pap'.[3]

This real jazz is often hard to find among the pap that is widely promoted in today's advertisement driven jazz media. Reading the magazines, and listening to much of the music programmed as jazz, it is sometimes hard to believe that anyone exists – musician, critic or fan – who thinks of jazz as an art any more. How many would subscribe to Francis Bacon's statement above? Or recognise themselves in the statement about contemporary literature by William Gass, which continues: 'Now it may be that in among these people are writers who are splendid. They are all very competent, but I don't think there's any pressure there at all. I'm upset when I read young writers who aren't upsetting me. I mean they're young.'[4]

And how many musicians would willingly accept, even in a non-literal sense, John Lewis' perceptive comment that 'the reward for playing jazz is playing jazz'?

REALISING ITS POTENTIAL

I see it as undeniable that jazz possesses 'a background hum', something that is constantly present, which permeates everything that is generally perceived of as being jazz. This background hum arises mainly from its marketing, which – once it has dealt with the new, usually good-looking, kids on the block – concentrates on increasing the popularity of those musicians who are 're-creators', and idolising those for whom technique is all. This is what jazz is for many people. It's what they're told it is. *All* it is. That 'virtuostic deconstructions and recapitulations are all we have to look forward to from here on in'.[5] It's my belief that this has a debilitating and pernicious effect on the music itself, making it extremely hard to move jazz away from this perception of what it is, and to move it back towards its true character.

However, one has to recognise that audiences have become confused by the sheer variety of music now presented under the name of jazz, as well as the ever-growing number of jazz CDs and downloads now available. Reflecting this confusion, and paraphrasing something I once read, 'who can we trust to tell us who we should listen to?' This is a point I will return to in *the jazz media* below. Many fans give up trying to keep up, relying on the familiarity of the past for their jazz intake, rather than taking a chance on something new. However, as many have observed, the internet has levelled the playing field somewhat by making independent music more visible, and allowing us to sample the wares by hearing short soundbites, buy single tracks, and find the free downloads of entire tracks that are increasingly being offered.

Part of that debilitating effect of the background hum is that many musicians seemingly don't want to 'deepen the game', for fear it will diminish their popularity. And the statement that 'you need to deepen the game to be any good at it' would be scorned by the hummers, the majority of critics and fans who are prepared to accept, without complaint, what is served up to them as jazz.

Deepening the game for them implies seriousness with strings, doleful melodies, pretentious titles and so on. But didn't Miles constantly deepen the game in his own playing, and in the surroundings he gave himself And one can see Dave Douglas, for example, is trying to deepen the game (but could be said to be spreading himself rather thin in his constant search for something different).

In earlier, very different times, Duke Ellington showed the way in jazz composing, and his successors, Charles Mingus and Gil Evans, deepened the game, too. Sadly, however, most of the writers who are *said* to be their successors – those who were discussed in *WHY WOULD WE WANT TO REPEAT IT?* – seemingly don't want to even consider the option.

I would go as far as to say that one of the big problems with jazz, a large part of its background hum, if you like, is the feeling that it 'ought to be popular'. The whole marketing and packaging (what we could call Americanising) of jazz implies that there is an audience we should be looking for, rather than an art we should be trying to work within. To forestall criticism I should perhaps add that the 'Americanising' of jazz I am speaking of has nothing to do with the music's roots, more to do with the way it – like many other things – is sold. No matter how good or bad the music is, it has become a product to be sold like a tin of baked beans.

It could be argued that the 'crisis in jazz' is not lack of record sales, lack of audiences, but that sales *per se*, audiences *per se*, are seen as important. As Derek Bailey says, 'To play in a manner which excludes the larger audience or, worse, *to prefer* to play before a small audience, is taken as an indication that the music is pretentious, elitist, "uncommunicative", self-absorbed and probably many other disgusting things too . . . . The propaganda of the entertainment industry and the strenuous, if futile, efforts of the art world to compete with it, combine to turn the audience into a body of mystical omnipotence. And what it seems to demand above all else is lip-service.'[6]

There are obvious financial implications here, but *is* jazz trying to be a stadium music – and selling its soul to do so – rather than concentrating on being an art? Jazz carries such a weight of being a 'popular music' that it often seems that this has dragged the music down to the level where it is seen as *only* a popular music (even by most of its participants), and the art, although talked about, is not striven for. Certainly, for the past twenty years or so, jazz – or what is marketed as jazz (a crucial distinction) – seems to be flailing around, trying to be popular, without attempting to realise even part of its true potential.

There is another problem as well: those (large) parts of the background hum which reflect the concern for tradition and an exemplary technique, are following ideas that permeate classical music. There, a high regard for technique, the desire to achieve an immaculate performance, and the promotion of a specific set of compositions and individuals as 'the canon', are accompanied by the belief that every musician must emulate those ideals. Certainly, jazz can learn from the way that classical music has no doubt that it is an art. However, aping classical music's methods contradicts what jazz *is:* a creative music that, because it uses the individuality of the players involved, has the possibility of being different from performance to performance.

In his famous essay on kitsch, Clement Greenberg, discussing whether a Russian peasant can appreciate Picasso in comparison to kitsch, makes the case that 'the peasant soon finds the necessity of working hard all day for his living and the rude, uncomfortable circumstances in which he lives do not allow him enough leisure, energy and comfort to train for the enjoyment of Picasso. This needs, after all, a considerable amount of "conditioning". . . . In the end the peasant will go back to kitsch when he feels like looking at pictures, for he can enjoy kitsch without effort.'[7] As Greenberg also said, 'Too many people simply refuse to make the effort of humility – as well as of patience – that is required to learn how to experience, or appreciate, art relevantly. Such people do not have the right to pronounce on any kind of art – *much less abstract art*.'[8] (italics added)

The opposite case was put, rather less elegantly, when, responding to Cecil Taylor's statement that, in order to listen to his music, people need to prepare, Branford Marsalis declared on television that this was 'self-indulgent bullshit'.

Having 'the right to pronounce on any kind of art', having to 'prepare before you can appreciate art', can seem onerous concepts. And even more difficult when we are discussing jazz, an art that, we are told, 'happens in real time'. Francis Davis has written about people nowadays being told what jazz is, and then going out to look for that kind of jazz – like Branford plays, one guesses – without needing to prepare, or indeed look any further. What they want is entertainment, and the difference between that and art is well summed up in this statement by art critic David Sylvester: 'I'll give you a definition I once arrived at, of the difference between art and entertainment. The entertainer is like the rhetorician: he wants to achieve certain effects which he is aware of wanting to achieve, and his mastery of the medium includes knowing exactly what effects he wants. The artist does not know what he wants to achieve; he goes into the thing with the desire to explore the subject-matter and see what happens.'[9]

THE JAZZ MEDIA

It is inconceivable that [the critic] will not be wrong a fair amount of the time. But being wrong is preferable to being irrelevant; and the recognition that everyone involved with contemporary art must work without certainty can only be beneficial in its effects . . . [and] it has the virtue of forcing the critic . . . to run the same risks as the artist whose work he criticizes.[10]

We're all critics. We decide what to buy – CDs, books, anything – based on previous knowledge, looks, cost and so on. A bandleader decides who will be in his band, a promoter decides whether or not to book that band, based on much the same things. (I should perhaps exclude looks, but in today's jazz world . . .)

A critic in the sense of one who writes for some kind of gain (of which more later) has to possess the first of these – previous knowledge. He shouldn't need to worry about the looks of his subject, although the editor may well have done that for him. And as for cost: 'For what shall it profit a man, if he shall gain the whole world, and lose his own soul?'

Somewhat serious all of a sudden, perhaps, but surely the least we as musicians can expect is that the critic treats the artist and his work as seriously as the artist himself does. The extract above, from a book about art, shows a different world from that inhabited by almost all of those who call themselves jazz critics today.

From a personal point of view I will admit that some critics have said useful things, useful mostly in the sense that they can be used in a CV, or to promote a record or gig, but it's rare indeed that they can be useful in any kind of creative sense, contributing to an artist's view of his music and of the world he works in.

It wasn't always like this. Brits of a certain age will have very fond memories of Charles Fox, who was what one might call a 'gentleman critic'. A joy to read because he not only wrote well, but knew about the traditions of the music, and what was being minted afresh around the next corner. Sadly Charles has passed on, but some of his comments have stuck in my mind. Writing about contemporary jazz composition he used the phrase 'participatory democracy', as opposed to earlier bandleaders who led their bands 'like feudal suzerains'. These comments were in a review about *Down Another Road*, an early album of mine. In the liner notes I had said that once one particular composition has been given to the band, it is 'out of [the composer's] control and sometimes develops, because of the band's performance, into almost a different animal'. Charles' review mentioned this and added 'it may be a different animal, but it always has its owner's name on the collar'. A very pertinent comment, beautifully put, and a mantra that has been very relevant to the core of my life, and one that underpins the message of this book.

As a subscriber at various times to most of the jazz magazines written in English, a follower of several dedicated jazz magazine websites, a searcher for jazz items in some on-line papers and magazines, I find little that lives up to Charles Fox's standard of writing and criticism.

Why is this? What accounts for the generally appalling standard of writing, not only in its critical content, but in the actual language used? I would say 'there go my good reviews' but I know that most critics, realising that they are among the select few who write well, will rise above this attack.

One reason that writing about jazz is so bad is that, increasingly, those involved are fans, with little or no writing experience, who want to write about the music. Nothing wrong with this in theory, and some may develop, as they have in the past, into good writers. But from a musician's point of view it seems perverse to put the fruits of his or her labour in front of someone willing to write for a name-check and a free CD, or for the paltry sums on offer from most of the jazz magazines. (An editor of *Jazz Times*, one of the best of the current jazz magazines, admitted to a colleague in 2005 that almost all their writers are fans writing for very low fees, or often for nothing at all.)

With very few exceptions it has always been the case that people writing for jazz magazines have been poorly paid (but, again with very few exceptions, so are jazz musicians). The internet has continued the tradition and it seems that the path to getting on to a major magazine may well start in the review sections of internet businesses such as Amazon: 'be the first customer to write a review'; or in the web-based magazines such as *All About Jazz*. Although lip service may be paid to some biographical background about the writer: 'I have written extensively for the press in my home town of Deadwood, Kansas . . . ' – it seems that anyone can take part. However as author and journalist Nic Jones says, 'I went with *AAJ* [*All About Jazz*] as an outlet as they were the only people who had the courtesy to respond to my proposals to become a writer . . . . As a general principle I think it's true to say that the internet, whether through the offices of Amazon or otherwise, has had an effect of 'democratising' that can be seen as detrimental, not least because it effectively amounts to open season for those who feel they have a right to express an opinion and who aren't going to let little things like ignorance, the inability to write persuasively or eloquently or downright inaccuracy get in their way.'[11]

One could quote many examples to support Nic Jones' comments but here's a brief extract from a *very* long review found on the web recently: 'Sound is a kaleidoscope of shapes . . . . Is it any surprise, then, that the music honks and hollers, spewing a volcanic steam of notes? But even as that happens, it relaxes into the calm of aftermath, soft shades that encompass interludes on the piano, a conversation with the drums, and moments of silence. A balance of sorts evolves. At the end of it all, the stentorious manifestations are primal to the cause, the results dazzling.'[12]

There are still some serious writers around: Francis Davis and Art Lange in the USA, Brian Priestley, Brian Morton, Chris Parker and Alyn Shipton in the UK, John Shand in Australia, Eduardo Hojman and Angel Gomez Aparicio in Spain, come to mind, but their outlets are shrinking. Most magazines seem to want to – they might say need to – fill their pages with articles – and pictures – of the latest photogenic 'star' served up to them by the record companies. And, look, there's a big ad on the back cover. What a surprise. If it's not a young beauty or hunk, there will be yet another article on Joe Lovano or Pat Metheny. And, look, there's another advert! And there will be more advertisements on the many pages of reviews filled cheaply by the aforementioned fans masquerading as critics. (Although one can understand the tie-in between adverts and current reviews, it seems that some magazines take this further and ask for an ad before they will guarantee that the CD in question will be reviewed . . . .)

In this regard, I can't resist quoting this, sent some time ago by a friend. It's from a spoof blindfold test which included 'Brandford Marsalis' 'Shopping Mall Blues" (with the name of Wynton's brother changed slightly, presumably to avoid litigation.)

'Hey, that's Brandford – you can't fool me with that. I picked up on that immediately he played that ascending fourths figure – also the sound of his horn. Yep, they all sound like that. Actually it could have been any one of about 100,000 tenor saxophone players with a college education and a mid-period Coltrane aesthetic. How did I know it was him? Because this is *DownBeat* which is mainly just advertising for Columbia, and Marsalis records for Columbia, and Columbia are giving him maximum hype at the moment. Quite simple really. And I see you got my cheque there, so I'll give it five stars.'[13]

Am I jealous of the coverage offered to Metheny and Lovano? Well, yes I am, although – it's the market, stupid – I do understand the reasoning behind it.

But would one want – do Metheny and Lovano want? – yet another sycophantic piece which to use Whitney Balliett's quote in a different context, 'says nothing at great length'? Probably yes, if it helps their sales, and who can blame them? Do the readers want them? Seemingly yes, if the magazines are doing their research properly. At times interesting people and CDs are covered, but what a collection of uninteresting, repetitive, stale material one has to wade through to find them. One longs for a literate magazine that is not in thrall to the market. There have been some and *The Jazz Review* (November 1958 to January 1961), edited by Nat Hentoff and Martin Williams, though short-lived was one of the best.

§ *I should also mention* Jazz Changes, *with its appropriately double-edged title, which has been drawn from at times for this book. Founded as the house magazine for the International Association of Schools of Jazz, this was run as a labour of love by my partner, journalist and author John Gill, and me between 1994 and 2001. We struggled along for seven years with a little help from the IASJ, and the Royal Academy of Music, as well as my own bank balance, but eventually market pressures forced us to close. There wasn't enough interest from advertisers in a magazine whose stated aim was to avoid conforming to the prevailing norm, and we had no money to hire professional ad agents, or a sales force. However, we ran some interesting articles and reviews and brought attention to a few scandals, such as an attempt by our far bigger sister organisation, IAJE, to encourage the jazz education market to get, in the immortal words of my co-editor's choice of headline, In Bed with Madonna.*

The 'background hum' spoken of above is, in the main, the responsibility of the critic. They may well have a point when they say that they are only responding to a demand from the audience, but how many of them are honest about what they see? I spoke earlier about the 'time-warp' aspect of the work of the Dave Holland big band, and that only one critic I have read pointed this out. Maria Schneider's albums have their moments, but they are raved about as though they are the second coming. In today's jazz media it seems that she is somehow above criticism.

Even what I see as the one well-justified criticism of Holland's work is couched in easy layman's terms. Has there been a deep analytical criticism of his music by someone who knows the subject? Of my music? Of anyone's music, apart from Walter van de Leur's book on Billy Strayhorn? In other words, can any jazz criticism live up to some of the art and literary criticism I have used, and will continue to use, to amplify various points in this book? At times one can barely credit what passes as jazz writing in many of the world's jazz magazines. Every critic, one assumes, is being published because someone believes they are informed and respects their judgement. In turn those judgements are expected to influence the readers' opinions and purchases. But here is an example where warning bells should surely have rung in the editor's office when a critic implied that she rarely listened to a CD twice, and started a review by saying 'Although I normally write the review while the CD is playing . . . .'

§ *Speaking of editors, in April 1985 the pre-wiggy* Wire *had 'Best [of] British' as a banner headline on the cover, with assorted names to illustrate what was in the magazine. Inside was an article on me by Roger Cotterrell which said that 'Graham Collier gets taken for granted in . . . Britain's reactionary cultural environment.' And guess whose name* wasn't *on the cover?*

What we, as fans and musicians, are entitled to expect is serious comment from experienced journalists who are, one would hope and expect, paid properly for their work. But one look at the major jazz magazines shows this to be a fallacy. Nor does it take long in the bookshop or library to see that the majority of books about jazz are collections of reviews, gathered from the critic's output over the years. Interesting for a light read, perhaps, but usually containing few insights about the musicians and their music. (Yes, I know I've quoted from some such compilations in this book, but only the pertinent comments from the better books!)

In a fascinating article, 'The Critic', James Lincoln Collier draws the distinction between journalists and scholars. In part he criticises almost all the major writers then, in the early 1990s, on the jazz scene, including Gary Giddins and Gunther Schuller. He observes, quite rightly, that a critic who wants to be taken seriously must know about music, and, where appropriate, be willing to do the mind-numbing research necessary to prove the theories he is writing about. 'But we cannot have it both ways. We cannot go on pretending we are doing scholarship when all we are doing is rummaging through the refrigerator for leftovers to run through the processor one more time . . . if we are to have a discipline of jazz studies worthy of the taxpayers' support, it must bring itself up to the standards of the academy.'[14]

Jim Collier, no relation, although a friend, is no stranger to abuse from the critics. Mainly from the Marsalis/Crouch camp when Jim correctly, but perhaps not advisedly, challenged the predominantly African American ethos at the Lincoln Center, but also for his slant on jazz history, both in general and with regard to the biographies he has written. However, as author William Howland Kenney says, 'the compulsion to castigate Collier's interpretations without doing the scholarly work necessary to fully develop another point of view comes repeatedly from writers who often have interpreted jazz outside any historical context.'[15]

§ *In connection with the abuse, I was once told by Ellis Marsalis, Wynton and Branford's father, that he had quoted from one of my books in his doctoral thesis. When, not knowing of the controversy, I modestly said, 'you must mean James Lincoln Collier', I was vehemently told 'What? Me quote from him? You've gotta be kidding.'*

Increasingly there is a genre of jazz writing being published that, at first sight, would appear to meet some of my complaints. I refer to the growing number of academic books, usually, but not always, from university presses. However, as you will see in the next chapter I have some criticisms of what can be found in many of these books. The language, though usually strong on research, often modulates into pretentious twaddle, seemingly written to guarantee tenure at the writer's university. When reading them one is often reminded of Duke Ellington's comment that 'such talk stinks up the place'. Of the many such books I have read I can single out Paul Berliner's *Thinking in Jazz*, as possibly the only exception. I would also point to Robert Walser's illuminating article on Miles Davis in *Jazz among the Discourses* as a model of what can be done, and how it should be done. In this brief example one could replace 'classicize' with 'review' and miss none of the sense: 'The most obvious failing of the movement to classicize jazz, however, is that it has never been able to do justice to the music; for example, it offers no means of accounting for why Miles Davis misses notes, or even of understanding what he is really doing the rest of the time.'[16]

THE HIDDEN PRESENT

Before doom and gloom set in completely, it needs to be appreciated that there is a parallel background hum, opposite to the marketed, 're-creative' and technique-driven world which most people see as jazz. This parallel hum will never supplant the first, but it is where the real music will survive. To be aware of it, it is necessary to ignore the marketing, and look for the 'hidden present', the real creative artists who exist in all countries. They have a small, generally local, following, and deserve to be far better known than they are.

Many non-American musicians, while recognising the genius of the great jazz musicians of the past – almost all of whom are Americans – have realised that it is not necessary to copy what Americans do in order to create real jazz. This will be discussed further in the next chapter, although, to develop Bill Shoemaker's remark above, non-Americans are just as capable of producing pap as Americans.

Demonstrably not pap are these two examples, one American, one not, which show very different approaches to the jazz trio.

The Norwegian trio Jøkleba were the subject of my *classic perform-ance* accolade in *JAZZ HAPPENS IN REAL TIME, ONCE* where some biographical information was given. The music they produce is a constantly changing kaleidoscope of different textures. All three musicians are constantly inventive, finding different levels from which to approach what the others are playing or singing.

A very different take on what three instruments can do is shown in the work of the Jimmy Giuffre 3. The veteran clarinet-tist Jimmy Giuffre (1921–2008) worked with Canadian pianist Paul Ble, and the bassist and fellow American Steve Swallow for over forty years. Their music has been called chamber jazz, possibly because it often lacks the constant pulse that so many find neces-sary for jazz. There was in the group a marvellous rapport. They produced music with a seamlessness, an intimacy, a delicacy, and at times a starkness and an acidity, which is very refreshing after the sheer in-your-face obviousness of much of today's jazz.

I guess Giuffre's name is reasonably famous in jazz terms but, sadly, he never achieved his due acclaim. His music lives on but certainly won't become part of the publicity-led 'mainstream' of jazz that has developed over the past twenty years or so. But I'm becoming more and more doubtful that this is a laudable aim. The aim should be to 'deepen the game'. To 'find a house that is lived in'. To add to the 'hidden present'. And for that to be judged, not necessarily as something marketable, but something that moves the few who find the music, and appreciate it for what it is. As the novelist and poet Conrad Aiken said (in his last letter, to a student fan) 'If there's anything good in my poetry people like you will find it. That's all we can hope for, and goodness knows it's enough. The effort alone is worth it.'[17]

Further examples of *the hidden present* will be found in *PART FOUR: SKINNING THE CAT*, but it has to be realised there is far more happening than anyone can be expected to know. I try to keep my ear to the ground, but when, some years ago, I asked three Norwegian students studying in London to present a talk on jazz from their country, I mentioned some of those I knew of, those from more or less my generation, Terje Rypdal, Jan Garbarek, Arild Andersen and so on. I was told in no uncertain terms 'there's far more than that'. And there was – and still is. Lots of it, and that in a country of only four million people. Proving, as the next chapter title has it, *IT AIN'T WHO YOU ARE (IT'S THE WAY THAT YOU DO IT)*.

CLASSIC ART

Jimmy Giuffre 3, 1961 *an ECM double album, re-releasing* Fusion *and* Thesis, *two classic recordings of the group from the midpoint of what I have called the revolutionary decade.*

Virtually any recording by Jimmy Giuffre with Paul Bley and Steve Swallow is worth listening to, but the best starting point would be this wonderful double CD. The records include several tunes by Carla Bley, and a stunning remake of what was once Benny Goodman's signature tune, Gordon Jenkins' 'Goodbye'. One doubts that the dancers of the 1930s would even recognise the tune, and, after Goodman's classically influenced sound, they would probably hate the often quirky distortions that Giuffre produces from the same instrument. But it represents an original, very personal take on the tune, and a reminder of what jazz is capable of. In the mid-1990s I played the CD to a group of students. In the hush at the end one said 'Jazz doesn't get any better.' Whether he meant the record was great, or that jazz hadn't improved since, was left open.

MORE ON JAZZ AS ART

For the reasons expressed above I am not recommending books on jazz as art, but, in their place, end with a quote from a book about Jackson Pollock, and with what seems an appropriate response, found on a jazz blog by noted critic Howard Mandel.

The dream of modern art may be an impossible one, and the wager unlikely – that individual freedoms can yield shared cultures, and that the apparent negation of tradition can rebuild something of equal worth, binding us paradoxically both to our time and simultaneously to the greatest achievements of the past – but in Pollock's best work, we feel, near the end of modern art's first century, that the gamble was redeemed. [18]

Where is Hancock as leader of this gang? Why can't or won't he make a statement, rally his troupe to focus its expression, reach out to the listeners, wrap us in the music and take us higher? If jazz doesn't do that, if it only wants to be admired, it's ready for burial now. [19]

10

IT AIN'T WHO YOU ARE
(IT'S THE WAY THAT YOU DO IT)

ON NOT BEING AN AMERICAN

dedicated to Jan Garbarek

I quite rapidly discovered that I was totally unable to play any of that clever shit that other people play, and I had to find something of my own . . . . You look inside yourself and see what it is that you can do . . . . I've worked on those so that I can present my view of the world – rather than something that sounds a little bit like somebody else.[1]

Like John Surman, whose remarks head this chapter, I'm not an American. Nor, as would be obvious from pictures of us, is either of us African American, or black. The distinction at the end of the sentence is not included for semantic reasons, rather to point, briefly, towards another aspect of this discussion. Namely, do black *non-American* jazz musicians have an advantage over their white counterparts when it comes to playing jazz? A question that became relevant in England some years ago, and made me wonder at the time how the pecking order works, and how far down it you have to be before you're beyond the pale, and would be better off taking up knitting.

I do have one advantage. I am male, although my being gay takes the edge off that for some observers.

These are serious issues, made more pointed by the increasing discussion in jazz magazines on American versus European jazz, women in jazz, black audiences for jazz and whether, as Stanley Crouch implied, gay musicians like Cecil Taylor can even *play* jazz. As we saw in INFINITE POSSIBILITIES, the opening up of the jazz language means that musicians are now free to be themselves. The widening of jazz to encompass all this individuality has its good and bad sides. Someone with the very personal approach of my dedicatee, Norwegian saxophonist Jan Garbarek, can become world-famous – helped, of course, by the backing of a strong record company and the international jazz press. The downside is that, without such support, no matter how good Garbarek's contemporaries may be (take Jøkleba as an example) they will be very lucky if they have any real following outside their own country.

This problem is linked to some of the areas that were explored but, unsurprisingly, not resolved, in DEEPENING THE GAME. But what concerns us here are the aspects of *belonging* to one specific group or another, in a music which, whether all involved like it or not, know it or not, has moved on and, ideally at least, should be able to include anyone.

ON 'NOT BEING EUROPEAN'

Writing about the rise of abstract expressionism in America at a time when art was seen as European, critic David Sylvester wrote, 'In the search for the absolute and commitment to the new, it was advantageous not to be a European, not to be steeped in a tired culture.' He quotes Barnett Newman, one of the great painters in that style, as saying, 'I believe that here in America, some of us, free from the weight of European culture . . . are creating images whose reality is self-evident . . . . We are freeing ourselves of the impediments of memory, association, nostalgia, legend, myth . . . we are making [art] out of ourselves, out of our own feelings.'[2]

This point is nicely developed by Sylvester, who says that Newman *was* influenced by Europeans such as Matisse and

Giacometti but 'it was they who had to deal with "the weight of European culture" and that it was because Newman was free of that weight that he could deal with Matisse and Giacometti and go on from there.'[3]

There are connections here with other arts. Literature was seen by Americans as 'European' but was looked at afresh by writers such as Faulkner and Hemingway. Cinema was seen as American, but was approached in a different way by Europeans such as Buñuel, Fellini and Godard.

Jazz, too, was born in America, and, like cinema, has been looked at afresh for many decades by non-American musicians. However, unlike the example of cinema, there is a distressing trend among some to think that America, and, often, specifically 'black' America, still 'owns' jazz, and that what is played elsewhere is something different – and somehow not as good. Indeed, Branford Marsalis is on record as saying, in a phrase that reminds us of his brother's convictions, that 'only those who have internalised the culture and way of life of African Americans can become jazz musicians. A prerequisite for this is to live in the US.'[4]

I should perhaps make it clear that I am not attempting to deny the prejudice that, in the early days of jazz, crowned white musicians such as Paul Whiteman the 'King of Jazz', and Benny Goodman the 'King of Swing', nor the bad taste left in the mouth when the latest hip white singing sensation is lauded far beyond his or her talent. But we only have to look at the case of many of the neo-classicist acolytes of Wynton Marsalis to see that reverse prejudice can and does happen. And, if more evidence is needed, there is Marsalis' odd answer when asked 'What do you think about European jazz?' His reply, 'If it is swinging and has some blues in it, I love it,' serves his agenda as he no doubt wished, but it implies that swing and the blues, those aspects of jazz vital to the music for Marsalis, are rarely found in European jazz. They're there, Wynton – and much else besides.

Drummer John Marshall, who has played in my various bands for many decades, made this interesting comment about the music that we were making in Britain in the sixties and seventies: 'although in many ways free jazz and rock music are diametrically opposed, they had a common point which allowed us, the Europeans, to get on with our own music.' And Stan Sulzmann, also involved in the scene at the time, said, after citing various influences, 'You didn't feel you were making a bad copy of an American record.'[5]

Some American musicians are aware that things have changed, both in the kinds of jazz that are played, and the attitudes to the music that are found elsewhere. As Quincy Jones says: 'The Europeans at this point are ready to say, "Hey guys, we'll just take jazz from here. You don't know what the hell to do with it." That's the way Europeans feel now. And I remember when they were just drooling over Bird and Diz and everybody. And now they have some amazing musicians over there.'[6]

In looking at what music is produced in the name of jazz, we can apply David Sylvester's point that the descendants of the creators of an art form may be carrying too much baggage from the past. And that those coming to an art form from a different direction, may be able to dispense with all or most of that baggage, and, in so doing, shed new light on the subject.

The baggage carried by American jazz has been dealt with by Miles and Ornette. As Kirk Varnedoe said about Jackson Pollock and Picasso 'each, in different ways and degrees altered the *international* languages of modern art.'[7] (Italics in the original.) They challenged the view that bebop was *the* language of jazz, all that could be used, all that should be taught. Much American jazz missed this epiphany and continued – and continues – to create music that could perhaps best be described as 'hard bop moderne'.

American musicians generally are aware of the great weight of jazz history behind them, and feel that they need to deal with it, to get it out of their system or, often, pun intended, to include it in their system.

It is, I believe, no coincidence that many non-American players, Garbarek for one, have taken much greater advantage of the
newly exposed potential of jazz, than many Americans have. As
pianist Bobo Stenson, a fellow Scandinavian, said, 'the American
jazz tradition is not so rigid for us as it is for American musicians
. . . and we can be freer in our approach.'[8]

When referring to non-Americans the jazz world usually means
Europeans, although, of course, there is good jazz being created
everywhere around the world. Jazz from these places sometimes
takes in local influences that would not occur – and would not be
appropriate – in much of American jazz. And, dangerous ground
here, it can be more personal. Echoing painter Barnett Newman's
stance, British saxophonist John Surman, in typical self-deprecat-
ing fashion, made the remarks that head this chapter. His work is
open and fresh and original and develops *from* the tradition rather
than staying locked inside it. As he says, 'I had to find something
of my own . . . I've worked on [this] so that I can present my view
of the world.'

In the same way, although almost all jazz composers readily
acknowledge, and show, the influence of Ellington, Gil Evans and
Mingus, it is usually the non-Americans who feel no need to carry
the baggage of the big band tradition. Composers such as the
Australian Paul Grabowsky and Austrian Christian Mühlbacher,
to be discussed below, demonstrate their respect for jazz traditions and for the 'big three' jazz composers mentioned above. But
their work shows a great deal of freshness and originality, and is a
long way removed from the greyness of much, but by no means all,
of the contemporary big band writing on display in America.

In trying to get away from the American big band tradition
they want to express themselves as what they are, Australian and
Austrian respectively, each with their own different palettes as
composers. In a similar way, during my time at Berklee, I wanted
to express myself as a European, and, importantly, as a European
jazz musician not influenced by the European classical tradition.
There is an odd dichotomy that, particularly in America, the

European classical tradition comes into many aspects of jazz: classical training, classical influences, the creation of an approved canon, and so on. There are sometimes good reasons for this, but I have more than a sneaking suspicion that much of it has to do with a misplaced inferiority complex among some jazz musicians and teachers.

That inferiority concept gets turned on its head when Americans are protecting their own view of jazz, as can be seen in the comment above by Branford Marsalis, as well as in many articles in jazz magazines and discussions on the internet. The consensus seems to be that Americans invented jazz, and all that musicians from other countries can do is to try – and by definition fail – to copy what has been achieved. To accept this, depends, of course, on how jazz is itself defined. For some, as Wynton Marsalis implies in his comment about European jazz, it *has* to swing and have the blues in it. Others, many outside America, accept these elements as being important ingredients for *some* jazz, but are less prescriptive when it comes to the whole.

Jazz may be seen as a broader church outside of America, but some of those involved have also been defensive about their approach to the music. Although their roots were in jazz, free improvisers such as Derek Bailey eschewed the style, and the word. Others tried to erect artificial barriers, proposing that American jazz is primarily note oriented, and European jazz is more interested in concepts of space, with Michael Brecker and Jan Garbarek presented as opposing examples. There is some truth in this, but if we look at John McLaughlin, European but very notey, and Bill Frisell, American but super-spacey, we soon realise that there are too many exceptions to posit any cast-iron rule. It might be safer to repeat what critic Bill Shoemaker said, when he got involved in a spat with British journalist Stuart Nicholson, an uncritical booster of most things European, 'The argument/discussion is not so much America versus Europe, as real jazz versus pap.'[9]

ON NOT BEING A (STRAIGHT) MAN

The implication by critic Stanley Crouch that Cecil Taylor can't play jazz because he is gay is offensive, showing a distorted view of humanity as well as of the music Crouch professes to support. Crouch also said – in *The Atlantic Monthly* of all places – that Wynton Marsalis was envied by critics because he 'had access to a far higher quality of female than they could ever imagine'.[10] And, to round off the circle, we hear that 'When asked what the [Lincoln] Center was doing to help young women learn the genre [Marsalis] responded by rolling his eyes and stating that he didn't have time for such political correctness.'[11]

These remarks paint a less than flattering picture of Crouch (and to a lesser extent Marsalis). Crouch, if it needs to be pointed out, is black, is someone who writes regularly and strongly about unfounded prejudice, and is, as though we need reminding, part of a music which, on the surface at least, prides itself on being inclusive.

Even ignoring crass antifeminism from figures such as Crouch, one still hears stories of women jazz musicians facing prejudice solely because of their gender. Or of being ignored, as by Marsalis, not having 'time for such political correctness'. The reasons for the lack of women in jazz (performers and audience) have been well rehearsed and, as society changes and, crucially perhaps, as the music changes, some, at least, of the many excellent women musicians are beginning to attract attention. Cynically, one is forced to add that it's usually the singers in our macho led society. In the words of a record company executive, they are 'prettier on an album cover'. But, strangely enough, the same could also be said of the many good looking young men who get record contracts, and are seen posing in advertisements, or on their CD covers. I know, 'it's the market, stupid', but what is being peddled here, music – or glamour?

And what is being peddled in the image of jazz musicians and critics who support – or at the least do not protest – these prejudices against women and against gays? As one woman educator said in the 'Women in Jazz' issue of *Jazz Changes*, 'I don't think that a lot of the young male [jazz education] directors I see are concerned about the subject. It's not part of their job description.'

In a seminar on *Gays in Jazz*, moderated by Francis Davis at the Village Vanguard in 2001, Grover Sales once again offered his theory, originally published in Gene Lees' *Newsletter* in 1984, that there are very few gays in jazz. 'I came to the conclusion back then that the percentage of male gays, not only among jazz musicians but among jazz audiences, was dramatically lower than the national average.' He also said, 'when I promoted Judy Garland's concerts, I would say, just on the basis of casual observation, that [the audience] was about ninety-five percent gay.' Even as a gay man it would be beyond my powers of casual, or even methodical, observation to reach Sales' ninety-five per cent conclusion, even at a Judy Garland concert. Perhaps the dresses gave them away . . . .

There are out gays in jazz, such as Cecil Taylor, Gary Burton, Andy Bey and Fred Hirsch, but others are completely or partially hidden, possibly because of concern about the prejudice which is, unfortunately, close to the surface in the macho jazz world. At the *Gays in Jazz* seminar, attended by Burton, Bey and Hirsch, one noted critic said, 'I would never dream about asking any of you . . . about your sexual behaviour for an article in *DownBeat*. Unless it has direct bearing on your music, I would ask that no more than I would ask somebody if they were a paedophile, if they beat their wives . . . .'[12]

The gays in jazz argument came a lot closer to home for some when David Hajdu, Billy Strayhorn's biographer, suggested in an article in *Vanity Fair* that Ellington might have had some sort of sexual relationship with his close musical colleague. As we all now know, Strayhorn was gay, an out homosexual at a time when it was rare. 'We all hid, every one of us, except Billy. He wasn't afraid. We were.'[13] Hajdu's claim that Strayhorn and Ellington may have been involved in some way, was backed up by Ellington's son Mercer, who told *Vanity Fair* that he always assumed that his father and

Strayhorn at least experimented together. 'I just presumed as much,' he said. 'So did the cats [in the band].'[14]

Such a relationship between Ellington and Strayhorn should not have been surprising if one realises the amount of time they must have spent together. Many a same sex couple have ended up in the same bed, possibly innocently, possibly not, after an evening's drinking, or, in Duke and Billy's case, work. Does it matter? (My reaction was to consider what songs they may have written in such circumstances with 'Things Ain't What They Used to Be' and 'Across the Track Blues' being among the main contenders.)

The attacks on Hajdu led him to respond in the newsletter of the Duke Ellington Society: 'I ask anyone unhappy with the piece to consider himself why. Is it really rational to accept if not glorify an artist's womanising as a component of his cool, yet horrible to accept the mere idea of intimacy between two people who were close for thirty years?'[15] This was reported – and attacked in its turn – in 'Vanity Thy Name Is Hajdu', a highly vituperative article by British critic Steve Voce.[16] Voce's prejudice in this offensive piece was on a par with his sniggeringly homophobic review of *AC–DC*, an album of (supposedly) gay-linked tunes, in a previous *Jazz Journal*, which caused much offence and comment at the time.

§ *I must admit that Steve Voce has been a supporter of my music, but I wonder if it would have made a difference if he had known I was gay? In fact, I have never encountered any problem with being out. Except peripherally, when ECM's annual catalogue reprinted my 'pick of the year' (Terje Rypdal's* Waves, *as it happens) from a jazz column I then wrote for* Gay News *(whose editor obviously disagreed with Grover Sales' view that very few gays were into jazz). One irate fan wrote to ECM asking if they knew what* Gay News *was, saying that he would never buy another ECM record again. As he had stated that his extensive record collection included classical composers such as Tchaikovsky and Benjamin Britten, we decided it was safe to ignore his ranting.*

ON THE BENEFITS OF AGE

Being young and good looking – female or male – does, of course, have certain advantages in marketing and media terms. That there is a concurrent disadvantage rarely seems to be noticed: in a music that could be said to depend on experience, they just don't have it.

Those with experience seem to fall into various camps. There are the elder statesmen like Ornette Coleman and Cecil Taylor, now accepted as genuine creators, still working, and in receipt of some of the largesse given out in grants in America. There are others who, although still wanting to be creative, are pushed out of the market-driven scene and end up, like trombonist Roswell Rudd, for example, working in a dance band in a New York State resort (although he does say he enjoys it). The third category is those content to coast on their past reputation.

But the question must be, how *can* one coast – at whatever age – in a music so demanding? Things change as one gets older, of course, but as conductor Kent Nagano has said, 'It takes a lot of effort to stay open and impressionable. The natural tendency is to become encrusted and cynical.' One could name many in the 'encrusted and cynical' group but, happily, there are also those, like Ornette and Cecil, who have remained 'open and impression-able', despite now being past their mid-seventies.

Few jazz musicians retire. Most can't afford to, but it's more than that. Speaking of the remote possibility that Ellington would retire, one of his musicians said: 'If he did, he'd be just like Dorian Gray. He'd age overnight . . . . Watch him some night in the wings. Those bags under his eyes are huge, and he looks beat and kind of lonely. But then we begin to play, he strides out on the stand, the audience turn their faces to him, and the cat is a new man. Pulitzer Prize? Who could *give* a musician anything to top what Duke already has?'[17] (For those unfamiliar with the history, the Pulitzer Prize committee rejected Ellington, then sixty-six, for a special award in composition. Duke's response was 'Fate is being kind to me. Fate doesn't want me to be too famous too young.'[18])

Some countries give awards for achievement to older artists. In each of the Scandinavian countries selected musicians are regularly given stipends to support them in the work they want to do. In addition, Denmark awarded the JAZZPAR Prize from 1990 to 2004, but this is now dormant due to lack of a sponsor. As their website says, JAZZPAR became an event from time to time mentioned as the Oscar or the Nobel Prize of Jazz and the winners, chosen by a panel of critics, have included Muhal Richard Abrams, Tommy Flanagan, Django Bates and Martial Solal. In America, large amounts of money are thrown, sometimes accurately, sometimes not, at musicians in the MacArthur and other awards. In England, sadly, there's none of that, apart from small project-based grants. You may be offered an honour from the Queen, as I was, but, with no money attached and seemingly no tangible result from it – although my mother was pleased – it was rather pointless.

§ *I was at the 1995 JAZZPAR ceremony in Copenhagen when the award was made to British saxophonist and composer Tony Coe. The audience was forced to listen to an interminable and very off-message speech from the assistant British Consul. (Something about tea parties up the Yangtse, as I remember.) His concluding remark, that like Denmark, Britain was a small country which valued its jazz musicians, was greeted by me with a cry of 'rubbish'. But being British did, at least, offer the opportunity of using our EU membership to escape painlessly to warmer climes . . . .*

There is one problem with being old (well more than one, but let's stick to the remit of the book). This is, that time moves on and eventually, like Ellington, like everybody, we get stuck in our chronological time. New things happen that we can't appreciate, perhaps just don't want to appreciate. I must be honest and say that there is a lot in the current jazz scene that just doesn't appeal to me. For once I'm not talking about jazz-lite, or the latest jazz singer – although they're still in my bad books – but of much of the experimentation that is around. Turntablists, hip-hop artists, excessive use of electronics. All popular, all gaining new audiences for jazz, but I just don't like the end results.

These new manifestations of the jazz spirit are another sign of the potential of the music that opened up all those years ago, and another sign that there is so much going on that no one can possibly like it all. This is something that has to be recognised by jazz artists, fans and critics of any age. Ideally, this will lead to more honesty in and about the music, and may mean critics and fans facing up to the reality that the new kid on the block – or indeed the legendary old musician – is, like the Emperor, somewhat lacking in clothes. To paraphrase something I've said before: why isn't a music that's meant to be honest, honest?

ON NOT BEING BLACK

When emphasis on universality is used to gloss over ethnic tensions or to deny the African American origins and leadership of the music, however, musicians are quick to emphasize the ethnic particularity of jazz . . . . To [clarinettist Don Byron] the music's originality is vitally related to its African American identity: 'I think the feeling of being outside the society is the ultimate inspiration . . . I just think the feeling of being conscious of yourself as part of a people that are both totally necessary to a society, only no one admits that, and totally reeling from it is the ultimate inspiration for doing something totally different.'[19]

That remark is, sadly, typical of many comments these days that exclude rather than include. Byron may see 'being outside the society as the ultimate inspiration', but it is his implication that one has to be in that position to do something totally different which doesn't ring true. If he means that those of us who aren't, can't, then that, to me, is a racist remark. And palpably untrue.

In saying this I am aware that I may, in many people's eyes, be going too far. That criticising one of today's leading jazz musicians, someone who has worked extensively with white musicians such as Dave Holland and Bill Frisell, for the racist tone of his remarks, is 'just not done'. But however much I examine the words I can find no excuse. There is, of course, truth in the implications he makes about being part of a race that is outside society. But to state, as he does, that this is *why* he is inspired as a creative person, has undertones that I find objectionable.

Perhaps he was misquoted, but Ingrid Monson, the author of the book in which the comment was found, takes this further. 'Since whiteness tends to be a sign of inauthenticity within the world of jazz, the appeals of white musicians to universalistic rhetoric can be perceived as power plays rather than genuine expressions of universal brotherhood.'[20]

She asserts that 'whiteness tends to be a sign of inauthenticity within the world of jazz'. Possibly among some African Americans – but even they might well make exceptions for Bill Evans, Gil Evans, John McLaughlin, Bix Beiderbecke and others. The rest of us take authenticity to be something we, as individuals, try to recognise from what is offered by other individuals. For me there is authenticity in Wayne Shorter and Jimmy Giuffre, but not in George Benson or Dave Sanborn.

Also what of Joe Lovano, Dave Liebman and Dave Holland – the highly praised whities (by many blacks also)? In whose jazz world are they seen as inauthentic? Also, if one accepts that there is a parallel jazz world where a lot of good stuff is going on – in Europe and elsewhere – that jazz world certainly doesn't regard whiteness as inauthentic. Unfortunately, Monson seems to be assuming that there is a specific 'world of jazz' (African American, of course) which has these powers to include or reject.

She continues ' . . . the appeals of white musicians to universalistic rhetoric can be perceived as power plays rather than general expressions of universal brotherhood.' By universalistic rhetoric I am supposing she means statements about jazz's acceptability by different people – its universal appeal. To regard them as *necessarily* 'power plays rather than general expressions of universal brotherhood' shows a breathtaking level of condescension. Why can't they be the latter? If Dave Holland, for example, says something about universality, does that mean he's making a power play to take over jazz? Surely all he is doing is making a general expression reflecting universal brotherhood. Which means including, not excluding.

Statements like the above from Byron and Monson – and many others one could come up with – are, for me, racial blindness and bullshit. One could not, and certainly would not want to, deny the African American claim to jazz's history, but claims that jazz is still only an African American music don't, can't, stand up any more. When the late-1950s Miles Davis band played black clubs with pianist Bill Evans in the group 'guys would come up and say "What's that white guy doing there?" [The other musicians] said "Miles *wants* him there. He's *supposed* to be there!"'[21]

In this respect it's worth remembering that 'Evans, according to [Stanley] Crouch was 'a "punk" whose playing could scarcely be considered jazz. He could not swing . . . and there was no blues in his playing.'[22] (Now where did we hear those qualifiers before?) Yet Wynton Kelly, the other pianist on *Kind of Blue* (black, if it matters) 'was influenced by Evans; according to his own testimony, he changed his ballad style after hearing Evans.'[23] Crouch's racism is so obscene because it comes from a seemingly intelligent man. But, really, how different is it from this remark made many years before to Duke Ellington by a white policeman? 'If you'd been a white man, Duke, you'd been a great musician.'[24]

One could not, and certainly would not want to, deny the American claim to be the birthplace of jazz, and the place where it developed, but claims that jazz is still only an American music have as little validity as saying that literature is still only European, or that film is still only American. Jazz is now a universal music. The changes of the late 1950s opened up the potential of the music so that, nowadays, real jazz, authentic jazz, is in the playing, rather than the skin colour or gender alignment, in the sounds rather than in any specific country. That the music can

now embrace what *anyone* has to offer should be a cause for celebration.

CLASSIC IT AIN'T WHO YOU ARE MUSICIAN

Django Reinhardt, who brought his gypsy background into jazz a
long time ago.

MORE ON IT AIN'T WHO YOU ARE

John Wickes, *Innovations in British Jazz, Volume 1 1960–1980* looks
closely at this important period of British jazz, including its connections to rock and free improvisation. An excellent read, and a
further instalment is said to be in the works.

Stuart Nicholson, *Is Jazz Dead? (Or has it moved to a new address)*. An
attempt by a British critic to deal with the current dichotomy
between American and non-American jazz. It has its moments,
but he over-eggs the pudding by ignoring much good American
music, and, while duly praising Norway for its jazz scene, manages
to miss much of what's happening elsewhere.

Linda Dahl's *Stormy Weather. The Music and Lives of a Century of
Jazzwomen* does a good job as far as it goes, but so much has
changed since the book was published in 1984 that a new book on
the subject is long overdue.

John Gill, *Queer Noises, Male and Female Homosexuality in Twentieth
Century Music*, a book by my partner which looks at the prevalence
of, and the prejudices surrounding, gays in jazz and other music.

PART FOUR

SKINNING THE CAT

11

NO MORE BLUES?

REASSESSING THE TRADITION

dedicated to Bill Evans for his sometime hidden hand in the making of *Kind of Blue*

[tradition should be present] like ghosts, or giving ghostly guidance.[1]

While few, if any, jazz composers have dispensed with *all* the traditions of jazz, many, like Miles Davis and Bill Evans on *Kind of Blue,* have changed or at least reassessed some, while allowing other traditions to g
ive 'ghostly guidance'. My intent in this chapter is to show *some* of the changes that have happened to the tune since the revolution of the late 1950s. I stress 'some' because, in keeping with what that revolution made possible, composers have taken very different views on what can inspire their fellow musicians. The tunes chosen are representative of some of the broad areas that have been explored. They are not new, but are among those likely to be known to most people involved in jazz.

Discussing the tune as a separate item, as I do here, isolates it from the other chapters of SKINNING THE CAT. They will discuss how the tune is looked at by some contemporary arrangers; how some jazz composers have tried to do more than write a vehicle for jazz soloing; and how some jazz composers prefer to give their musicians very little, if anything, to work from.

THE COMMON PRACTICES OF JAZZ

- traditional forms of the blues and thirty-two bar AABA standard song
- new melodies over borrowed chord progressions
- melodic development by use of repetition and transposition
- use of functional harmonies
- overall form of theme-solos-theme
- quintet or sextet instrumentation, or that of the conventional big band
- small group solo order of front line first, then the rhythm section
- solos generally accompanied by the full rhythm section
- rhythm section playing around a constant pulse, usually 4/4
- tunes played as separate items

When we listen to much of the jazz that has been created since the late 1950s – including *Kind of Blue* – it is easy to see, despite my slightly mischievous question mark in the title of this chapter, just how much of the traditional way of doing things musicians continue to use. Speaking of Don Cherry's time with Sonny Rollins, Ekkehard Jost, author of *Free Jazz*, remarked, 'It is likely that one of the most important lessons he learned was that traditional models and improvisational freedom are by no means incompatible.'[2] Or, to re-use the Clement Greenberg quote that ended *INFINITE POSSIBILITIES*, and which heads this chapter, tradition should be present 'like ghosts, or giving ghostly guidance'.

The combination of freedom and tradition is vital for jazz, and is well illustrated in *Kind of Blue*. It uses a traditional small group instrumentation of three front line players, here trumpet and alto and tenor saxophones, plus the usual piano, bass, drums rhythm section. The rhythm section plays, as a group, around a constant pulse in each of the tunes. With the exception of 'Flamenco Sketches', which doesn't have a tune, the themes are played at the beginning and end, within an overall theme-solos-theme form.

The solo order is traditional – usually front line players first, then piano – although in a slight deviation from this, Miles, as leader, sometimes takes the first and last solo. Each tune is treated as a separate item.

Three of the tunes on *Kind of Blue* follow the traditional route fairly strictly. 'Freddie Freeloader' and 'All Blues' use the twelve-bar blues form, 'So What', the thirty-two bar AABA standard song form. The two blues tunes use a very basic blues chord sequence, albeit with some small but important alterations. 'So What', as we have seen, strips away functional harmony and uses one mode only.

All three have simple melodies, using traditional repetition and transposition ideas, with 'So What' also using call and response, one of the basic building blocks of jazz. 'Freddie Freeloader' and 'So What' are in 4/4 throughout, while 'All Blues' is in 6/8, a time signature that will be discussed further below. However, unlike 'Freddie Freeloader', which stays with the twelve-bar blues form throughout, 'All Blues' uses the opening four-bar vamp as an interlude between each of the solos. This device opens up the form, allowing breathing space between the solos, both for the listener, and for the soloist who has time to prepare for his own entry.

Although they follow some of the conventions laid out above, two of the tunes have less obvious traditional aspects. 'Flamenco Sketches' is not a tune at all, simply a collection of five scales, each to be played as long as the soloist wishes. But there is a constant pulse, the rhythm section play together all the time, each of the horns takes a solo in turn, and so on. Much may be traditional but, *in respect of its starting point*, 'Flamenco Sketches' radically opened up new ground, which will be best covered below in TAKING A CHANCE.

The other out-of-the-ordinary tune, 'Blue in Green' is, as Bill Evans said in the original liner notes, 'a ten-measure circular form following a four-measure introduction and played by soloists in various augmentation and diminution of time values'. The harmony, although it has some functional touches, is intriguing, and the melody is simple. The resulting performance is beautiful, especially Evans' out of tempo interpretation of the final theme. As Miles implies, the form is somewhat difficult to follow at times: 'You can tell where it starts [but] you can't tell where it stops . . . . I love that suspense. Not only does it sound good – it's unpredictable.'[3]

'Blue in Green' is usually credited to Miles Davis, sometimes jointly to Miles and pianist Bill Evans. The truth – which becomes apparent if one compares it to the other tunes on the record – is that it was written by Bill Evans. But, true perhaps to Duke Ellington's precedent, it was copyrighted by the bandleader, Miles Davis.

Evans was certainly more involved than the other musicians in the ideas behind *Kind of Blue*. He was brought back to the band to replace Wynton Kelly, then Miles' regular pianist, on all the tracks except 'Freddie Freeloader'. Miles thought Evans' approach was more in keeping with the effect he wanted, something more open, more spacious than Kelly's funky style was suited to. But Evans' influence went deeper. Miles later said of *Kind of Blue*, 'Evans' approach to the piano brought that piece out',[4] while, as we saw in *INFINITE POSSIBILITIES,* 'the ideas and music were mostly where Bill was coming from'. Bill Evans himself has reported that 'That morning before the date I went to [Miles'] apartment. I sketched out 'Blue in Green', which was my tune and I sketched out the melody and the changes to it for the guys. 'Flamenco Sketches' was something Miles and I did together.'[5]

As far as I know Evans never claimed co-ownership of 'Flamenco Sketches', but he did complain about the writing cred-its on 'Blue in Green'. It's said that when he asked about royalties Miles gave him a cheque, but only for $25! The situation now seems to be resolved – after both musicians are dead and, I am sure, much to the delight of the lawyers. The Bill Evans website carries this note: 'though the writer's credit still usually goes to Miles, the Miles Davis Estate has finally admitted in 2002 on the official web site, that Evans wrote the tune.'[6]

It should be admitted that, with the one exception of 'Blue in Green', none of the tunes on *Kind of Blue* is distinguished, either melodically or harmonically, in the same way as, say, 'Sophisticated Lady' or 'Stella by Starlight'. This is, in some ways, intentional, or, perhaps more accurately, is an unavoidable by-product of the approach taken. As a result of this approach, the tunes are much simpler than most jazz tunes, as simple, one could say, as 'C-Jam Blues'. Their strength is that they breathe a different air. 'Freddie Freeloader' is a bone-simple basic blues progression and melody yet, as Davis biographer Ian Carr says 'the feeling which infuses it has become more subtle, more refined, more evocative'. It is this simplicity and the feelings it evokes, which is the focus of the album, the source of its greatness, and the inspiration for some wonderful improvising.

Ashley Kahn surmises that 'there have been close to one hundred and fifty covers of 'All Blues' and 'So What', almost one hundred of 'Blue in Green', and (surprisingly) only fifteen or so of 'Freddie Freeloader' . . . 'Flamenco Sketches' has been covered only five times.'[7] As for the record itself, it is said to have 'sold twelve million copies worldwide, most of them in the past decade or so'. Ashley Kahn quotes a presumably happy record label head as saying 'during the Christmas season last year [1998] I remember *Kind of Blue* was hitting as much as twenty-five thousand [copies] in a week.'[8]

Historically, *Kind of Blue* marked a move away from the complexities of bebop, and the lack of flexibility in bebop tunes. The simplicity of the melodies, and of the underlying ideas, between them create a sense of space that had generally been lacking in recent jazz, allowing each player to present a more individual approach to their solos. Each improvisation can be different, and does not need to rely, as in the main the beboppers largely did, on an improvising language based on a string of eighth notes with little or no space. As such it was one of the most important aspects of the changes of the late 1950s, allowing many of Miles' infinite possibilities to happen.

From the point of view of a jazz composer it could be seen as ironic that the biggest selling jazz album of all time, everyone's favourite jazz record, is based on very simple material. The fact is that the tunes became great jazz compositions because of the *performances*. And, in the case of 'So What' and 'All Blues' in particular, *other* great jazz performances have been produced from that same material. These simple tunes have become other, *new*, jazz compositions and prove, by their example, what jazz composition is. The real irony lies in the fact that many jazz composers have still not recognised this.

NEW APPROACHES TO THE TRADITION

A year or so before writing the music for *Kind of Blue,* Miles was exploring the territory with his modal tune 'Milestones', and his work on Louis Malle's film *Ascenseur pour l'Échafaud (Lift to the Scaffold).* His 'score' for the film was improvised from some scraps of ideas, straight to tape while watching the film being projected. Pierre Michelot, bassist on the session, has said that 'save for one piece . . . we only had the most succinct guidance from Miles'.[9] As Ian Carr has said, 'For perhaps the first time, it became clear to [Miles] that it was possible to create absorbing music with neither formally written themes nor any real harmonic movement.'[10] This approach was at least partially responsible for 'Flamenco Sketches' and had a significant effect on jazz composing, which will be discussed further in TAKING A CHANCE.

During the next few years, in an intriguing offshoot from the ideas of *Lift to the Scaffold,* Miles continued to develop the idea of improvising from scraps of melody. He became so adept at distilling the essence of standard songs, as well as his own material such as 'So What' and 'All Blues', that at times little of the original melody survives. But what remains is still immediately identifiable as being *that* tune.

'Milestones', the title track of a 1958 Miles Davis recording (Columbia Jazz Masterpieces), anticipates the ideas of 'So What'.

The form is AABA, but the tune is forty bars long, not the usual thirty-two. Again, modes are used – the Dorian, as in 'So What' for the A sections, and the Aeolian mode (the C scale starting on A) for the bridge. However, unlike 'So What', there is a change of mood *inside* the piece. The first eight bars are based on a very tight rhythmic figure. The bridge, which is, unusually, sixteen bars long, has a more sustained feel – which at times seems to slow down because of the slight displacement of the long notes played by the saxes and Miles. These changes of mood are an important part of the approach of the whole band to the playing of the tune, and in the subsequent solos, although Cannonball Adderley is, as usual, something of an exception.

Five years after *Kind of Blue,* saxophonist and composer Wayne Shorter joined the Miles Davis group. It was a mutually beneficial relationship. Shorter's more oblique way of soloing complements Miles', but, like Miles, he knows how to develop just a few notes into an interesting solo. Conversely, as a composer Shorter was, as we will see, a great influence on Miles.

Shorter contributed many tunes to the recordings the band made, such as *ESP, Miles Smiles,* and *Nefertiti* (all recorded for Columbia in the mid-1960s). I stress recordings because, interestingly, on live gigs at that time, the band was mostly playing standards (although 'So What' and 'All Blues' were still in the band's repertoire). Following the approach I discussed above, much of this material was played in a sketchy way, radically different to the norm, and this will be discussed further in *DON'T BE AFRAID . . . .* (This way of sketching melodies may have some bearing on the intriguing remark Miles is said to have made to Shorter, 'Do you ever get tired of playing music that sounds like music?'[11]

Speaking of the process of composing, Wayne Shorter said, 'You know those songs came really fast . . . 'ESP', 'Nefertiti' and 'Fall' . . . . One night I'm sitting at four o'clock in the morning with candlelight and it ['Nefertiti'] came. And 'Fall' was like that, I just drew my hands up and there it was. I had to be careful with these pinkies. I said "Wait a minute." And they moved at the last minute and then resolved, and then the next one. I said "Oh-oh, here it comes."

'You wait, and you imagine, and then you hear. And then something elusive comes and you go for it. You say "If I can make it, I don't care how long it takes . . ." And something that is elusive stays longer than something that gives instant gratification, that's right in front of you and is like "blang, blang, blang".'[12]

With tunes such as 'Fall', 'Pinocchio' and 'Nefertiti' Shorter had turned away from writing *tunes*, solely designed as a framework for solos, and was writing real *compositions*, which consistently blurred the line between what was written and what was improvised.

The aspect that most distinguishes Shorter's work from that of many others is his use of harmony. My guess is that he would subscribe to the following, said to be Debussy's comment 'to his mystified fellow-students': 'The chords: Where do they come from? Where are they going to? Is it absolutely necessary to know? Just listen, that is enough.'[13]

The approach to harmony shown in that remark is very liberating for the jazz composer. It allows a move away from the set rules and formulae of Broadway songs – the functional harmony discussed elsewhere. It encourages the use of harmony as units of sound, as patches of colour, which do not need to resolve in a conventional way. 'The harmonies . . . no longer represent anything but blocks of *sound qualities* maintaining new relationships with each other. Their function has been displaced towards the domain of *timbre*.'[14]

Shorter took, and still takes, advantage of this. His tunes use recognisable chords, often with many alterations and extensions, but uses them in a non-functional, non-tonal, way. 'Iris', from the album *ESP,* is a good example of this, and of his penchant for tunes with no bridges and no turnarounds.[*] It is a beautiful six-

---

[*] The lack of a bridge (which in standard material usually necessitated a change of approach by the soloist), and the absence of turnarounds (a set of chords at the end of one section designed to turn the tune back to its

teen-bar melody with many long notes, giving the tune a very spacious air which carries over into the solos. In an intriguing approach the solos are first based on the chords as written, then, while the pulse stays the same, the time each chord lasts is halved. Shorter also worked within common forms and harmonic structures. 'Footprints', a twenty-four bar 'long blues', is built, in the main, over a loping 3/4 bass figure. It has its own twists and turns, but is much simpler than many of his other tunes, and this has helped make it an established favourite among jazz musicians. Reflecting the changes we are discussing, Shorter's later versions of the tune sketch the melody rather than definitely state it, and work into a collective improvisation, rather than the theme-solos-theme form heard on the original *Miles Smiles* recording.

Tunes like 'Footprints' have become part of the current jazz repertoire, joining material by other contemporary jazz musicians such as Keith Jarrett, Herbie Hancock and Chick Corea. Their melodic lines are distinctive, while their generally non-functional harmonies provide a base for improvising that is seen by some musicians as being a more satisfactory starting point than more open modal forms.

The tunes composed by Ornette Coleman were somewhat different – more angular, more dissonant, more unusual. As was discussed in *INFINITE POSSIBILITIES*, Coleman, like Gerry Mulligan, changed the normal jazz group instrumentation by dispensing with a chording instrument. But, unlike Mulligan, he also dispensed with the harmonic base that such an instrument would normally supply, allowing those who improvise on his tunes to be much freer. For example, 'Congeniality', one of Coleman's better-known tunes, contains many different ideas. It 'is neither happy, nor sad, nor hectic, but all three together. It is up to the

---

starting point) means that the improvisations can be much more flowing than those over the more common thirty-two-bar form. This approach – which could be said to be a halfway point between modal composition and more standard material – was welcomed by Miles, and was an influence on his own writing.

improviser to choose from the reservoir of emotional content. 'Congeniality', therefore, is a free-jazz theme in the truest sense of the word.'[15]

Coleman's approach to melody can be seen in 'Lonely Woman', my classic moment in INFINITE POSSIBILITIES, where I spoke of hearing it played by a solo tuba. It appears today to be a beautiful tune, full of sadness and heartache, but at the time it offended many. Such people may still not like it, but I am reminded of what the poet and art critic Frank O'Hara said about the way time has affected our view of Jackson Pollock's paintings, 'when seen only a few years later . . . the violence had been transmuted into a powerful personal lyricism. *The paintings had not changed, but the world around them had.*'[16] (Italics added.)

'Lonely Woman' uses the common AABA form but, depending how you count the freely played melody, the A sections are *fifteen* bars long, while the bridge, which is played in time, is a more normal eight bars. The melodic phrases of the main theme are written to be played 'elastically', being bent and smeared by the player, a style particularly appropriate to my lonely tuba player's interpretation.

On the recording, an active, urgent, rhythmic feel is set up by the bass and drums before Coleman and trumpeter Don Cherry, using deliberately individual phrasing to avoid a 'written', unison feeling, play the much more slowly paced melody. This creates a separate *level*, an important but little recognised device which is discussed further in 'PLAY A RAT PATROL SOUND'. Unusually, two-thirds of the performance uses composed material, with only one short solo sandwiched between the two long theme statements.

The shadowing effect seen in the deliberately individual phrasing of Coleman and Cherry, the ideas that themes, whether originals or standard songs, could be sketched by the musicians rather than being played exactly as written, all served, and still serve, to lessen the importance of the theme statement in some jazz performances. However, as Coleman shows, the *influence* of the theme should be, and perhaps needs to be, paramount. It's all about context and I would generally agree with Thelonious Monk's view that what is played in the solo, should have some relevance to the tune it is based on. But not always. Miles Davis' version of Monk's 'Straight, No Chaser' on *Milestones* is simply a very good blowing blues, where the solos are based on the blues chords, not the melody, nor what the melody suggests. The result is a great jazz performance, which I admit with some trepidation is more acceptable to me than Monk's own.

Thelonious Monk was, of course, around before and after *Kind of Blue* and his place in the pantheon of jazz composers is secure. Pantheon or not, I must confess that, for some reason, his work has always been a blind spot for me. I can appreciate that his pianistic touch is very different from many others, but I find his playing, and his tunes, too dry, too 'quirky' for my tastes.

I can't deny that Monk's tunes, such as 'Straight, No Chaser', 'Well You Needn't', 'I Mean You', are well-crafted small melodies often built around the development of a single motif, repeating it, transposing it, displacing it. They are based on traditional forms and have interesting harmonies. As such most musicians enjoy playing them and many highly praised performances have happened. But for me they usually stay as tunes, followed by solos. Both tune and solos are too knowing, too self-referential, and, ironically given their common source, seem to be separate entities. I have rarely found them to be, or become, jazz compositions in my sense of the phrase – where something is created which is more than the sum of the tune and the different solos. Given Monk's reputation I can see the critics lining up to disagree even as I write, but, although I can appreciate his approach to jazz, and realise it's my loss, all I can say is that I don't have to like it.

I wrote above of the influence of the theme being lessened in much contemporary jazz. But there were, and are, composers who take the opposite view, who still wish to present a well-crafted tune that would inspire improvisers and arrangers. One early example was John Carisi's exquisite 'Israel', one of the most interesting blues ever written. First heard on *The Birth of the Cool*

(Capitol) and later recorded by Gerry Mulligan's Concert Jazz Band (Mosaic Records), its loping melodic line seems endless, and its harmonies show what can be done to enhance the basic blues chord progression.

Charles Mingus' 'Goodbye Pork Pie Hat' is another blues with a similar 'never-ending' line and an interesting slant on extending blues harmonies. Titled after Lester Young's customary headgear, the tune was, we are told, partially sketched out on the bandstand of the Half Note Café when Mingus heard that Young had died. The band 'were playing a very slow, minor blues and, in the middle of the tune, a man came in and whispered to Charles that Lester Young had died. And his response was, immediately, to start fashioning what became 'Goodbye Pork Pie Hat', and, by the time they were finished, the germ of it was there.'[17] The tune is recognisably Mingus, but also has Lester's style in it somewhere, aptly matching Mingus' one word definition of Lester Young as 'sensitivity'.

Although only a blues head, Mingus' 'Goodbye Pork Pie Hat' becomes a very fine jazz composition in the original recording by virtue of the arrangement and the sensitive John Handy tenor solo. It's all very simple, almost all unison saxes on the theme, inside a theme-solo-theme form. It's a brilliant example of Mingus' genius and shows his awareness that he could stamp his identity as a composer on a piece, while allowing the soloists to add their own. Other Mingus works will be discussed in all three chapters below, reflecting his status as the next great jazz composer after Ellington. (And his importance to me as an exemplar.)

Critic Nat Hentoff coined the apt phrase 'profiles built on essences' to describe tunes such as 'Goodbye Pork Pie Hat', and the phrase can be applied equally well to John Lewis' classic tune 'Django', an elegy for the gypsy guitarist Django Reinhardt, my classic non-American in *IT AIN'T WHO YOU ARE*. The melody, wholly derived from the initial two-bar motif, aims to capture the strange mixture of sadness and rejoicing seen in the New Orleans funeral tradition. Unusually for the time, Lewis sets out a different chord sequence, and a different form, for the solos. This 'soloing chord progression' is, as one would expect from Lewis, well constructed. It opens with a sixteen-bar section with unusual chord movements, a twelve-bar bridge with different chords over a repeating F pedal in the bass, and a loping, cowboy-like bass pattern repeated for eight bars. This bass pattern was much used in Gil Evans' treatment of the tune, to be discussed in DON'T BE AFRAID . . . .

As well constructed as it is, this chord progression would seem a long way from the openness of Ornette Coleman, but it is a mark of how different approaches to the challenge of integrating what is written with what is improvised have been devised by contemporary jazz composers. For many composers it is no longer sufficient to write a theme for the soloists to 'just blow' on. In Wayne Shorter's 'Fall', for example, the soloists are expected to play specific fragments of the theme, in unison with the other horn, in the same places in each chorus. As one might expect, this isn't done slavishly by the band, but is varied, both in the arrangement – who plays what when – and the interpretation of those fragments. In this way, the performance becomes a *collaboration* between composer and performers.

Shorter's tune 'Nefertiti' is another example of such a collaboration, again in a very fresh way. It's a perfectly good melody with interesting harmonies, yet it was in the initial performance, on the album of the same name, that it attained a relevance to jazz beyond that of being just a tune to blow on. It is arranged in such a way that the melody repeats over and over, first played by Shorter on saxophone alone, then joined in unison by Miles, then in what I have called 'shadowing', with each musician interpreting the phrases in his own way. (See ROLLED STEEL INTO GOLD for more on this.) As an accompaniment to this constantly repeating tune, drummer Tony Williams improvises freely, and magnificently, taking his layering approach to playing one step further. On this, as in all the tunes on the *Miles Davis Quintet 1965–1968* box set (Columbia), he plays amazingly, supplying a seemingly independent but complementary layer to what the soloists are doing.

Williams' approach reverses the expected roles of front line and rhythm section. When Joe Zawinul, who was to join Miles some years later, first heard this track he told an interviewer, 'that he kept waiting for the music to start (since there were no conventional solos). And only when the tune reached its end did he realise that the music had been happening all along.'[18]

Joe Zawinul's comments on 'Nefertiti', Ron Carter's on 'So What' detailed in INFINITE POSSIBILITIES and, I am sure, many other comments from musicians that went unreported, show how the radical approach Miles was taking in this period – between the late 1950s and the mid-1960s – confused some of his observers, even the musicians who were to play with him later. It could even be argued that Miles himself didn't see the full potential of some of his ideas until some years had passed. If we listen to the subsequent recordings of 'So What' and 'All Blues' (the other tunes on *Kind of Blue* were never, as far as I know, played again by Miles), we can see that not only did the whole approach of the rhythm section change, but also, as I've noted above, the approach to playing the tune itself. This approach, of sketching the melody rather than playing it as written, of allowing each player, even when playing with someone else, to interpret what was on the paper in his own way, gives a great sense of freedom to the later recordings. This too passed into jazz practice. It can be seen in Miles' approach to standards, to be discussed below, and in the looseness of some musicians' approach to what is written that we will see below in TAKING A CHANCE and throughout PART FIVE.

THE CHANGING ROLE OF THE SOLOIST

Given the openness of the concept behind *Kind of Blue* and the other changes that developed from the late 1950s on, it was perhaps inevitable that the role of the soloist would change. When, as in bebop, there are complex melodies and fast-moving chord changes, it's a brave soloist who would play long notes and take time out to allow the solo room to breath. Most took the accepted route – and, to be fair, tried to keep their solo in context – by playing lots of notes while keeping up with the chord changes.

§ *I once asked a student why he took his trumpet away from his lips during a solo. He answered 'because I can't think of anything else to play'. That answer, the one I had hoped for, echoes Miles' comment when John Coltrane said he found it difficult to stop playing: 'try taking the saxophone out of your mouth.'*

The three front line players in 'So What' illustrate, as I have already mentioned, the freedom allowed by the basic modal underpinning. Miles' own solo is simple, using many notes from the underlying mode, and leaving plenty of space. In complete contrast, John Coltrane's solo uses lots more notes but 'indicates the direction that Coltrane's music was to take during the 1960s, more so than 'Giant Steps'. He became more and more concerned with structural aspects of improvisation; as he did so, he concentrated more exclusively on modal backgrounds, which gave him the time he needed to develop his ideas at length.'[19] Fitting snugly between them is Cannonball Adderley, who 'takes a more fluid and melodic approach'. As pianist Dick Katz commented, 'Cannonball was just playing Cannonball.'

Simplistic though it may sound, it is this freedom, this opportunity for the soloist to express himself without having to meet fast-changing chordal deadlines, which is the main legacy of *Kind of Blue*. It has had a tremendous effect on jazz as we have seen, and will continue to see. In a way, Ellington foresaw it. Admittedly, the improvising language was much simpler, but Ellington's *control* of his musicians, and their willingness to be controlled without giving up their freedom to be themselves, has an echo in what we see coming out of *Kind of Blue*. One musician who took this freedom further was Ornette Coleman, who can be said to typify the area we are discussing. His work has been discussed above, and will return at the end of this section, but first a look at some of the other ways in which the role of the soloist has changed.

For a start, solos are now much longer. But as Charles Mingus said, 'I could never get Bird to play over two choruses. Now, kids play fifty thousand if you let them. Who is that good?'[20] Solos are longer on record because of the advent first of the long-playing record, then of the CD. They are longer in performance because . . . well, because the idea has sprung up that long solos are good. Perhaps Miles' advice that Coltrane should 'take the saxophone out of his mouth' in order to stop should be written above the door of most jazz clubs and all jazz classrooms. So should the phrase 'soloing is about context' – an approach that is, as Francis Davis says, 'at odds with most American and European jazz musicians, for whom improvisation is an end in itself.'

Long solos are not always a bad thing, of course, and the openness that musicians such as Ornette Coleman brought into jazz has allowed solos to become very lengthy indeed. But any extended solo needs a well-developed sense of form. There should be some subconscious internal logic underpinning it, and it should come to a satisfactory end. In this respect there is a connection between some aspects of modern literature and contemporary jazz solos. As critic Nicholas Kostyleff, writing about poetic inspiration, said: 'the initial stimulus, the stimulus which first set the language habit to work, is soon lost sight of in the wealth of other language associations which are evoked from the subconscious.'[21] And as critic and poet Conrad Aiken said about William Faulkner's long sentences: the 'purpose is simply to keep the form – and the idea – fluid and unfinished, still in motion, as it were, and unknown, until the dropping into place of the very last syllable.'[22]

When it works, in jazz as in Faulkner, it is what critic Charles Fox called 'the sudden transformation of the unexpected into the invitable'.[23]

The traditional way of soloing – front line players first, then piano, usually followed by the bass, and then by 'fours' with the drums – has largely disappeared. Even groups who rely on the bebop approach to jazz have realised that this format can be boring in its predictability and have changed things around. Not everyone needs to be featured on every tune. Not everyone needs to play the main theme, and, as we see with 'So What', the theme can even be played on the bass. Drum solos, as in 'Nefertiti', needn't be unaccompanied, but can be placed over and around, complementing or in opposition to, the statement of a melody.

Collective improvising, one or more front line players improvising together, is hardly a new concept. It was a very large part of traditional jazz, although there each musician had his own role. It disappeared in the swing era, and was never part of bebop's thinking. It has, however, resurfaced since the late 1950s, and will be discussed further in TAKING A CHANCE.

Another aspect of improvising which was rarely if ever seen in bebop, was the soloist as observer. There are precedents, once again, in the work of Duke Ellington. His soloists are often accompanied by, or accompany, a very strong melody, and their role can be said to be to act as observer, listening to what else is going on and commenting on it. Contemporary jazz has taken advantage of the new thinking and developed this concept much further. Pieces have been written where, instead of being expected to interpret a chord sequence, or a set of modes, the soloist is left to decide what he should do. His job is to listen to what is going on around him and react to it when he feels he should. This allows the possibility of a much closer integration between what is written and what is improvised, and was undoubtedly the approach used in 'Nefertiti', with Tony Williams observing and commenting on what was happening to the melody.

Stan Getz always excelled in the observer role when accompanying singers, and reached perfection in his two collaborations with Eddie Sauter: *Focus* (Verve), the album which showed that strings *can* be used effectively in jazz, to be discussed in DON'T BE AFRAID... and the music to Arthur Penn's film *Mickey One* (Verve). In the film, Getz's sardonic saxophone commentary as Warren

Beatty's down-and-out character suffers a church service in order to be fed, is worth the price of admission alone.

Getz had something outside of the music to improvise from, but, as we saw with Sonny Rollins 'motivic' way of improvising in WELL MAN, WE JUST BLOW, other musicians delve deeply into the music itself. Speaking of Ornette Coleman's approach Gunther Schuller wrote, 'Little motifs are attacked from every conceivable angle, tried sequentially in numerous ways until they yield a motif-ic spring board for a new and contrasting idea, which will in turn be developed similarly, only to yield yet another link in the chain of musical thought, and so on until the entire statement has been made.'[24]

THE CHANGING ROLE OF THE RHYTHM SECTION

I've come to feel increasingly inhibited and frustrated by the insistent pounding of the rhythm section . . . Not having [the beat] implicit allows freer thinking.[25]

The role of observer could be said to be at the core of the work of a good rhythm section. I should perhaps say 'contemporary rhythm section', as their role, like that of the soloist, has changed dramatically since the late 1950s. Jimmy Giuffre's comment that 'not having the beat implicit allows freer thinking' is a crucial part of these new ideas.

Rhythm is rightly seen as one of the basics of jazz. It comes in two forms, the subtle rhythmic variations of a jazz musician's play-ing, and the underlying 'pulse', usually four beats to the bar, which is still seen by many to be a prerequisite of the music. A musician's rhythmic subtlety is, I feel, essential to jazz, but the absence, or disruption, of the usually constant pulse can be a useful device inside a jazz performance. There is an effective absence of a stat-ed pulse in the stop-time sections of some early jazz, and, in a dif-ferent way, in some contemporary performances, where the music may have no pulse at all.

The pulse can be disrupted by superimposing a new time against the prevalent pulse, or altered by changing rhythmic moods. Much more rarely, the pulse can be deliberately sped up or slowed down. This is seen in some of Charles Mingus' work, particularly *The Black Saint and the Sinner Lady*, to be discussed in *I HEAR A SYMPHONY*, while Betty Carter had a wonderful trick of encouraging her rhythm section to get faster, or slower, very gradually, until they reached the tempo of her next song.

The norm with the rhythm section is everybody playing all the time – and, all too often, not listening to each other, or to the soloist they are meant to be accompanying. This, as was discussed earlier, produces a kind of live play-along record. After the changes of the late 1950s, rhythm sections were used in a much looser way. The pulse, if it exists at all, is not necessarily played by all members of the section, and rhythm section players have realised that they can contribute to the textures by using their instruments not as time-keepers, but as sound resources.

As we have seen, 'All Blues' is in a somewhat unusual time signature in that period, although some composers had been using time signatures other than 4/4 for many years. To state the obvious, unusual time signatures must sound natural to work effectively, and be as capable of swinging, as capable of being moved away from, as anything in 4/4. 'I was fascinated with 'All Blues' because, being a drummer, having to master 3/4 time [*sic**] was something we wanted to do at an early age. But [Miles'] interpretation was not stiff, it was flowing like a river, effortlessly . . . There wasn't any stop and go.'[26]

Dave Brubeck experimented with different time signatures, one of the most popular being his 'Blue Rondo a la Turk', an

---

* In the absence of written music, 6/8 and 3/4 time signatures can seem to be interchangeable. For me, and for those who have transcribed the melody and solos, the 6/8 feel in 'All Blues' is obvious. Intriguingly however, Ian Carr's biography states that Miles told critic Ralph Gleason 'I wrote it in 4/4 but when we got to the studio, it hit me that it should be in 3/4. I hadn't thought of it like that before, but it was exactly right.'[27]

adaptation of Mozart's *Turkish Rondo* into 9/8 (grouped not as three threes, but as 2+2+2+3). This was an effective change, but one rather dissipated when the band went into a normal 4/4 twelve-bar blues for the solos. By far the most popular jazz composition in a different time signature has been 'Take Five', written by Brubeck's saxophonist, Paul Desmond. As 'the biggest-selling jazz single of all time' it is said to have earned over four million dollars in royalties for the American Red Cross, Desmond's legatee.[28] Its listing by the NPR [National Public Radio] website as one of the '100 Most Important Musical Works of the Twentieth Century', should perhaps be taken with a good dose of Desmond's own renowned wry humour.

Apart from Brubeck, one of the best known – and most persistent – experimenters with unusual rhythmic patterns was bandleader and trumpeter Don Ellis. Their use was often unsubtle, with the pulse usually being pounded out relentlessly. Few of the soloists, apart from Ellis himself, were able to cope with the challenges presented by the unusual time signature. As a contemporary review said: 'Bad jazz is bad jazz, whether it's in 4/4 or 17/8.'

§ *In the early sixties 'Sixty Two Talbot', a modal piece of mine, in 7/8, disturbed most of my fellow students at Berklee. However, it was greeted with enthusiasm by trumpeter Dusko Goykovich who said: 'It's one of my native time signatures'. His composition 'Macedonia', named after his country of origin, then part of Yugoslavia, is one of the most natural sounding 5/4 tunes I know.*

In much jazz, there is a tendency for medium tempo tunes that are played regularly to get faster, and Miles Davis' later versions of 'All Blues' and 'So What' are no exception. The originals seem very sedate now, compared to the later performances, particularly those from the time the band's personnel changed in the mid-1960s. This also reflected a change in the approach of the rhythm section to playing time. The original recordings featured a rhythm section which was still firmly rooted in the ethos of all working together to set a smoothly swinging background that the soloists could rely on. The players in the later rhythm section were more intent on being individuals, part of the group but acting as observers to what was going on. Allowing themselves to contribute something to the solo rather than just accompanying it.

In all the ways listed in this chapter, and many more too numerous to mention, jazz musicians and composers have tried to do something new while keeping one eye on what went before – but few were forgetting the past entirely.

THE CLASSIC NEW TUNE: 'SO WHAT'

Miles Davis' tune, first recorded on *Kind of Blue*, is, as we have seen, based on traditional form and the traditional building block of call and response, but it has had such a variety of performances from Miles' groups alone, that it still has the feeling of being a new tune. Which should be the mark of any true jazz composition. There may not be much to it as tune-qua-tune, but, to restate one of the mantras emerging as this book progresses, the tune is there to provide the basis for a good jazz performance not, necessarily, to be an entity in itself, not necessarily to be a jazz composition in itself.

MORE ON NO MORE BLUES?

As we have seen, contemporary tunes continue to use accepted forms as well as exploring new ideas. Collections of these tunes, sometimes including transcribed improvisations of the solos produced from them, are increasingly available. Any attempt to make a comprehensive list would be pointless given the constantly changing situation, but collections of each of the major composers I have mentioned – Miles Davis, Wayne Shorter, Ornette Coleman, Thelonious Monk, Keith Jarrett, Chick Corea – are currently in print.

12

DON'T BE AFRAID . . .

ADVANCED ARRANGING

dedicated to Gil Evans

People are tired of hearing . . . [big bands with] a rhythm section pounding away 1-2-3-4, 1-2-3-4, as though the audience has no sense of rhythm or beat in its mind. And still playing arrangements as though there were only three instruments in the band: a trumpet, a trombone and a saxophone, with the other three or four trumpets, three or four trombones and four or five saxophones there just to make the arrangement sound louder by playing harmonic support to the leading trumpet, trombone and saxophone. What would you call this? A big band? A loud band? A jazz band? A creative band?[1]

Charles Mingus' diatribe sets the tone of this chapter, as do the two phrases I have used in naming it. Like Mingus, what I want to do is draw attention to the great disconnect between what *can* be done with the resources available to a jazz composer, and what, in general terms, *is* being done.

Hence the main title and the subtitle can both be seen as slightly tongue-in-cheek, but also cautionary. As a listener, as a sometime critic, and most of all as a composer, I think that I am entitled to ask, why is it, that all these years after Duke Ellington, the Gerry Mulligan and Ornette Coleman Quartets, Charles Mingus' various groups, not to mention my dedicatee, Gil

Evans, why is it that so much grey music is still being produced? I guess it could well be 'the money, stupid'. It could also be lack of ambition, lack of interest, lack of what's needed to be fully creative. Or a fear of the unknown.

Harsh words, but, as Mingus' full song title says, 'Don't Be Afraid, The Clown's Afraid Too'. I can guess at the meaning Mingus intended, but the sentence could also be said to encompass what artists such as those I mention above, and many more, have had to fight against as they try to do something different. And, in case anyone needs reminding, to do something different in an art that is meant to be creative.

One wonders what Mingus would have made of the use of his title in the Lincoln Center Jazz Orchestra record, *Don't Be Afraid, The Music of Charles Mingus*, which was released as I was writing this chapter. Can we surmise that Wynton Marsalis, the leader of the orchestra and artistic director of the Lincoln Center's jazz programme, really is afraid of Mingus? Probably not, but it is possibly nearer the mark to think that he assumes that his audience might be. The safe programming at the Lincoln Center has been a bone of contention among jazz musicians for many years. Pianist D. D. Jackson wrote an open letter, sadly unpublished, saying what a difference could have been made to jazz if someone less conservative than Marsalis had been given the Lincoln Center job. And, a colleague adds, the ear of Ken Burns, whose series of documentaries on jazz have undoubtedly brought some benefits to the music, as has Marsalis' Lincoln Center stewardship. But, in both cases, rather than a continuing look at what jazz once was, one would have wished for a wider appreciation of what jazz is, now.

ACHIEVING BEAUTY

In Mehldau's hands the song [Paul Simon's 'Still Crazy After All These Years'] achieves, in that moment, a beauty akin to being the best ballad ever.

That comment, found on the web and used in full in SOMETHING
BORROWED, SOMETHING NEW, points up the 'fact' – proven to me –
with which I ended the last chapter: 'The tune is there to provide
the basis for a good jazz performance not, necessarily, to be an
entity in itself, not, necessarily, to be a jazz composition in itself.'
Following the example of Billie Holiday, Sonny Rollins, and many
others, Mehldau proves that a silk purse can be made out of a
sow's ear. To misquote Bob Dylan, 'the tunes they are a-changin'.'
But ultimately what matters in jazz is that a good performance is
created, whatever starting point is chosen.

An equally unlikely song for jazz treatment would seem to be
'My Favorite Things'. But when performed by John Coltrane it
became an excellent illustration of what I call 'advanced arranging'. A saccharine song. In the original *Sound of Music* setting, the
tune was transformed by Coltrane radically thinning it down, taking what he wanted and discarding the rest: 'The piece is built,
during several measures, on two chords, but we have prolonged
the two chords for the whole piece.'[2] As Miles Davis said, 'Only
he could do that and make it work' and in so doing Coltrane created a framework from which his group created many great jazz
performances.

'Still Crazy' and 'My Favorite Things', however inappropriate
they may once have seemed, have become jazz compositions,
capable of being changed from performance to performance.
However, there are some tunes that may seem to have had their
definitive performance, as Coltrane's suite *A Love Supreme* can be
said to have done on its 1964 recording. The compositions of
Charles Mingus would seem to be another case in point. Mingus
himself performed most of them many times and managed to
keep them alive, but other bands often find them difficult to deal
with. Even the various Mingus tribute bands (officially sanctioned
by his widow and very popular) lack the master touch – the energy, the sheer excitement – that Mingus brought to his own work.
As someone once commented, 'I like my Mingus with some
Mingus in it.'

While lacking in actual Mingus, Hal Wilner's *Weird Nightmare, Meditations on Mingus* (Columbia), is a wonderful tribute to Mingus the composer, to the strength of the material, and to its ability to be looked at afresh. Unlike most tributes these are not pale undemanding copies of the original, a reminder of something once loved, but something new which acknowledges the greatness of the source.

In creating his fascinating CD-length composition made out of many diverse Mingus themes, Wilner went outside of the box in a big way, going to extremes not usually available to jazz musicians. He used instruments that had been invented by the eccentric American composer Harry Partch, and, in among the jazz musicians such as guitarist Bill Frisell, pianist Geri Allen and clarinettist Don Byron, were several rock musicians, all admitted Mingus fans, such as Keith Richards, Elvis Costello and Leonard Cohen.

Bobby Previtte's typically zany arrangement of 'Open Letter To Duke', for example, has a bluegrass feel to it, with an instrumentation that includes banjo, harmonica and spoons. As far removed from Mingus and Duke as we could be, but it works. As does Bill Frisell's meditative look, again typical of his approach elsewhere, at 'Self-Portrait in Three Colors', with the instrumentation here including bass marimba, 'marimba eroica' and 'surrogate kithara' (all instruments invented by Harry Partch). The result is weird, but I am sure Mingus would have approved.

The achievement can be summed up with these words by author Mike Heffley discussing the Globe Unity Orchestra's tributes to Jelly Roll Morton: 'It does suggest a kind of benign, even affectionate nod by the players to the material, not a condescension so much as a kindly salute from those whose serious jazz dues are paid in full and whose credentials as hip and creative intellectuals are well established.'[3]

UNBEARABLE LIGHTNESS

The solos . . . are often framed by softly stated chords of countermelodies that throw the soloist into even bolder relief, while discreetly reminding him that he is still part of a group. The result is a relaxed, intricate busyness that is a pleasing contrast to the widespread practice among modern jazz musicians of allowing soloist after soloist to perform at excessive – and generally vacuous – length, supported by an inevitably metronomic rhythm section. [4]

As so often, Whitney Balliett hits the nail on the head with his contrasting of a creative thinker, in this case Gerry Mulligan, and the 'widespread practice' that existed around him. In both small group and big band areas, Mulligan demonstrates the attributes Balliett credits him with, and epitomises what I have called, borrowing the phrase from Milan Kundera, 'unbearable lightness'.

Using the term shows off my readerly credentials, but also allows me to continue to stress the point that what is unbearable is not the lightness, but that so little of what Mulligan showed us has been adopted by others. To continue the analogy there is a heaviness in much contemporary jazz, created by plodding rhythm sections, too much writing, too many notes in the solos, and by the lack of room in which the performance can breathe. As always there are reasons – and exceptions. The main reason is that bebop has left jazz with a legacy of a technique-driven music, with little space around it, and seemingly little opportunity for the emergence of less technically inclined players. These effects were countered, as we have seen, by the approach seen in *Kind of Blue*, and by such small groups of the fifties and sixties as the Modern Jazz Quartet and the piano-less groups of Ornette Coleman and Gerry Mulligan.

The lack of piano gave the last two groups some room in which they could achieve lightness. This was increased in Coleman's case by his decision that he would not follow the form of the tune, but improvise from its mood, a concept which has been of great importance to many contemporary musicians. The Gerry Mulligan quartet's lightness came from the interweaving contrapuntal lines between the leader's baritone sax (sounding far less heavy than the instrument had usually been heard before) and his accompanying front line partner, most famously trumpeter Chet Baker. All this over a light rhythm feel, part of his chosen players' style, but made even lighter by the absence of piano. Mulligan's original compositions were always interesting, and his treatment of standards was fresh and individual. The group's music remains highly attractive to this day, with 'Moonlight in Vermont', with its intriguing voicings, including a harmony part sung by the bassist, being an outstanding example.

Mulligan's lightness of feel was carried over into his big band writing. His early arrangement for Gene Krupa's band of 'If You Were the Only Girl in the World' (another seemingly inappropriate song for jazz) is a gem, as were the arrangements that he and others did for his wonderful Concert Jazz Band of the early 1960s, whose recordings were collected in a four CD set by Mosaic in 2003.

As well as the lightness of Mulligan's overall touch, it is interesting to note that one of the strong aspects of the band was its spontaneity. Echoing the approach of the Count Basie band discussed in WHO DOES WHAT WHEN they made up parts of their arrangements during the performance. As the band's bassist Bill Crow said, 'The thing that I really liked about that band was that we had a good riff-maker in each section: Clark [Terry] and Bob [Brookmeyer] and Gerry . . . pretty soon we had a new head arrangement . . . it would really expand the charts and make them so interesting.' But, sadly for those who never heard the band live, 'we never recorded much of that.'[5]

Although it was Mulligan's band he wrote fewer pieces for it than most of his other writers. In a cri de coeur well known to many bandleader/composers, Mulligan said later: 'The reason for having a band in the first place was to have a vehicle to arrange for. And of course, there's enough business involved trying to put a band like that together – I didn't really have time nor the frame of mind to be able to do it. So much for having a band to write for.'[6]

But his influence was strong, and whoever was responsible for each arrangement, the sounds came over as being similar in style and direction, with all the attributes, and none of the problems, expressed in the Balliett quote above. Al Cohn's gloriously titled 'Lady Chatterley's Mother' is a case in point, as is Mulligan's own arrangement of 'Come Rain or Shine', which, featuring Zoot Sims, at times does seem to achieve an unbearable lightness.

One band that Mulligan did get to write a lot for was, somewhat surprisingly, Stan Kenton's, which despite some good points was never known for its subtlety. Mulligan, alongside Bill Holman, one of the other writers for the Concert Jazz Band, gave the hitherto loud, brash and heavy Kenton band a lightness which many thought could never be achieved. Both writers had an enviable gift for counterpoint (of having different groups of instruments play interesting independent lines) usually colourfully orchestrated. Mulligan's 'Young Blood' and Holman's 'Fearless Finlay' (*Kenton Showcase,* Capitol), are great charts, and examples that should have played a larger role in the post bebop development of the big band than they did. But many writers preferred – and prefer – to take the grey route.

GREY VERSUS CREATIVE

My argument rests on the case that there is, and seemingly forever will be, a coterie of musicians whose small group work is clichéd and predictable, those, that is, who are not 'paying tribute' to someone from the past. Alongside them is a group of arrangers who between them has produced, and continues to produce, a very large pile (the word is used advisedly) of arrangements that are, to put it frankly, boring. Both approaches have their fans, as I have discussed above, but in comparison to the very best jazz playing, the very best jazz arranging, whether for large or small groups, this music lacks creativity, lacks life.

grey music: The instrumentation is that of the classic big band or of the usual quintet or sextet. If a big band, the voicings are as formulaic as Mingus says in the quote used at the head of this chapter. If a quintet or sextet, unisons or some basic voicings are the norm.

creative music: If the instrumentation is that of the classic big band, the voicings are more interesting, more colourful, often voicing across sections as Ellington did. If the classic big band line-up is changed, it is to add new instruments such as different reed instruments, some strings, more percussion, electronics, in fact anything that works for the arranger. The classic jazz quintet or sextet is rarely used, but if it is, it is used in a much more creative way. New instruments, groupings and approaches are introduced, such as those seen in the Ornette Coleman, Gerry Mulligan and Modern Jazz Quartets from the past, and many others in the present.

grey music: The theme is very recognisable, with only some smallish, obvious changes from how it was originally written.

creative music: The theme, and its subsequent development, may undergo serious transformation, either at the hands of a soloist or small group, or by an arranger.

grey music: Soloing is often a separate thing, distinct from the tune or what has been written by the composer. Backgrounds are often bland, or the opposite, very busy, seemingly designed to inhibit the soloist. Solos are generally accompanied by all the rhythm section, playing around a regular pulse.

creative music: The integration of the soloists into what has been written is of great importance. The soloist is set up, introduced properly, with effective backgrounds that stimulate and support, and is given time and space to present himself, while conforming to the demands of the composition. Solos can be in time or out, be accompanied by the rhythm section in full or in part, or be totally unaccompanied.

In essence, grey music, whether for small group or big band, often sounds heavy, solid, earth based, with little real variety, while creative music has textural change, and integration of what's written with what's improvised. Above all, in every area of creative music, it seems that there is room to breathe.

One could suggest that, at this juncture, in order to give this chapter room to breathe, readers should be encouraged to take time out to put on a track from each of two CDs: one from any of the grey writers I have mentioned above, and one from Duke Ellington or Gerry Mulligan. And, while listening, to read the next two paragraphs.

As Gunther Schuller said in a quote I used in WHO DOES WHAT WHEN there was a drastic swing of the pendulum in the 1930s, away from the polyphonic New Orleans style, with five or six players improvising together, towards the block chord section writing of the swing era big bands. As he rightly concluded 'to this day [the pendulum] has never swung back fully to re-embrace polyphony in the large-ensemble context.'

Quite why it has never swung back fully can be seen as the $64,000 question. How did we get to all this heaviness, all this grey music, when there are examples around such as those we have mentioned? Gil Evans may have used some instruments not usually seen in a jazz setting, but Ellington and Mulligan didn't. They used the normal big band line up, like the grey men and women, but they used it with a sense of grace, and lightness. Nor is it that their music is far out, it's very accessible, not disturbing as, perhaps, Mingus might be at the Lincoln Center.

One can understand that writing fresh, creative music for a big band is not easy, nor is finding the money to play it and record it.

Critic Max Harrison has made the point that, for very obvious reasons, the touring schedules of the swing bands 'stood in the way of further orchestral developments'. Harrison, following critic André Hodeir, also points out that Ellington was so far ahead of his contemporaries 'that for many years there was no question of the underlying principles of his writing influencing them'.[7]

But why, in the words of Whitney Balliett, do big bands *still* sound like 'a plump, highly regimented expansion of the traditional New Orleans instrumentation'? Why, again in the words of Balliett, do they ignore the example of Ellington who 'had begun replacing conventional big-band devices in the mid-thirties with new harmonies, his own brilliant melodies, and little concerto-type structures built around one soloist'?[8]

My guess is that the rot in jazz arranging came in with the rise of jazz education, and the increasing need for arrangements that could be played by, and in some ways be used to educate, a growing number of 'stage bands'. This term was a misnomer given to early college big bands in post-war America to avoid using the dreaded word jazz. In some ways the arrangements produced for them could be said to have done their best to avoid any connection with the dreaded word also. Based on block voicings, and all the ills enumerated by Mingus in my opening quote, the space for soloing was limited. Also limited, for the obvious reason that the arrangements were, by definition, written for anonymous players, was any sense that real people were involved. The factory had come to jazz.

Churning out charts for college bands became a living for many arrangers, and formulaic writing became the norm. The appeal of disciplined ensemble playing grew, both in the bands who played it, and in the audiences they attracted. Professional bands developed whose reputation was built on these premises and the result has been that one-trick writers like Sammy Nestico are highly praised and performed widely, and one-track bands like the Thad Jones–Mel Lewis band are seen as role models.

FLORENTINE GLASS

Critic Bill Mathieu's comment that Gil Evans' scores should be 'preserved under glass in a Florentine museum' has already been mentioned. The reason is Evans' masterly use of colour, his ability to add texture to a tune or to a simple phrase. While in no way wishing to denigrate that aspect of Evans' talents, which I will go into further below, I would say that concentrating on that alone, as some observers have tended to do, runs the risk of not seeing the wood for the trees.

His version of 'Summertime', from the *Porgy and Bess* collaboration with Miles Davis, provides a good starting point. His take on the tune was to find a simple riff and repeat it – almost always with a different orchestration – under Miles' theme statement and solo. The repetitive motif is a bow to the head arrangements of the swing era, which were discussed in WHO DOES WHAT WHEN. The fact that he decided to change the orchestration almost every time could be seen as showing off, but is a mark of just how talented he was in this area. The realisation that a riff *could* be constantly changed orchestrally is something that, I believe, had a great effect on the way he worked later in his career, which will be discussed further below.

Above all, though, 'Summertime' is a prime example of using simple ideas to provide a fresh approach to something we thought we knew, an approach that transforms the chosen material into a new jazz composition.

Selecting from the given material is a distinguishing characteristic of Evans' work. One can see a connection between this approach and Miles 'sketching' the melody of standard songs and tunes such as 'So What'. And, as Francis Davis pointed out, there is a connection with the approach of certain improvisers. 'Like Rollins, [Evans] tends to isolate and expand discreet elements of his source materials – an especially provocative passing chord, a rhythmically insistent vamp, an unexpected melodic ellipsis – and discard the rest.'[9]

This aspect of Evans' genius is very evident in his re-compositions of two tunes which have been discussed above, Jelly Roll Morton's 'King Porter Stomp' (on *New Bottle Old Wine*, Pacific Jazz) and 'Django', John Lewis' elegy for Django Reinhardt (on *The Complete Pacific Jazz Sessions*, Blue Note Records). In 'Django' Evans pays tribute to the original, not least in the opening where the lines he creates from Lewis' block chords, notably an independent tuba line, seem to be suspended in space. Towards the end, with a bow to earlier head arrangements, he isolates, and expands, the loping cowboy-like bass pattern discussed in *NO MORE BLUES?*, before his darkly scored brass version of the main theme returns us to his suspended opening and Lewis' original sorrowful elegy.

There's a lot of Morton left in Evans' version of 'King Porter Stomp', but enough of Gil to make it into a new composition. What's missing is one of Evans' trademarks, and, as so often, there are precedents in Ellington's work. This is what's known as an 'arranger's chorus', where the composer writes and then orchestrates his own improvisation on the chords. In Ellington's 'Cotton Tail' the saxophone section play an arranger's chorus (and a half) towards the end, and there is a particularly good Gil Evans' example in his arrangement, early in his career, of 'Donna Lee' for Claude Thornhill (*Tapestries*, Affinity).

Undoubtedly, Gil Evans' masterworks were the three albums he recorded with Miles Davis for Columbia between 1957 and 1961. *Miles Ahead*, *Porgy and Bess* and *Sketches of Spain* are, deservedly, classics. Classics in the way they are orchestrated, classics in the way that generally known material is transformed into something new, and classics that demonstrate the deep understanding that developed between soloist and composer. Evans had been involved with Miles in *The Birth of the Cool* and even had some input to *Kind of Blue,* but it was in their collaboration on these three albums that arranged jazz, orchestrated jazz, came of age.

As critic Bill Mathieu said in a rave review in *DownBeat* of *Sketches of Spain* ('one of the most important musical triumphs that this century has yet produced'), these three records 'form a kind of terrifying triumvirate. If there is to be a new jazz, a Shape of Things to Come, then *this* is the beginning. To Davis and Evans goes not the distinction of five, ten or a zillion stars in a review rating, but the burden of continuing to show us The Way.'[10] (Capitals in the original.)

Those three records are also 'classic' in that they marked a very unusual commitment from a record company to an artist. Producer George Avakian has said that the idea to record *Miles Ahead* came because of his fondness for *The Birth of the Cool.* Evans was the obvious choice to do the writing, and the project was given what must have been a huge budget for a jazz album. Inevitably, however, it was not enough and one can hear mistakes happening that should not have been allowed to pass. Some of the problem is down to union-imposed restrictions on prior rehearsal, but as one of the musicians told critic Max Harrison in a private correspondence, 'The crux of the matter is that Gil did not rehearse carefully enough . . . . In pieces which are scored as sensitively and as intricately as Gil's, it's a shame to let the performances cancel out half of their effectiveness. Many details of the scoring simply could not be – or at least were not – touched upon in the sessions I was on.'[11]

Such an approach meant that much editing – and some over-dubbing – was needed after the recording. More will be said on this, and how it affects the 'jazz happens in real time, once' mantra, in *I HEAR A SYMPHONY,* where Charles Mingus' even more radical approach when assembling *The Black Saint and the Sinner Lady* is discussed. However, regardless of how much of *Miles Ahead* was made afterwards using technical wizardry, the end result is wonderful, and the large budget would seem to have been justified by the great success of the recording. Quite probably it was more successful than many of the classical projects that Columbia were recording at the time, where, the cynic in me is forced to point out, big budgets were, and to some extent still are, the norm.

§ *Many years ago in an attempt to educate myself I attended a season of operas at the Royal Opera House in London. I enjoyed some of the them, but at times jealousy took over as I counted the scores and scores of people who would come on to the stage only once or twice during the performance, and calculated just how much I, or any other jazz composer, could have done with a fraction of the money that was being spent.*

More recently, a comment piece in The Guardian *from an orchestral musician headed 'Why we look so miserable', revealed what many of us had long suspected. While the orchestral players are paid around £100 for a concert, some of the 'maestros' who conduct them are able to command a staggering £100,000 per concert. A thousand times more. An obscene amount which, without doubt, would require public subsidy in order to be met. Subsidy which is then lost to the arts for ever, going as it does to support one man's inflated ego and lifestyle.*

The instrumentation Evans chose for *Miles Ahead* had its roots in *The Birth of the Cool*, which, as we saw in INFINITE POSSIBILITIES, was itself derived from the Claude Thornhill band of the 1940s, for which Evans had written arrangements. There were five trumpets, three trombones, bass trombone, two french horns, tuba, bass and drums and four reed players using various combinations of saxophone, clarinet, bass clarinet, oboe, flute and alto flute. Although there were the precedents that we have noted, the use of some of these instruments was unusual at the time. Nowadays, they, and individual string instruments, are in common use, both in terms of enhancing orchestration possibilities, and as soloing instruments.

These resources gave Evans an incredible palette of colours to work with. A palette to which he added harp and bassoon for *Sketches of Spain*. But, brilliant though the results are, at times he seems to be dipping into his paintbox a little too often, and there are just too many colours occurring.

As I have mentioned above, there is a sense that Evans' use of orchestral colours in his arrangement of 'Summertime' led him into new directions.

One can see the result of this very clearly in his composition 'La Nevada' as heard on the album *Out of the Cool* (Impulse!). Most of the performance is improvised, with the form probably decided in the studio. He adds layers of melody, using fragments of what is only a four-bar theme, and rhythm, including the use of maracas as the sole timekeeper for a while. 'La Nevada' was recorded in 1960, just eighteen months after *Kind of Blue*, and, in working this way, Evans demonstrated his awareness of how a new kind of jazz composition could be created by writing *just enough*. This was a concept that he used increasingly, and which will be discussed further in TAKING A CHANCE.

Not that everyone agreed about the importance of 'La Nevada': 'the observation that Gil Evans avoids overwriting seems to be an understatement. It's the absence of composerly structure in 'La Nevada' which results in poorly constructed jamming . . . one is left with the impression of music which takes itself rather seriously but lacks the substance to support the posture it adopts.'[12]

To complain of 'lack of composerly structure' is to assume a starting point that Evans deliberately avoided, and if it does 'take itself rather seriously', it does so as a *jazz* composition. Mark Gilbert's view is, however, countered in Max Harrison's excellent essay on Gil Evans' work (details below and in the bibliography) which includes the comment that 'every note, every vibration, carries significance.' He also points out that the album also 'contains a hypnotically prolonged 'Where Flamingos Fly', whose acute melancholy is etherialised, dissolved. Such pieces well accord with Claude Lévi-Strauss' view of music as "a machine for the suppression of time", and embody a more authentic modern sensibility than a lot of more overtly dissonant jazz.'[13]

While Gil Evans did, at times, use massive resources, they are not necessary to achieve what we can call orchestral sonority. Ellington managed it with the normal big band line-up. His ability, as we saw, to blend the textures of a clarinet, a trumpet, a trombone to produce the sounds heard in 'Mood Indigo' should put the peddlers of grey music to shame. In Duke's music one constantly hears combinations of instruments that puzzle the brain as to how they have been devised. The band 'never needs to use strings or oboes or bassoons, yet sometimes sounds as if it's got them'.[14] (And see the André Previn observation in ONE PLUS ONE MAKES THREE.)

The Mingus quote used in the introduction is the basis of my comments about grey music. It draws attention to the lack of colour in the average jazz big band, or, at least, the inability of arrangers to find the colour that Ellington and Strayhorn were able to find. They found it partially because, unlike many of their successors, they 'shared a fascination for orchestral sonority, harmonic richness, and formal balance'.[15] But also because they had in the band *a group of individuals whose sounds they explored fully*.

One writer who seems to share this fascination for orchestral sonority is Maria Schneider. While recognising this, and her skill as an orchestrator in the Gil Evans mould, I'm afraid I have my doubts about the end product. There is more compositional sense than some of her contemporaries, but it is still essentially a block sound, still a big band language, rather than an improvising group language. This is what she wants, of course, but I find that such music is more or less predictable. The 'sound of surprise' that is evident in Ellington and Evans (and in the classic re-compositions I discuss below) is missing. Even though we know that the majority of Ellington and Evans is written – when they all play together for example – it sounds as if it *could* be improvised, because what we hear is so fresh, so unexpected. Which, with some exceptions, is not true of Schneider's charts. And, I should say, that despite the serious misgivings I am expressing, I find her work much more interesting than any of her contemporaries.

The arrangements are usually in tempo for all or most of the time. Each of the solos is given very full backing, backings that seem like mild updates of Basie's style. She does write some good Ellington/Evans-ish voicings, but relies on them too much. She often allows the soloists to go on too long, without them being properly integrated into the composition. There is no doubt, however, that her charts are technically challenging and attractive to musicians because of this. But, to me, like so much of this kind of music, it's all surface excitement. Where's the depth?

With Schneider, and many of her contemporaries, I am never very sure as to what role improvising plays in the overall charts. At times it seems to have been introduced because 'it's jazz and we must have some solos'. In connection with this it was interesting to see this comment in a *New York Times* interview from Bob Brookmeyer, one of her mentors: 'My first rule became: The first solo only happens when absolutely nothing else can happen. You don't write in a solo until you've completely exhausted what you have to say. If you give a soloist an open solo for thirty seconds, he plays like he's coming from the piece that you wrote. Then he says, "What the hell was that piece that I was playing from?" And the next thirty seconds is, "Oh, I guess I'll play what I learned last night." And bang! Minute two is whoever he likes, which is probably Coltrane.'[16]

It appears from this that Brookmeyer, no mean improviser himself in his early years, is, as a composer, using a strange kind of soloist. This point, already raised in WELL MAN, WE JUST BLOW in connection with a Roscoe Mitchell quote, will be discussed in more depth later. My unshakeable view, and I follow Ellington in this regard, is that a great part of the jazz composer's craft is choosing his soloists, who they are, and where they are asked to play. If you ignore that, you're not writing jazz.

CLASSIC ADVANCED ARRANGEMENTS

*Paul Grabowsky's 'Strange Meeting' (*Ringing the Bell Backwards, Origin Records*) and Christian Mühlbacher's 'Over the Rainbow' (15-04-98, Extraplatte).*

There are many examples one could give of notable advanced arranging, but here are two that sum up most of the strands of this chapter and of the book as a whole. The first, written by an

Australian, uses, again, a seemingly totally inappropriate tune for jazz, and uses instruments and approaches far removed from grey music, integrating the vision of a composer with the soloing skills of his musicians. 'Strange Meeting', Paul Grabowsky's version of the Vera Lynn Second World War song 'We'll Meet Again', is a masterpiece of re-composition.

I use the word masterpiece advisedly. I was floored when I first heard it, as everybody else I have played it to has been – musicians, jazz fans, and those who profess not to like jazz. Vera Lynn's wartime classic is very aptly retitled 'Strange Meeting', and from this unpromising basic material Grabowsky (who speaks of his take on the old tune as being 'post-imperial') creates a tour de force of different ideas. 'It's as though he has given the theme to, say, Gavin Bryars, Duke Ellington, Philip Glass, Gil Evans and David Byrne and then applied William Burroughs' cut-up technique to the results.'[17]

Among the disparate elements are the brilliant opening violin improvisation, a minimalist percussion pattern over which the melody is first introduced, a heavy jazz-rock section with the melody still peeking through at times, electronics, a distorted 'Land of Hope and Glory' and, finally, a very sentimental piano ending, complete with the occasional deliberate wrong note. This may seem a very odd combination of ideas, but from them a stunning *composition* emerges, unlike anything I have ever heard from any writer anywhere. The fact that Grabowsky didn't write the original tune is immaterial. His arrangement, allied with the Australian Art Orchestra's performance, *recomposes* the tune, making it as much of a jazz composition as anything he, I, or anyone else could have written. Vera Lynn is, at the time of writing, still with us, and one can only wonder at what she would think of this particular makeover of the song she made famous.

As well as wondering what Vera Lynn would think of Paul Grabowsky's 'We'll Meet Again', one can also wonder what Judy Garland, if she were still alive, would have thought of Christian Mühlbacher's 'Over the Rainbow'. (I should perhaps point out

that, despite Gene Santori's comment on many gay people liking
Judy Garland, quoted in *IT AIN'T WHO YOU ARE*, I am among the
many gay men who don't!)

Mühlbacher, an Austrian percussionist and drummer, manages,
uniquely as far as I know, to record one album a year, always on
5th April. His version of 'Over the Rainbow' on *5-04-98* is a masterpiece of postmodernism, from the very distorted harmonies of
the opening through the seemingly never-ending repetitions of
the already repetitive melody in the bridge. They finally resolve
into a multilayered patterned background, inside which random
versions of the tune's motifs appear and disappear. It's recognisably 'Over the Rainbow', in the same way that Picasso's paintings
of guitars are recognisably guitars, but something new has been
created.

Although almost certainly unknown to most jazz fans, there is
no doubt that the innovative writing of Paul Grabowsky and
Christian Mühlbacher, and that of many others I could name, is
world-class, and as far from grey music as it's possible to be.

MORE ON ADVANCED ARRANGING

Fred Sturm *Changes Over Time, the Evolution of Jazz Arranging.* An
aptly titled analytical comparison of different arrangements of
four well-known jazz tunes. Although somewhat confusingly laid
out, it is nevertheless an intriguing look at how arrangers such as
Don Redman, Fletcher Henderson, Billy Strayhorn and Gil Evans
looked at 'King Porter Stomp', 'Chant of the Weed', 'All of Me'
and 'Take the 'A' Train'.

Max Harrison on Gil Evans in *a jazz retrospect.* A fascinating essay
on Evans' work from possibly the only jazz critic who can use
Claude Lévi-Strauss, Ralph Waldo Emerson and Mallarmé in an
article without sounding pretentious.

Larry Hicock, *Castles Made of Sound.* A biography of Gil Evans
which covers his life well, and, as I will say in *TAKING A CHANCE,*

includes many interesting observations, particularly from the musicians involved, on just *how* Evans constructed some of this later works.

Jack Chambers, *Sketches of Miles Davis and Gil Evans*. A review with soundbites of *Miles Davis & Gil Evans, The Complete Columbia Studio Recordings*. Originally in *Coda*, now on the web at *www.chass.utoronto.ca/-chambers/miles.html*

Gil Evans Collection (Falk Symposium). A folio of fifteen Gil Evans scores from throughout his career, including 'Jambangle', 'La Nevada', 'Sunken Treasure' and 'Zee Zee'.

13

I HEAR A SYMPHONY

PAINTING NEW PICTURES

dedicated to Charles Mingus

The composer who is good enough can set up something that takes the improviser beyond his own clichés, gives him musical information and structure, a spiritual dimension, a philosophical dimension, that is really a great human thing.[1]

I want to get to the point where everyone playing something of mine will be able to think in terms of creating a whole, *will be able to improvise compositionally so that it will be hard to tell where the writing ends and the improvisation begins . . . . When I get enough players who can do that, I'll be able to write that two-hour symphony that's been in my head – all the parts of my life, like a book.*[2]

For a jazz composer to 'hear a symphony' he must want to do something more than just write a tune to blow on, or dress up a previously written tune, even one of his own, in a big band arrangement. The second quote above, from Charles Mingus, shows that he had ambitions to write a symphony, and he could be said to have written a mini-symphony with 'Goodbye Pork Pie Hat', and Paul Grabowsky's new take on 'We'll Meet Again' is, as he almost said himself, a post-imperial epic.

Hearing, or writing, a symphony is not meant to suggest that those writers who do want to go further, are *necessarily* wishing to ape classical music. Some do, and I will touch on them below. What concerns me here are those writers who, like Mingus, like Grabowsky, want to say something more *within the jazz language*. Unlike those composers we will discuss in TAKING A CHANCE, who relinquish some or all control to the improvisers, these writers want to keep *composer* control, want their vision to be the one that is captured in the music. They want to write *for* improvisation, rather than simply allowing it to colour their work. As the German saxophonist Ernst-Ludwig Petrovsky says above, 'that is really a great human thing'.

There is, however, a problem with this. Once the composer finds the idea, whether abstract or representational, and gets it on paper, he has, if he *is* writing jazz, to find a way of including other creative talents. I mean, of course, the improvisers, who may not have the same picture in mind that the composer has. As Jaki Byard, a long time Mingus collaborator, said, 'I can do without the dictator approach in music . . . I like to play a certain thing, but sometimes I don't have that feeling, and when it's forced on me, it becomes another thing entirely.'[3]

How the composer gets over this, is one of the great problems of jazz, and may go some way to explaining one of the great mysteries which I keep returning to: the high incidence of grey music within the creative art which is jazz.

DOING MORE

'Star-Crossed Lovers' from *Such Sweet Thunder*, 'Saeta' from *Sketches of Spain*, and *The Black Saint and the Sinner Lady*, are all examples of compositions that go some way outside the box of just being a tune or an arrangement. There are, of course, many more examples I could have chosen, either from the three writers whose work I have selected, Duke Ellington, Gil Evans, and Charles Mingus respectively, or from many others. But these three pieces, ranging in length from four to almost forty minutes, will serve as examples of great jazz compositions. And even a superficial listen, even a cursory look, will serve to point out why they are not, in any way, grey.

Each of the pieces was written with at least some specific performers in mind. Depicting the 'Star-Crossed Lovers' in Billy Strayhorn's composition are the saxophonists Johnny Hodges and Paul Gonsalves, accompanied by the Ellington band of the time, which, as we have seen, was the main source of orchestral inspiration for Strayhorn and Ellington. *The Black Saint and the Sinner Lady* uses a larger band than Mingus normally had, but he would have chosen all the musicians himself, and the featured soloist, Charlie Mariano, was one of his favourite improvisers. (It's interesting to note that when asked why he used Mariano, if, as he often said, he disliked white people, Mingus replied 'He's not white, he's Italian.')

'Saeta' features Miles Davis in a highly unusual role that will be discussed later. The other musicians were typical studio musicians, many with jazz credentials, and almost certainly known to Gil Evans beforehand. 'My arrangements don't sound right unless they're played by a certain group of players, and unless I've rehearsed them. They're very personal, and they're not so highly stylized that it's easy to catch on to what I have in mind right away.'[4] When he couldn't get the players he wanted, there could be problems, as Miles Davis reports: 'In the beginning, we had the wrong trumpet players because we had those who were classically trained. But that was a problem. We had to tell them *not* to play exactly like it was on the score. They started looking at us – at Gil, mostly – like we were crazy . . . they knew we must be crazy talking about "Play what *isn't* there".'[5]

The common ground is that in each case the composer was using people known to him. The soloists were put into situations that drew on their individual strengths as improvisers, and using the other musicians' individual sounds allowed each composer to fashion a personal textural palette which was unique. And by no means grey.

Each of the pieces has a 'reason for being'. 'Saeta' is part of the aptly titled Miles Davis/Gil Evans collaboration *Sketches of Spain*, and represents Gil Evans' take on a Spanish religious procession. *The Black Saint and the Sinner Lady* was written by Mingus as a fairly abstract piece, but one that has, judging by the titles and subtitles of the separate movements, significant racial and sociological overtones.

The most obvious of the three, 'Star-Crossed Lovers', has a clear connection to Shakespeare's *Romeo and Juliet,* and can easily be read as a perfect musical representation of the message of the title. The melody is ravishing, young love at its most romantic, and though one wouldn't want to take it too far (remember, the Ellington police may still be with us) one can read something of this in the passionate playing of Hodges and Gonsalves.

But, as we saw earlier, not everything is as it seems. Originally called 'Pretty Girl', it was credited to Billy Strayhorn and had lyrics. By the time it was included in *Such Sweet Thunder*, it had lost its lyrics, gained a new title, and was credited jointly to Ellington and Strayhorn. Such legerdemain could be said to illustrate the aptness of the comment 'thinking of a better way'. Additionally, it draws attention to an interesting aspect of 'painting new pictures'. Just how much significance, how much effect, does a title have?

Quite a lot I would say. There's a joke too long to be repeated here in full, which deals with a 'beautiful ballad' played by a tramp whenever he could get near a piano. When asked why he didn't sell the song and change his life, he said nobody wanted to publish it because it was called . . . . You can fill in your own obscenities, but it points up the way that titles do affect the way we think about music. The song formerly known as 'Pretty Girl' is a lovely tune, whatever it is called (well, remembering the tramp, almost whatever it is called). But putting it in a suite inspired by, and named after, Shakespearean ideas and characters, makes its new title apt and, one might say, inevitable. It works musically, thanks to the arrangement and the well-chosen featured soloists, and that title will be forever associated with the composition.

In fact, Ellington often changed his titles, and in many cases added them later. On his private recording sessions he often referred to new tunes by four letter code names, such as TAGM and LELE, which, one would imagine, only he understood. And the same happened with some Miles Davis tunes. We are told in Ashley Kahn's book on *Kind of Blue* that 'Flamenco Sketches' was just called 'Spanish' on the tape box. (What Kahn isn't able to explain however is one of the great mysteries of that record, one that even lived on in a couple of later editions of the album: how 'All Blues' and 'Flamenco Sketches', totally different tunes based on totally different ideas, could be misnamed in the liner notes and the listings. The 6/8 'All Blues' was described as a set of five scales, while the set of five scales was described as a blues . . . . Strange!)

One of Ellington's (own) most famous pieces was 'Harlem Air Shaft'. As once described by Ellington himself, 'You get the full essence of Harlem in an air shaft. You hear fights, you smell dinner, you hear people making love. You hear intimate gossip floating down. You hear the radio. An air shaft is one great big loudspeaker . . . . You smell coffee. A wonderful thing, that smell . . . . One guy is cooking dried fish and rice and another guy's got a great big turkey.'[6]

Whether, prompted by the title and some imagination, one can sense these things from the music is, as we shall see, a matter of opinion. However, it is said that Ellington's description 'was concocted, probably in reply to an interviewer, to stimulate interest in a piece which was originally intended to be called, according to the Victor record company files, 'Rumpus in Richmond'.'[7] Did Ellington realise the composition represented one thing better than the other and change its title? Or was it, like 'Star-Crossed Lovers', a piece that was a close enough fit when something new was needed? Or was it, like the *Kind of Blue* mislabellings, just a record company cock-up?

Regardless of any of that, what we get is a piece of vintage Ellington, and this would be true whatever he called it. Like 'Star-Crossed Lovers', 'Harlem Air Shaft' does *seem* to fit its title and description – once we know them, but opinions differ on just how well tune and title match. Ellington biographer James Lincoln Collier makes a good case for the representational side of the composition, while, on the other hand, the liner notes to *The Blanton-Webster Band* box set say 'there is little correspondence between [Duke's] words and his music'.

Most composers in jazz use some kind of descriptive title for their work, recognising that it sets up a pact with the listeners, allowing them to approach the composition with some degree, however small, of implied foreknowledge. However, this view has its detractors. As saxophonist Geoff Warren says, 'Why do jazzers have to give title when straight composers can get away with opus numbers? Are we still thought of as part of the pop scene? . . . . The danger is that the piece may not live up to the *pictorial* expectations of the listener. I remember junior school music teachers describing the pictorial aspects of classical records which gave me the idea that classical music was just a rather imperfect way of doing landscape painting.'[8]

Almost certainly Ellington's musicians would be aware of what sounds could be heard in a Harlem air shaft. But this correspondence between composer's idea and musicians' knowledge is unusual, and raises the question as to whether titles affect the way musicians play; whether the musicians are consciously affected by what the composer or leader may tell them, or whether they are subconsciously influenced by their own feelings about the title and the mood of the piece.

Or, whether they 'just blow' regardless.

If the latter, then any possible collaboration between composer and soloist is doomed from the start. However, achieving the right fit of composition and soloist, integrating what's written with what's improvised is an important aspect of jazz composing. One that raises expectations about what the art is capable of, and raises concerns about how, in the wrong hands, it can easily turn into grey music.

Although we could reasonably expect Ellington's musicians to have some knowledge of a Harlem air shaft, and that Gonsalves and Hodges could respond appropriately to a beautiful ballad like 'The Star-Crossed Lovers', one wouldn't expect Miles Davis to have any knowledge of Spanish women singers and their role in religious processions. It is part of Gil Evans' genius in 'Saeta' that he saw that Miles, uniquely among his peers, could provide the emotion that the piece required, and part of Miles Davis' genius that he fits the role so well.

'The *saeta*, in flamencan music, is "the arrow of song". One of the oldest religious types of music in Andalusía, it is usually sung without accompaniment during Holy Week . . . . It tells of the Passion of Christ and is usually addressed to the image of the crucified Christ that is carried in the march, or to the Virgin Mary. As described by Gilbert Chase, "The singer, usually a woman, stands on a balcony overlooking the procession, grasping the iron railing firmly in both hands (the grip tightens as the emotion grows). The procession stops so that the image which is being addressed remains stationary while the *saeta* is being sung. A fanfare of trumpets gives the signal for the procession to move on."'[9]

Miles said '['Saeta'] was the hardest thing for me to do . . . . To play parts on the trumpet where someone was supposed to be singing . . . . Because you've got all those Arabic musical scales up in there, black African scales that you can hear. And they modulate and bend and twist and snake and move around. It's like being in Morocco.'[10] As well as Miles' playing, what is fascinating is the way that Evans accompanies Miles with a sustained but slowly pulsating carpet of sounds over somewhat menacing snare drum rolls, depicting the small movements of the band musicians while they stand for the ceremony. He also captures the feeling of the street procession with the notes of the fanfares, some deliberately cracked, being played on separate trumpets to give the idea of bugles.*

What we hear in 'Saeta', as well as Arabic scales, fascinating textural backgrounds, and evocations of something 'Spanish', is jazz composition being moved into new realms of possibilities. Miles Davis' portrayal of the singer is magnificent, eminently believable, and still jazz. The collaboration with Gil Evans on this piece showed the way to something new in jazz composition. Something that is much more than a tune or an arrangement. A composition that has different aims than the integration *within* accepted jazz traditions of what's written with what's improvised. A composition in which composer and soloist combine to portray an idea *outside* jazz. 'Saeta' inhabits a different world, and is an achievement that has rarely been equalled.

The difficulty of incorporating soloists into a composer's vision is, as I have said, one of the major problems of writing more than just a tune or a simple arrangement. Some composers give their soloists compositionally important fragments of melody or scales to use as starting points for their solos. At times, these may come from a totally separate part of the composition and therefore help to meld the piece together, and blur the dividing line between what is written and what is improvised.

Ideally, of course, the soloist is aware of all the written elements of a composition, working with them, away from them, or towards them, integrating the motifs into the solo as though they were their own invention. In the first part of George Russell's 'All About Rosie' the stunning piano solo by Bill Evans is interrupted

---

* Interestingly, there is an alternate 'full' take of 'Saeta' on the *Complete Columbia Studio Recordings*. The take that was used has the procession fading as the band disappears into the distance. The 'full' version has Miles returning to improvise over some sustained sounds. Even in normal jazz terms, where such a 'doodle 'til faded' return from the soloist might be expected, this is not always a good idea. In a piece as brilliantly conceived and executed as 'Saeta' it just doesn't work, and was rightly dropped.)

by a band phrase that seems to have arrived because the band, magically, cottoned on to what Evans was playing. It was, of course, Evans who worked towards that moment, and who works away from the written elements after the band's contribution has gone. (This track, originally from *Modern Jazz Concert* recorded at the Brandeis Festival in 1957, can be found on various compilations including *The Birth of the Third Stream*, Columbia Legacy).

§ *It is, of course, desirable, even essential, that the soloist be fully aware of what's happening in the music around him. But sometimes events get in the way. Because of the band set-up in one particular venue, the soloist, who had to contend with my placing any one of five ensemble cues against what he was playing, was unable to see my signals to the band. He commented afterwards that soloing under those conditions 'was like walking through a minefield'.*

MINGUS, MINGUS, MINGUS

I play and write me, the way I feel .... If someone has been escaping reality, I don't expect him to dig my music .... My music is alive and it's about the living and the dead, about good and evil. It's angry, yet it's real because it knows it's angry.[11]

There is a story that on the day Charles Mingus died – at the age of fifty-six in Mexico – fifty-six whales beached themselves on a nearby coast. Such cosmic recognition of a jazz musician's genius is, it must be acknowledged, somewhat rare. But, if anyone deserved it after Duke and Jelly Roll, both of whom he appreciated greatly, it was Charles Mingus.

One can be forgiven for wondering why the cosmic recognition couldn't have happened sooner, giving Mingus the support he often lacked to enable him to present his music more often, and in settings more conducive to his ambitions. Maybe it would have given him the opportunities – and the temperament – that enabled Ellington to subsidise his composing ambitions by running a band full-time. Or perhaps, in some magical way, it could have snuck him a tiny percentage of the royalties earned by the pop and rock stars who, even today, openly acknowledge his influence.

Unfortunately, none of this happened. The jazz composer who was there to take advantage of the changes of the revolutionary decade, who, as I have already said, in many ways helped make those changes happen, had all the disadvantages of a genius existing in hard times. Which could have been why he was hard to get along with. 'Mingus had a volatile temperament that could lead from one explosive extreme to another . . . . He would vacillate between feelings of high exuberance on the one hand and total depression on the other. He felt deep down that he was a hunted man, oppressed by his environment, and his feelings of vulnerability and hurt were often converted into uncontrollable rage and tyrannical behaviour to others – at times even those closest to him.'[12]

Many of Mingus' compositional trademarks, were, as I've said elsewhere, directly influenced by Ellington. Like Ellington he realised that a jazz composer should write for the people in his band; that their ideas in putting a piece together could be important; that what was written down wasn't sacred and could be changed in rehearsal or on the bandstand. (If indeed it was written down. Mingus' way of teaching the musicians by singing musical lines to them has been discussed above).

But he was also influenced by others. As Ekkehard Jost has pointed out, 'By working as sideman of such dissimilar musicians as Kid Ory, Louis Armstrong, Lionel Hampton, Red Norvo, Art Tatum and Charlie Parker, Mingus got intimately acquainted with a broad spectrum of styles. In fact, it is doubtful whether any other musician has ever had quite the same amount of direct access to so many different kinds of jazz.'[13]

One can also see influences of New Orleans music in Mingus' interest in collective improvisation, of Count Basie in his use of background riffs, and of Ellington, again, in his abiding interest in orchestral textures. As Mingus biographer Brian Priestley says: 'the aspiring jazz composer must be open to so many potential influences that the process of absorption is, as with Ellington, much more subconscious and protracted.'[14]

Priestley also makes the point that 'both Mingus and Ellington were often thought of by their contemporaries as standing outside the mainstream of jazz development, and Duke, indeed, had to wait until he was in his sixties for the historical significance of his work to be fully understood. In this respect, Mingus was more fortunate, by a decade or so, but without the kind of mass popularity that kept Ellington going he had some hard times ahead.'[15]

Because of his chronological time, Mingus was able to take Ellington's ideas further, and in doing so he produced a body of work unequalled in pure jazz composing. His example, even more than Ellington's, is the one many contemporary jazz composers, including myself, have followed. The main reason is that he is nearer our time, and, because of this, he was able to use a language which is freer than Ellington's. To connect back to the argument of *IT AIN'T WHO YOU ARE*, Ellington had to deal with the baggage around him, including the entertainment aspects of the music. Mingus could learn from, and move on from, what Ellington had developed.

Following Ellington's example, however, Mingus realised that a jazz composition can be continuously revised, sometimes with the help of the musicians, sometimes in the performance itself. 'As long as they start where I start and end where I end, the musicians can change the composition if they feel like it. They add themselves, they add how they feel, while we're playing.'[16]

Which, once more, raises the question of jazz form, to be discussed further below.

Even though Mingus did not, could not, have a regular band as Ellington did, he had – as with all contemporary jazz composers – a group of musicians with whom he worked regularly. One of his main collaborators, unsurprisingly given their related roles, was drummer Dannie Richmond. In a very interesting chapter on

Mingus in Ekkehard Jost's *Free Jazz* Richmond says, 'Mingus and I feel each other out as we go . . . . The best way I can explain is that we find a beat that's in the air, and just take it out of the air when we want it.' Jost adds: 'This may sound a bit mystic but it hits the mark. It is doubtless this "feeling", this intuitive response, that has given Mingus' music part of its tension and fascination.'[17]

This tension and fascination is seen in all of the tracks on *Mingus Ah Um* (CBS), recorded with an eight piece band in 1959, shortly after *Kind of Blue*. The whole range of Mingus' 'miniatures' are on display, including tributes to Ellington, Morton and Lester Young, as well as two of his very popular gospel-tinged numbers, 'Better Git It In Your Soul' and 'Boogie Stop Shuffle'. Somewhat different in concept is 'Self-Portrait in Three Colors', originally written for the John Cassavetes film *Shadows*, which may account for the fact that there is, in the final saxophone flourish, only *one* bar of what one could call improvising. But the playing of the main melody (six + nine bars long), and the two other very strong lines that accompany it, are sufficient to make it a strong jazz composition.

Mingus' example, in all the pieces I have mentioned and many more, also means that jazz *composers* can exist. Not just as tune writers – although the opportunity to write something new in this area is still there, as Mingus often showed. Not as arrangers or orchestrators – areas in which much interesting work continues to be done (and areas in which, in the accepted sense, Mingus did *not* excel). Not as recomposers, another fertile area for Mingus and many of today's musicians. *But to exist as jazz composers, pure and simple.* Composers who want to put their own stamp on a piece, while using the textural and individual resources of the musicians involved to 'paint a picture' together. Not that the musicians were always grateful. As trombonist Jimmy Knepper said about his time with Mingus: 'I used to get very depressed. Good god, I'd say to myself, I'm stuck with this guy for the rest of my life. His music was so difficult, with all those time changes and different sequences . . . . It seemed written to trip you up. I wanted to relax and play standards.'[18]

The Black Saint and the Sinner Lady is a work that typifies Mingus' methods. In six movements, and thirty-eight minutes long, it is one of the most successful longer works in jazz – and has a lengthy liner note from Mingus' psychologist to prove it! This note includes Mingus' own comment that the use of the Spanish guitar 'was meant to mirror the period of the Spanish Inquisition and El Greco's mood of oppressive poverty and death'.

While the flamenco guitar does give the feeling of Spain, there is no doubt that this is a jazz composition. The ensemble sounds are drenched with Ellington references, the strongly featured – and brilliant – alto soloist Charlie Mariano constantly evokes Johnny Hodges, and there are obvious echoes of Harry Carney in the ever-present baritone. Yet Mingus' identity is apparent all the way. Themes are often repeated, as can be seen in Priestley's almost indispensable analysis referred to below, but it is the close-knit textures, remarkably obtained from only a ten piece band, that seem to hold the whole composition together. It's a very kaleidoscopic piece, which constantly seems to be happening, to be alive, justifying my mantra that jazz happens in real time, once.

Which in a way it did, and in a way it didn't. It was assembled in the studio by Mingus and producer Bob Thiele who commented, 'there were literally fifty splices to be made after the date – all in Charlie's head.'[19] And, to thicken the plot, Mariano's solo parts were apparently dubbed on a week later. As Priestley says, *The Black Saint* 'marks the first occasion in any field where the combination of overdubbing with creative editing determined the nature of the product.'[20]

The 'product' is a jazz suite made up of a series of shortish sections created 'live' in the studio, and assembled later by Mingus. This assembling and overdubbing could well have been something of a necessity given the difficulties of recording a complex piece in anything like its entirety in a studio. However, I think there was more than that going on. My guess is that Mingus used a combination of 'jazz form' – put together in the studio, or pre-conceived in his head – allied to a healthy dose of Ellington's 'thinking of a better way'. Towards the very end of the recording there are three consecutive takes of the same piece of music. They are played differently and orchestrated differently, but the fact that each uses the same kind of increasing tempo, starting from a similar very slow base, is a strong indication that to use them *consecutively* must have been an inspiration in the editing suite.

Many of the other solos were recorded with the band and rhythm section in the studio together, but Mariano's overdubbing allowed a different approach. The idea wasn't to have Mariano and a rhythm section creating together, but that Mariano should observe and comment on what the band had previously recorded. The soloist, and Mingus himself, were allowed the luxury of time to determine exactly when the soloist would stop and start, and probably what the content could be, with, presumably, the opportunity to try a few different takes. (I am reminded of a time when, asked for recommendations for a sax player by Irmin Schmidt of the German experimental rock group Can, I suggested Geoff Warren. Geoff told me later that he was asked to improvise over some pre-recorded tracks. He did this 'many times', was paid, and went home, leaving Irmin to decide which solos, or *parts of solos*, best fitted his concept.)

These ideas were new to jazz in 1963 and have, for somewhat obvious reasons, not been used much since. Indeed *The Black Saint* was never played again by Mingus. The first half of the piece was attempted by a repertory Mingus band but, as Francis Davis reported, 'The performance's most agonising flaw was its lack of Mingus-like vehemence . . . . As a result, this wasn't Mingus.' Which neatly illustrates my contention that it's the performance that matters, and that in the case of the *Black Saint* recording, jazz *did* happen in real time, but there were a few real times needed to make it into the masterpiece it undoubtedly is.

CLASSICAL INFLUENCES

Once words such as symphony are used, one enters, or at least veers towards, the territory of classical music. Not always a bad thing, but an area that has to be treated with more caution than many jazz composers allow. Why caution? Put simply, because it's a different ball game.

§ *Some critics have used the word symphonic to describe my work. It's not a word I'm keen on, in that it has too many connotations with classical music, which, as readers will have realised, I see as a totally different music. But if those critics mean that there is space for things to develop, then I'll go along with them.*

However, I do have to admit that one of my pieces is called A Symphony of Scorpions. *The title came from the phrase 'a symphony of scorpions, a procession of flying grand pianos and cathedrals' found in Malcolm Lowry's novel* Ultramarine. *The imagery evoked was too good to pass up as a title and as a source of inspiration. Although when it came to the writing, having no scorpions or cathedrals and only one grand piano, I decided against being too literal.*

Writing an ambitious work such as *The Black Saint* could be said to be an influence from classical music. Jazz composing generally starts, and often stops, with the tune, a piece of music in a simple form such as the twelve-bar blues, or the AABA thirty-two bar standard song. Classical music has its miniatures, too, but it also has its grand symphonies and concertos, and some jazz composers have been tempted to emulate this kind of thinking. But, compared to jazz composers, classical composers have different ideas on how to fill all that space. And different ideas on how to use their resources.

When classical influences are apparent, the question, at least for me, is whether the end result is jazz or not. This is tricky ground. Some people say there are only two kinds of music, good and bad (though I would add a third, 'indifferent'). But for me this begs all sorts of questions. Although finding the dividing line may be difficult, there is a difference between, say, Charles Ives' *Fourth Symphony* and Charles Mingus' *The Black Saint and the Sinner Lady*. Both great pieces of music, but each designed and written for different ends. They speak different languages, indeed, inhabit different worlds. Ives' aim was to produce an extended orchestral composition using his language of contrasts and levels, and the resources of a full symphony orchestra in a four-movement form. Mingus' aim was also to write an extended composition, drawing contrasts and levels although from a much smaller group, by using *jazz* resources within his chosen form. As part of his language he was using the musicians in his band as specific, individual, colours. Ives wrote everything down with only some interpretative areas left to the conductor. Mingus conceived the idea and wrote some of it down, but left sufficient space for the soloists to contribute to the whole, and for ideas to be developed in the studio and also in the subsequent editing.

When listening to a composer such as Charles Ives one realises that it is just not possible to do what he is doing in jazz. Nor is it possible with Ives' language and approach, to do what jazz is capable of doing. With classical music, the challenge lies in making technical and musical sense out of a lot of notes. With jazz the challenge is very different: making something personal out of the ideas – often very simple ideas – that are presented.

This could be seen to be restrictive but it is, I would argue, part of the music's real strength, and to think otherwise can be seen as a throwback to classical conditioning. For me, jazz should provide a feeling that something new is happening, not because of what is on the paper – though of course, that can help – but because of the occasion: *the performance has life and freshness because of the contributions and interaction of all those involved.*

There is, then, one area where something of a line can be drawn between jazz and classical composing. If it's all written, there's no space for soloists, no opportunity to use that unique resource of the jazz composer, his musicians. There's a difference in language, too. The classical language has its own strengths, not least the ability to create fascinating textures from the available resources. But the classical language, almost by definition, ignores the inflexions of jazz, the rhythmic feel of jazz, the possibility of blending individual colours created by individual jazz musicians. Everything, that is, which makes up the jazz language.

Although the term has gone somewhat out of fashion, compositions that attempt to merge jazz and classical music are usually referred to as 'third stream', a term coined by Gunther Schuller and once unkindly likened to 'two nearby radio stations merging together'. I've never been happy with the term, nor with the works produced using these ideas, and, as might be imagined, I have some arguments about even making the attempt.

Many of the works written under the banner of third stream have the same characteristics. To take an example from one of the musicians I have previously praised, I am sorry to say that I find Ornette Coleman's *Skies of America*, for the Coleman quartet with full symphony orchestra, to be both pretentious and long-winded. It contains more juvenile writing for an orchestra than I had ever expected to hear outside of a beginners' orchestration class; yet it, like other examples of this genre, is regularly salivated over by jazz critics and fans who, when faced with such fusions, seem to leave their critical facilities at home. Such compositions throw out the best of both musics and end up being a hybrid that should satisfy nobody. That Coleman has been highly praised for that particular work is one of the mysteries of life that I guess I'll have to learn to live with. (Except for *Sound Grammar* [Phrase Text Inc.] I've not been too fond of much of his later pure jazz work either: it may not be pretentious, but it's certainly long winded, and seems to be based on the premise that unrelenting mono-textured sounds can be attractive.)

One place where an orchestra (of strings only) was successfully used in jazz was *Focus*, the Eddie Sauter/Stan Getz collaboration, recorded for Verve in 1961. It remains the classic lesson in how to use strings in jazz, and how to use jazz when strings are around.

Sauter realised that, as Bartók and Stravinsky had already proved, strings *can* make their own rhythms; and that using a string quartet as the cornerstones of the orchestra, would meld the group together in a way that has its relationship *to the way jazz works*. Stan Getz's contribution was as an observer, listening to what the strings were playing and commenting on it, a role in which, as we have seen, Getz excels. Apart from the rhythmic attack of the strings no attempt was made to make the orchestra swing. The only time anything like a conventional jazz feel is heard is in 'I'm Late, I'm Late', where Roy Haynes' freely improvised drum accompaniment adds another layer.

§ Focus *was the inspiration for my only attempt to work in this genre when, some years ago, I was one of three composers commissioned by Westdeutscher Rundfunk in Cologne to write a composition for symphony orchestra and our own choice of jazz soloists. My composition,* Plain Song and Mountain Birds, *took as its starting point the Gregorian chant I had heard sung – 'hanging in the air' – in Cologne Cathedral on a previous research visit, and the fact that mountain birds were said to roost in the cathedral's spires, the highest point around. My two soloists, sax and flute player Geoff Warren and guitarist Ed Speight, acted, in programmatic terms, as mountain birds, observing what was happening in the orchestra, whose history had started with music like the plainsong I had heard in the cathedral.*

The audience acclaim for my piece was, I must admit, somewhat eclipsed by a good, but very poppish, arrangement from one of the other composers, but that's life! Interestingly though, the third writer, ignoring the (different) precedents which I and the other writer had followed, went down a route which has rarely if ever worked. He used a jazz-rock rhythm section with the orchestra, and, finding the inevitable problems of 'moving the orchestra' too hard to handle, had to withdraw one movement of his piece during rehearsals.

Any comparison between jazz and classical music is often confused by the exaggerated praise from both sides of the divide.

What are we to make of Bob Belden, respected jazz composer, compiler and annotator of Miles Davis collections, when he said in a *Jazz Times* article 'the sheer magnanimity of what they (Rachmaninov, Prokofiev, Wagner, Holst or Verdi) did compared to what jazz musicians do, there's no comparison?'[21] As I wrote in a published response: 'He misses the point. His cited composers, strange bedfellows but it's his choice, may have had magnanimity, but surely Ellington, Miles and many others also have that same 'greatness of soul', only in a different ball game.'

But looking at it another way, what are we to make of Anthony Braxton's remarks: 'For to understand what has been raised in the progression of creative music as it has been defined through the work of the Ellingtons–Hendersons–Minguses–Colemans–etc, is to be aware of the most significant use of the orchestra medium in the last hundred years (and some).'[22] Is Braxton really saying that his quoted examples used the orchestra medium more significantly than Berio? Stravinsky? Shostakovich? I hope not. (And see my remarks on Coleman's orchestral writing above.) What he is saying (I think; Braxton's prose style is not the easiest to understand) is that jazz musicians have brought something different to the orchestra medium, and that this should change the way we think about the potential of the idiom. I agree, but that's a different argument. Berio and Ellington have both used the orchestra medium significantly, and any discussion of one is not best served by denigrating, implicitly or explicitly, the other.

The feeling by many in the classical field that jazz is not as good as classical music is confusingly apparent in the increasing number of 'crossover' performances and events that (dis)grace our concert halls and airwaves. Some years ago the London Philharmonic Orchestra, playing some Ellington material alongside Shostakovich's *Jazz Suite Number One*, called the programme *Take Jazz Seriously*. What the (expletive deleted) do they think jazz musicians do?

THE QUESTION OF FORM

It's clear why you like those pieces and composers. They appear to share a similar aesthetic to yours at least in the space and sweep of the mood, things are not crowded with events and everything unfolds in general in a more organic way. [23]

This comment from guitarist and promoter Paul Nash, on why I had suggested certain pieces by other European jazz composers for him to select from for a concert in New York, sums up, as he says, my own approach to the question of form. But this is a matter for my subconscious. Some composers use accepted forms such as 'symphonic form', 'sonata form', 'song form' but these are just starting points and how any composition reaches its final form is a matter of mystery, even to many classical composers. But, with jazz, there are the added ingredients of the soloists, and the contributions of the other musicians, as well as the application of the concise and very apt comment made about Ellington, 'thinking of a better way'. That phrase can also be applied to the methods of Charles Mingus, and, as we will see in the next chapter, is also relevant to the way Gil Evans worked in his later years.

These factors have led me to coin the phrase 'jazz form' to describe – or attempt to describe – something that happens in jazz (in real time, once, remember), but which is so amorphous that it is almost impossible to grasp. To simplify matters, and admitting that it is probably a cop out, I'll settle for a very basic definition for now: jazz form is what works for jazz over an extended time frame. By which I mean the ability of a jazz composer, with the help of his musicians, to create a piece of music that hangs together over an extended period of time, a composition that incorporates the talents of the musicians without overwhelming them, or allowing them to overwhelm the composition. To write a piece of music that says, unequivocally, 'this is jazz', with enough content and interest to justify its time scale.

The idea that there is such a thing as jazz form has become increasingly interesting, increasingly important, as I have worked through this book. It will be discussed further in the next two chapters and will be summed up, alongside a discussion of space and levels, in the penultimate chapter, '*PLAY A RAT PATROL SOUND*'. The quotes that end this chapter – some with editorial comment – circle around the subject, and will go some way to explaining what jazz form can be.

'Jazz is too rigid, too narrow in all phases of expressive nuance to allow for formal growth. I believe this poverty to be technically inherent.' [24]
(There may have been some truth in that in the early days of jazz, but at the time this was written, by composer and teacher Robert Cowley in 1959, many of the new possibilities were becoming visible, if not yet totally obvious.)

'Jazz has too many strangling qualities for a composer.' [25]
(Charles Mingus' statement should perhaps be taken with a grain or two of salt. Certainly much of his work belies that remark, as does the quote which follows. But one can also read the remark as a reaction against much of the jazz that was going on at the time (and probably achieving more success than his own). It could also be seen as a pointer towards the arguments covered in *IT AIN'T WHO YOU ARE*, that perhaps even Mingus could not get rid of all the baggage that was carried by American jazz musicians.)

Although not so precisely demanding of his performers as, say, Milton Babbitt or [George] Russell, Mingus takes greater risks . . . . ['Revelations'] extends itself as a succession of moods, feelings, atmospheres, melting into and out of each other. This was something which had not then been widely attempted in jazz, although music, like poetry, is well equipped for it, good examples being L'Après-midi d'un faune – both the Debussy and Mallarmé versions. [26]
From Max Harrison's review of *Modern Jazz Concert* reissued as part of *The Birth of the Third Stream* (Columbia Legacy).

The conversion of the canvas into an active 'field' represents a major revolution in the art of painting . . . . Instead of moving toward a resolution the field remains open, to attract an indefinite quantity of data seemingly placed at random.[27]

The piece is pure development . . . the form becom[es] a succession of moments without ending.[28]

What is indispensable and counts most, in music as well as literature, is inner, emotional, dramatic form . . . . [Form] can be recognised only emotionally not intellectually. That is, it is a question decided by taste.[29]

The first sentence of any novel should be 'Trust me, this will take time'.[30]

CLASSIC *'JAZZ SYMPHONY'*

Escalator Over the Hill (2CD set, JCOA/ECM)

Called a 'chronotransduction' by its composer Carla Bley, and lyricist Paul Haines (no, I don't know what it means, either), *Escalator Over the Hill* is a very ambitious work, painting a picture that goes outside jazz, and largely succeeds. Initially inspired we are told by Bley hearing the Beatles' *Sgt. Pepper's Lonely Hearts Club Band* and deciding to match it, the large cast includes Jack Bruce and Linda Ronstadt as well as jazz musicians such as Gato Barbieri, Don Cherry, Charlie Haden, Dewey Redman and John McLaughlin. A sprawling work, as close to an opera as I've heard in jazz, but without the warbling and overstaffing, it is more successful than much of her later work, where, I'm afraid, she seems to have slipped into whimsy. But *Escalator* is good, great at times.

For a breakdown of what happens over the almost two hour length of the work go to this somewhat over the top article from critic Marcello Carlin, in which he (self-admittedly) tries to justify his claim that *Escalator* is 'the piece of music which I regard as the greatest ever made, the gold standard against which I qualitatively measure all other music, the definitive record which, thirty years after its original appearance, may still render all other records redundant.'[31]

As he says – and who am I to argue? – 'We have now arrived at the end of side four of the original six-sided vinyl edition. So far we have witnessed an unprecedented, certainly pre-post modern collision (more fission than fusion) between avant-pop, European light opera, post-Darmstadt electronica which also foresees the *Iceman Cometh* atmosphere which was to drench everything from Sonic Youth's *Daydream Nation* to Portishead's *Dummy*. Not to mention foreseeing John Zorn. Or David Thomas. Or indeed the whole fucking No Wave scene . . . .'[32]

MORE ON HEARING SYMPHONIES

Brian Priestley, *Mingus: A Critical Biography*, unusually for jazz biographies contains much about the actual music, including an indispensable analysis of *The Black Saint and the Sinner Lady*.

Ekkehard Jost, *Free Jazz*, includes an illuminating chapter on Mingus' work and influence.

Charles Mingus. More than a Fake Book, a collection of fifty-five Mingus compositions edited and with musical analyses by Andrew Homzy, who, in collaboration with Sue Mingus, has been heavily involved in preserving the complete Mingus catalogue.

14

TAKING A CHANCE

RELINQUISHING CONTROL

dedicated to Steve Harris [*] and ZAUM

*I am not . . . even to the least extent, counting on the possible creative
ability of the performers . . . . I do not wish, even partially, to relinquish
the authorship of the music I have written.*[1]

*The problem of the big band in free jazz lies first and foremost in
employing the sound potential of a large apparatus structurally . . .
without having to reduce the individual creativity of a majority of the
players to merely reading notes.*[2]

The first comment, Witold Lutosławski talking of his forays into
aleatoric music, is a valid viewpoint for a classical composer – it's
what they do. They write music so that it can be played by any
group of the same size and instrumentation, and expect the end
result to be a fairly exact representation of what they, as composers, believe the piece will sound like. As we saw in the last
chapter, some jazz composers also want to work, at least partially,
in that area. But there are those who have gone the opposite
way, writing little or nothing to inspire the musicians, relying

---

[*] While on the final revision for this book, news of Steve's early death
at fifty-nine reached me. He will be much missed as a friend and as a
great musician.

instead on what happens when they as individuals, alone or in a group, start to improvise. The second quote, by Ekkehard Jost, illustrates the challenge they set themselves, especially in terms of the large group.

JUST FIVE SCALES

As we know, Miles, with help from Bill Evans, took some scraps of paper into the recording studio for *Kind of Blue*. Some control was exercised in deciding who would play what when, but, in keeping with a practice he continued for much of his career, Miles, like Duke before him, allowed the musicians to make suggestions as to how a tune should develop. The development was, with some variations, along theme-solos-theme lines, and the inherent looseness in the tunes was not explored fully until some time later.

However, one of the scraps of paper, seen in all its torn glory on Cannonball Adderley's music stand in a picture in Ashley Kahn's book, was somewhat different. There was no melody, no chords, simply a set of five scales, 'each to be played as long as the soloist wishes until he has completed the series.'[3] 'I thought that . . . we could move through two or three or four or five levels that would relate to one another and make a cycle . . . we worked at it at the piano until we arrived at the five levels we used.'[4]

To use such an idea as the basis for a composition was breathtaking in its simplicity, and in its vision. 'Flamenco Sketches', as the recorded performance came to be called, is the distilled essence of jazz. It illustrates, perfectly, that anything – or nothing – can, because it results in a great jazz performance, be a great jazz composition.

Given the newness of the concept it is not surprising that the soloists did not go too far out, remaining fairly close to the usual four- and eight-bar phrase lengths. As Herbie Hancock said, 'It was as though they were walking into this unknown territory and being very careful where they stepped. Nobody played too much – there was a minimalist approach to the material.'[5]

However, it could well be argued that the minimal approach was 'in the air', not only in the sparse theme statements of the tunes on *Kind of Blue*, but in the approach to melodies of Miles and John Coltrane at that time. As Ekkehard Jost says, 'Coltrane's 'India' picks up the concept of 'My Favorite Things' . . . and carries it further. Again the theme is only of secondary importance for the progress of the piece. It sets the emotional mood, without providing a rhythmic, harmonic or formal foundation.'[6]

It is only a small step from this sparseness of approach to doing without a starting point altogether.

JUST BLOWING

I'm suggesting that if anyone in the production of a music event is dispensable, it is the score-maker, or the 'composer' as he is often called. My 'ideal music' is played by groups of musicians who choose one another's company and who improvise freely in relation to the precise emotional, acoustic, psychological and other less tangible atmospheric conditions in effect at the time the music is played.[7]

This chapter's dedicatees, Steve Harris (1948–2008) and his group ZAUM, have created, in their live performances and in their CDs, sets of miniatures that show distinct compositional form, with some moments of aggression, alongside some moments of pure beauty. To my ear they could have been composed, yet I am told that they were completely improvised in performance. Some of the sounds are undeniably jazz, some could have been created from music written by a contemporary classical composer. They provide a completely satisfying experience in an area where, for me – because of the risk taking? because of my preference for some kind of underlying form? – this is rare.

'We really don't prepare for performance or recording in the conventional sense and certainly don't pre-plan. In fact I have a rule that we don't play together (the briefest of soundchecks where necessary) before a performance . . . in a relatively large group like ZAUM there are lots of possibilities operating in cells within the group, we don't all need to be following one idea and when this is happening I, like any of the musicians, can chose to move around reinforcing or subverting different ideas. That's when it's working the best . . . I always stress the importance of looking for endings, for me a consensus on an ending between all the players somehow determines that they've all been playing the same piece of music.'[8]*

One reason why I find a lot of the avant-garde's music unsatisfactory could be summed up in the famous comment by George Santayana, 'those who forget the past are doomed to repeat it'. The free approach to jazz has been around a long time, and there are many times when I feel I've heard it all before. Mainly in the sixties and seventies. It's an odd phenomenon when today's so-called free music is, at times, so redolent of the past that, hearing something called 'free' today, one seems to relive an earlier experience, as if it were Duke Ellington in Coventry Cathedral, or Ben Webster in Ronnie Scott's club.

As Steve Lacy said, 'I had a group in 1966 with Enrico Rava and Johnny Dyani and Louis Moholo and we played completely free music; we dropped the tunes, the rhythm and the harmony, one by one, until we were completely free of all those things. But after a year, it all started to sound the same – it wasn't free anymore. So we started to structure the free, started to put limits on it. That was the beginning of the whole period that's flowering now – the post-free, the poly-free, *controlling* what we learned in that sixties revolution.'[9] (Italics added.) Miles' view was along similar lines. 'You have [to have] some kind of form. You have to start *somewhere.*'[10]

One result of the changes of the late 1950s was the emergence of different improvising languages. Not always clear-cut, of course, but there have been two distinct paths. Some musicians keep to a recognisable jazz language, but often exaggerate aspects of it. Others use an improvising language that is, at least in part, derived from classical music. It is 'purer', less individual, and at times seems designed to show off technique rather than individuality of approach.

Some of this can, no doubt, be put down to the situations in which these musicians have improvised before, and to what Heffley calls 'the tyranny of the composer'. He speaks of Stockhausen, who, 'having "liberally" bestowed freedom on his players . . . would reserve the right to declare which "free" improvisations "worked" and which did not.'[11]

Looking at jazz from another angle, Polish composer Krzysztof Penderecki was inspired to write *Actions* after hearing the Globe Unity Orchestra, an all-star free improvising group. The piece was given its first performance, under the direction of the composer, at the Donaueschingen Music Festival in 1971, by a group made up of many Globe Unity members plus other free improvisers. However, it is apparent, when comparing the score and the recording of *Actions* (Don Cherry/Krzysztof Penderecki, Philips LP, Intuitions CD) that, by and large, the band 'just blew'. What was written seems to have been the honest reaction of a classical composer to what he *heard* from a band such as the Globe Unity Orchestra, but it seems that he had little idea how this was achieved.

§ *I conducted* Actions *as part of the Royal Academy of Music's Penderecki festival in 1986. The players were mainly students on the then-new jazz option course, with some added guests, two of whom had been involved with the original Globe Unity performance. I was told by the composer that 'only five per cent is written, the rest is up to you', but this wasn't true. The music requires that the players react to strictly written fragments and achieves its success by its weight of textures, leading to an intensity which one classically influenced observer called 'truly orgasmic'. Our performance, although not of the standard heard in the recording, was, however, much closer to what was written in the score.*

At the final rehearsal I waited – with some trepidation, I admit – for the composer's comments. He walked from the back of the hall to the stage, paused for a while and said only, 'I think the last chord could be a little longer'. Which, as I had already indicated that to the band, proved that perhaps I was a better conductor of other people's work than I'd ever pretended to be, or that Penderecki, as he had earlier almost admitted, had forgotten the work and was surprised to find it on the programme.

The German free saxophonist Ernst-Ludwig Petrovsky, whose comment about how composers can inspire improvisers was used in *I HEAR A SYMPHONY*, feels that Lutosławski and Penderecki 'appropriated more than collaboratively incorporated the improviser's sound world and process'.[12] A point elaborated by trombonist Johannes Bauer: 'the possibilities of soundmaking are taken much further in improvised than in interpreted music. This development of the soundworld itself is something I think improvised music does far better than composed music seems able to do.'[13]

Some musicians move easily between different improvising languages, those playing in ZAUM being a good example. Others completely shun the trappings and soundscapes related to jazz. The musicians mostly come from the classical improvising world, and the groups they play in don't want a swing pulse, don't use recognisable forms, and avoid set harmonies. Sometimes they just blow, relying on the talents of the individuals and their collective feelings to get them through. At other times the controlling factors can be anything from written guides using notes or symbols, to conceptual starting points.

Trombonist George Lewis, for example, although well known in jazz circles, doesn't call his compositions jazz, speaking instead of 'the creative improvisers orchestra'. (Is there a *non-creative* improvisers orchestra' lurking somewhere?) There are some written passages in his music, and some are said to use 'graphic shorthands that walk the tightrope connecting improvisation with indeterminacy'.[14] I find this a strange construct. He probably means that, without an underlying form, or chord progression, his improvisers are free to make any sounds they wish, and the art, as always, is making them sound 'inevitable and right'.

The proof of the pudding is in the listening experience, and what I hear, in his work, and in many other groups who work in this genre, is a series of generally individual sounds, mostly pleasant, sometimes not, which drift through the piece, sometimes solo, sometimes in groups. Those involved seem set on deliberately *not* creating jazz sounds. There is no tempo as such, and few rhythmic inflexions of any kind. There is little or no ensemble playing, and often no 'power', either that of the conventional big band, or the aggressive power seen in some avant-garde groups.

Where there are jazz musicians involved – as in the Globe Unity Orchestra, for example – there will probably be a different set of parameters. They may well just blow, but may start with a sketchy theme or, as in some Anthony Braxton compositions, the inspiration may be from a complex drawing. (Yusef Lateef commented that he was once faced with a drawing of a coffin on one of Mingus' scores. 'And that was the substance on which I was to improvise.'[15]) Both music and drawings serve as starting points, which set a mood from which the performance should flow. During the performance there will be individual solos, or duets, or trios, usually interspersed with the whole group improvising together. These formats can be pre-planned, but are often improvised during the performance. As author John F. Szwed says, 'Can't mood, feeling, emotional climate, tonality, harmonic infrastructure, rhythm, and tempo be expressed without a composition? . . . . One of the lessons of free jazz was how shared musical conventions can be activated by the slightest allusion.'[16]

Such effects have been created in free music by a conductor – a better term might be director – improvising *with* the musicians. Perhaps the best-known of these, Butch Morris, has devised a complicated series of gestures (apparently patented) with which he makes up performances. He calls his system 'conduction', a word he trademarked. Directorial control is exercised on every aspect of the music, not on every note played but on each musician's approach to the note or group of notes: how long or short, how loud or soft and so on. Such matters can be controlled by writing things down, or they can be left to the demands of the piece and the resources of the musicians.

Or the two approaches can be combined as they are in the work of composers such as Ellington, Mingus and Gil Evans. But Morris wants to be 'in charge', and while what he attempts to do may appear to be close to my 'jazz happens in real time' mantra, I usually have some misgivings about the end results. This is mainly because of its lack of underlying structure, its lack of what I have been calling jazz form, and its lack of awareness of how jazz can work. There is a report of German improvisers 'bristling' at Morris 'for presuming to direct their free expressions in any way',[17] and I am told that Derek Bailey lasted five minutes in a London version of Morris' band before packing up his guitar and leaving.

However, there is no doubt that the experience of working with Morris and those using similar methods will be interesting to musicians who have no particular improvising language or jazz skills. His work has been highly praised for using improvisational methods with classical orchestras, ethnic groupings, choirs and other 'non-jazz' people, but usually it seems it is not judged on whether it is good music or not, but regarded as sufficient that it is being done at all.

Although many of the results of the free jazz and free improvising approaches I have been discussing are interesting and enjoyable to listen to, one feels at times that the freedom may be exaggerated. There can be too much of it and many of the things that give 'pure jazz' its identity – and which draw me and many others to the music – are deliberately *not* used. Among these are the use, in what's written and what's improvised, of a contemporary jazz vocabulary; the use of passages in tempo, but not necessarily all the time; the sheer power of an ensemble playing together; and, most importantly perhaps, some sense that there is an underlying form, an underlying idea, an underlying concept, which holds things together. But, to be fair, as Evan Parker's statement which opened this section implied, that's not their aim. Their aim is to create something *purely* from what the improvisers, whatever language they are using, bring to the performance space. Other composers and musicians want that, but with just a little more added.

JUST ENOUGH

There isn't much to it. You just have to create an environment in which people can create. [18]

All my life I'd been sitting in front of that piano trying to figure out another way to voice a minor seventh chord . . . . It was such a lonesome thing that I decided I needed adventure, and the only way to get adventure was to get a band together. [19]

Before addressing Gil Evans' later work, and how he changed from what I have called 'advanced arranging' to working from just a scrap of paper, developing 'an environment in which people can create', it's time to consider the case of Sun Ra, another composer who saw his role as forming a creative environment. Sun Ra named himself after an Egyptian god saying, among other things, that he was a descendant of the ancient Egyptians, or that he was born on Saturn. 'On this planet', as he would have said, from 1914 to 1993, Sun Ra's dates are roughly contemporary with those of Gil Evans (1912 to 1988). Like Gil Evans he was involved with highly scored pieces earlier in his career, which, for Ra, was during his time with Fletcher Henderson. Throughout his life his concerts included performances of pieces in that style (often dramatically exaggerated recompositions of tunes connected with Henderson such as 'Limehouse Blues' and 'King Porter Stomp') along with original material.

In a way somewhat similar to Ellington, Sun Ra had a band available to him most of the time, while Evans, once he decided on his adventure to form a band, took the more contemporary and practical route of playing occasional gigs and tours, with musicians drawn from a regular pool. However, unlike Ellington's band which lived together 'on the road', constantly touring, Sun Ra's band was based in his house, actually living together, constantly rehearsing, constantly discussing music and, we are told, cosmology and other subjects far removed from jazz as we earthlings know it. Relative to the amount of time they rehearsed, the band did not work much, but made over a hundred albums, mostly self-recorded and self-distributed.

Given such a huge recorded output, often on *very* obscure labels, there can be few who know Sun Ra's work in its entirety. My problem is that, of what I have heard, there is very little that I actually enjoy. I like his piano solos, somewhat reminiscent of Cecil Taylor at times, and I can also relate to many of his somewhat drastic re-compositions mentioned above. Where I tend to part company is with his original compositions, which, while they can be interesting at times, I can't seem to get a handle on, can't grasp what they are about. I find nothing that grabs me – either solo-wise or melody wise or sound-wise. It all seems somewhat distant – not communicating . . . . (As an experiment, after listening to *Heliocentric Worlds, Volume 1*, one of Sun Ra's most praised albums, I put on a random track of ZAUM, the free improvising group mentioned above. I immediately felt drawn in to the sound world, and sense of form, that Steve Harris and his musicians were creating, an effect which had passed me by when listening to Sun Ra. I should add that I have seen Sun Ra live and enjoyed the spectacle hugely, and most of the music, but have not, for the reasons mentioned above, become enough of a fan to follow it through.)

I can see that I must be missing out. Like my dislike of most compositions written by Thelonious Monk and George Russell, I can only say that I have tried, and stress the personal pronoun in saying that what he was doing has 'passed *me* by'. I realise that I am pitted against a barrow-load of critical praise and audience acclaim, but can only, once again, repeat that a listener doesn't *have* to, probably can't, like everything. And, to be realistic, new music is always emerging, and it has to be accepted as a fact of life that some musicians, however highly praised by others, will be rarely taken off the record shelf, or, when there is a chance, listened to in concert.

Gil Evans' later work also created what we can describe as soundscapes, largely derived by means of improvisation, a drastic change of approach after his magnificent, highly orchestrated scores for Miles Davis. He was working in a much freer way, creating – in performance – lengthy pieces, at times derived from something written on 'a scrap of paper produced from his back pocket'. Undoubtedly this approach was in some part economically driven, but, more importantly, it was also a response to the new opportunities that were to be found in jazz from the late 1950s on. Ideas that he had helped develop in his work with Miles Davis on *The Birth of the Cool, Kind of Blue* and, as is now becoming more widely known, the sextet library of the 1960s. (His widow, Anita Evans, claims, without anger, that Gil was never paid for his work on the latter. 'It was just something they did together.'[20])

Evans' new approach relied far more on the musicians than ever before. 'On a job anybody can play and they usually do. I try to think of music in which everybody has some way of expressing himself. That's why we play a lot of heads now. Sometimes something will come from that: everybody will start filling in around it and maybe veer off in some way – and all of a sudden I have an improvised arrangement.'[21] Trumpeter Henry Lowther, a member of Evans' British band, has said, 'There were fragments of music, not neat and tidy charts . . . . There were few instructions about who was going to solo and for that reason there was a lot of collective playing. With us, John Surman took over the direction as we found Gil's visual cues no use at all. I enjoyed it immensely but at times I felt the need for more structure.'[22]

When compared to Henry Lowther's view, Gil's explanation of his own role is interesting, as are the qualms mentioned. 'I've never really played like this before, never had good enough surroundings so that I am covered if anything happens. I know what my role is with this band. It's more like I'm the cheerleader. I'm on piano and if the music goes this way or that way, I try to say RA-RA. It's a gamble here with us you know. We have enough of an intimacy established that it's like technically foolproof. It doesn't mean it's always gonna be great – some nights, some tunes are better than others. It's based on the ideas that anybody can play anything they want at any time. That's a touchy thing. You can wind up with two extremes. Either someone is too shy to do anything or you wind up with someone who feels it's a duty to improvise. That duty's the worst thing in life.

As Gil Evans said, 'Well . . . we have our times and we don't have our times. It's never terrible, we teeter on the edge of formlessness sometimes, but somebody usually can't stand it and brings us out of it.'[23] However, given the success of his collaborations with Miles, it is not surprising that Evans' later work has had its detractors. Critic Francis Davis for one: 'By 1970 . . . his music had left perfectionism behind in a quest for greater expansion. His later output has suffered from laxity . . . . The Gil Evans Orchestra is an anomaly: a big band led by a great arranger, but ruled by his soloists, which, given their prolixity, may be leaving far too much to chance.'[24]

Even some of the musicians agreed. As Airto Moreira said: Some musicians, they didn't really like that, because they wanted to play chops, they were there to show off . . . . And that was not what the band was about. The band was about *ensemble*.[25]

The comments above, about the prolixity of jazz soloists, and some wanting to 'show off', point up one of the dilemmas faced in live performances of music where a large part of the control is passed to the musicians. The problem lies in controlling the soloists, both in what they play, and in the length of the solo.

§ *The temptation to sit back and enjoy a great solo which is going on too long, is something that any leader has to learn to avoid. Many years ago Conny Bauer, a wonderful trombonist, was in the band I assembled for* Hoarded Dreams. *Reflecting his usual home in free jazz groups, he played an absolutely staggering, but very long, solo cadenza. It was far too long for the situation, but I could find no sensible way of stopping him, and it was so good that in some ways I didn't want to. But I was aware that, at least as I saw it, he was spoiling the shape of the piece. So, in an attempt to move the piece on, I brought the band in. One critic picked me up on this – in a way rightly, but if I hadn't, I suspect he might have still been playing!*

On another Hoarded Dreams *gig I let three of the soloists go on too long, for much the same reasons. This led some other members of the band to say that I should resist the temptation: 'The audience haven't come to hear the musicians as though they were playing in a club. They've come to hear your composition.' Comments somewhat sobering for a bandleader, but encouraging for a composer.*

As we saw in I HEAR A SYMPHONY composers with the urge to write more have to find a way of controlling their musicians' own talents and instincts. But, as this quote from Roscoe Mitchell shows, the problems are still there, and in some ways exacerbated, for composers who want to 'take a chance'. 'As a composer, you never really have that much control over what happens to your piece once the part you've written comes to its conclusion and the solos begin. All you can hope for is that the improviser will be having a good night and stay within the guidelines you've provided. Usually, that doesn't happen, especially in free music. Cat's playing and you don't know *what* he's playing! It may be a fine solo in terms of its own vocabulary but not relate at all to the piece you've written. To me, this is a sign of immaturity, both as a player and as a human being. You can't even suppress your ego long enough to concentrate on the task that's placed before you.'[26]

When I used the first part of that quote in WELL MAN, WE JUST BLOW, I said that there were some points that I disagreed with.

I would argue that a jazz composition need not *have* a clear distinction between 'the part you have written . . . and the solos.' Nor should a jazz composer work with immature people who 'can't suppress their ego'. If you have to, as with students perhaps, then their instincts – usually to play too many notes and ignore the context they are in – need to be controlled. One may also have to remember Strayhorn's crucial point about Ellington 'exchang[ing] parts in the middle of a piece because the man and the part weren't the same character.' In most circumstances, however, the jazz composer should be writing for people he knows and respects, and that respect should be, as it almost always is, reciprocated, and demonstrated by the musicians' reaction to the music.

§ *Every composer who wants to do something different – in any field, including classical music – will have anecdotes of incomprehension, ignorance, outright hostility, even sabotage, towards them from musicians who 'just don't get it'. One example: a Dutch trumpet student came up to me at a workshop and, without any preamble, flatly told me, 'I like Clifford Brown.' When I said, 'so do I,' it came out that the point she was making was that she didn't like my music. I made the obvious response: 'Try to understand what we are doing. If you can't, it will all be over in a day or two. And, if this is the worst music you'll ever be asked to play in your career, you'll be very lucky!' She did the gig, and still didn't like it, but as I said before, that's life.*

Undoubtedly, at times, Gil Evans did let the soloists go on far too long, and this lessened the impact of some of his music. More structure, more leadership, more pre-planned form, would have helped also. When his approach comes off, as I believe it does in 'Zee Zee', my *classic chance taking performance* below, it achieves something that equals, although in a totally different area, his classic work with Miles Davis.

This different area was an exploration of one aspect of what I have called 'jazz form', a totally live application of Ellington's 'thinking of a better way'. Beginning in the 1970s, 'Gil developed a unique style of merging highly spontaneous music with his highly organised written scores. It started with Gil passing his charts out with particular ensemble sections identified by a name or number. When he wanted to hear one of these sections, he would simply call it out. Often, these ensembles were sections taken from his earlier arrangements – the bridge from 'Gone' or 'Summertime', for example. They might be played as written, or they might contain newly written voicings or playing instructions. Either way, the players had to remain loose – but alert. Airto Moreira: "Let's say it was a piece that was written. In the middle of the piece of music he'd write, 'Free – play out', or whatever. So everybody would just go totally crazy. And then while they were doing this, he would choose *another* song . . . one by one we would stop playing and put up that page . . . . And when everybody was ready he would start the band . . . . It was an incredible thing".'[27]

'[I]t wasn't a show; it was a real creative experience . . . when you afford that kind of freedom, you also have the nerve to know that plenty of times it's *not* going to work.'[28]

Gil Evans' methods developed in even freer directions over the last period of his life, but that comment from trumpeter Lew Soloff sums up the chance he was taking. Evans' statement to his musicians 'play what *you* want to hear, not what you think *I* want to hear'[29] is similar to Mingus' attitude and takes jazz composing to a different level. Like Miles playing 'Stella by Starlight', Coltrane playing 'My Favorite Things', Mingus playing 'Goodbye Pork Pie Hat', performance is all. The music has truly been moved off the paper.

CLASSIC CHANCE TAKING PERFORMANCE

Gil Evans 'Zee Zee' *Svengali* (1973)

'Zee Zee' is just a blues in 5/4 and the rhythm I got from a Basque rhythm which they dance very fast. It's called Zort-ziko . . . I just started fooling

around with that rhythm and I played a melody and I just made a blues out of it . . . 'Zee Zee' is . . . the first half of the blues – four bars of one [the tonic chord] and two bars of four [the subdominant chord] and we just keep playing that over and over. [30]

To make such a simple idea work, and to sustain it for over eleven minutes, as two of the three recorded versions do, demands the full involvement of the musicians as well as skill – one might even say luck – in shaping the performance. The earliest version, a studio recording from 1971 released on *Where Flamingos Fly*, doesn't come off for those very reasons. The main soloist, trumpeter Johnny Coles, for whom, in different settings, I have a great admiration, is not a free-enough player and fails to get to grips with the space he is given. And one feels that Evans himself lost his nerve by allowing the background pattern, the brooding presence of which makes the piece in the other performances, to be too stressed at times, to disappear completely part way through, and to be subverted by the drummer's urge to 'do something'.

The two later versions, the one I have chosen from *Svengali*, and another from *Live at the Public Theater New York 1980 Volume II*, come off well, producing wonderful jazz in the process. One surmises that Gil, and his musicians, had learnt to deal with such open situations in a better, more creative way. In both versions the supporting musicians very subtly enhance the constantly hovering background pattern with changing textures. The soloist on both performances is trumpeter Hannibal Marvin Peterson, a far better choice than Coles, given his free credentials. Using the space he has been given in a very innovative way, he carves out a well-constructed solo each time. The solo seems to exist as a different independent level to the background, but a level that never loses contact with the piece as a whole. (The subject of levels, fascinating but rarely discussed, will be covered in 'PLAY A RAT PATROL SOUND'.)

Although there is not much to choose between the versions on *Svengali* and *The Public Theater*, I feel that the latter version goes on a little too long, mostly because of Peterson's cadenza-like ending, which is somewhat self-indulgent. But these are among the problems that this kind of 'taking a chance' music making creates. What it allows for, and why it should be cherished, warts and all, are the new possibilities that can be opened up *in performance*. Both performances are worth listening to. In the one I didn't choose, the 1980 version, there are more colourful changes of texture from the supporting musicians, and an incredible, seemingly unending, trilled passage in Peterson's solo which resolves itself in an upward flurry that is just stunning.

As Gil Evans said, there is very little to 'Zee Zee' on paper, or conceptually, but there is just enough for these two great jazz performances to be created.

MORE CHANCE TAKING

Ashley Kahn's book on *Kind of Blue* has a section on 'Flamenco Sketches' including a photograph of Cannonball Adderley's scrap of music in, as I have said above, all its torn glory.

Ekkehard Jost's *Free Jazz* (which includes a section on 'Flamenco Sketches') and Roger Dean's *New Structures in Jazz and Improvised Music since 1960* are both interesting surveys of the developments which created free jazz and 'improvised music'.

Mike Heffley's *Northern Sun, Southern Moon, Europe's Reinvention of Jazz*, as the title implies, places great stress on European developments in the area of free jazz.

Larry Hicock, *Castles Made of Sound, the Story of Gil Evans* includes many interesting observations, particularly from the musicians involved, on just *how* Evans constructed some of this later works.

More about Zaum can be found at *www.steve-harris.info/*

PART FIVE

DIRECTING 14

JACKSON POLLOCKS

15

ROLLED STEEL INTO GOLD

A BASIS FOR CHANGE

What the hell does conducted mean anyway? . . . sometimes it doesn't mean anything more than handing rolled steel to Jack Bruce and watching as he turns it into gold in front of thousands of people.[1]

As we saw in the previous section contemporary jazz composers have taken different routes in pursuing their art. Some continue writing tunes, some write arrangements using new instrumentation and orchestration ideas, some compose ambitious long works, while others write very little. The aim of the last group – the one that, no surprise, I have most sympathy with – is to create compositions that, by relying on the improvisers and what happens during the performance, have the potential to change each time they are played.

The contributions of the improvisers, acknowledged up to this point more in the breach than in the observance, are summed up in Kip Hanrahan's beautifully expressed acknowledgement, which heads this chapter. The rest of the jazz composer's art can, I feel, be best expressed in these statements which have formed the backbone of this book: Clement Greenberg's 'Each art had to determine . . . the effects peculiar and exclusive to itself'; Duke Ellington's 'Music saves time. It provides a basis for change'; and my own mantra 'Jazz happens in real time, once.'

These statements, and my recognition of the truth behind Kip

Hanrahan's observation, have shaped my direction as a composer. They go some way to resolving the issues that face what one critic has called 'one of those problematic beings, a "jazz composer"'. But from where I'm sitting it's not problematic at all; rather, as Duke, Gil, Mingus and countless others have shown, a calling that has the potential to produce a way of making music that is different from any other, and is as rewarding as any other art form.

This chapter, following on from the mostly philosophical arguments of the book so far, is a look at some of the ideas and techniques I have developed during my work as a composer. Relying on my own work in this way is an acknowledgement of the truism that any composer knows his own work best, and, practically, that I have complete knowledge of what the musicians were given to start from. But admitting this does not negate the fact that many of the ideas can be universal. As Jackson Pollock said, 'Technique is just a means of arriving at a statement.' The ideas presented are not meant as complete solutions, but rather as indications of what *can* be done; of what is possible when one thinks of jazz as an open concept, not as something closed.

There is, though, something else nibbling at the margins. This can be seen in my decision in the paragraph above, to call myself a composer, without adding jazz to the noun. As I've said above, I don't believe that I am a 'problematic being', and am normally anxious to use the full description. It is, after all, what the book purports to be about. However, while I believe that there is something called a jazz composer, they shouldn't, despite what I may have implied elsewhere, be separated *too* far from their classical colleagues. As a Finnish critic wrote: 'Though Collier is usually only considered a jazz composer, his musical scale is much wider that that. It is clearly more appropriate to call him a modern composer who has been highly influenced by jazz, and who attributes great importance to improvisation.'[2]

What all composers do is to create music by using their available resources. The point is that for the jazz composer these resources are different.

ROUNDING IN THE FREEFALL

His laid back attitude was totally at odds with the full frontal sound of the music. He appeared to casually stroll around the stage, giving directions to these fantastic musicians by hand signals . . . . It was a bit like someone directing 14 Jackson Pollocks. The result was absolutely fantastic. Quite how much he was controlling everything I'm not sure, but individuals went into apparent freefall only to be 'rounded in to the whole phenomena.

It was a complete texture of sound – massive sound . . . . How the hell does he write this? Or how much does he write and how much is improvisation? No way of knowing. How does he recall non pattern musical events? Anyway, however he does it, the end result was fantastic . . . . The performance was awesome.

It's strange how you can cope with non-figurative art and yet with music your perception longs for a 'catch' or 'tune'. Last night that all went into the bin and the music was so great that you just went with the flow and enjoyed it. You didn't come out singing but realised you'd had an exceptional audio experience.[3]

Not normally a jazz fan, and attending a concert of mine for the first time, the writer, an artist friend of a friend, intuitively appreciated that I try to live the two truths of jazz: that it is about individuals, a lesson demonstrated long ago by Duke Ellington, and that it happens in real time, once, as Miles Davis and many others constantly show. It has been quoted at length because it shows a deep understanding of what jazz is, or should be, about. And of 'what I do', capturing my approach to performing, which reflects my approach to jazz composing. Her felicitous observation that I was 'directing 14 Jackson Pollocks' provides the overall title of this final section, and became the title for the CD of that concert, the source of some of the examples used below. (Other examples are drawn, as will be seen below, from various other easily available CDs. Additionally all the examples can be heard on *thejazzcomposer.com*.)

Such an understanding of my methods has eluded many of my critics, whether their criticism has been favourable or not. In their defence it should be said that they have often made remarks in ignorance of my methods, thinking perhaps that, as with most other jazz composers, most of what they hear (apart from the obvious solo sections) is written down. Were they to see a performance, as the Pollock fan did, they might realise that I am controlling the piece, directing most of the sounds, drawing the creative side out of the musicians and treating their contributions, whether it be a solo in front of the band, or as part of a textured background, as something vital to my work.

The principles underlying what I am trying to do, and common, I believe, to all good jazz, can be seen in this statement by literary critic Malcolm Cowley: 'I might suggest that the story proper, if it is complete, will include four elements. A *person* (or group of persons) is involved in a *situation* and performs an *act (or series of acts, or merely undergoes an experience)* as a result of which *something is changed.*' [4] (Italics in the original.) The application of those concepts to what, in Cowley's words, we might call 'complete' jazz is obvious: a group, in performance, plays a piece and something is affected by that performance. What is affected can be the players, the audience, the piece itself – or any combination of them.

In a 'complete performance', the way I see it, *all* of them will be affected. The players, by the fact that their contributions make up something more than the sum of the parts; the piece, by virtue of the fact that a *different performance* is created each time from the given elements; the audience, because they realise that they were present when 'something happened'.

One of the unique strengths of jazz lies in how what is written down is treated and developed during a performance. The music used is, in the main, incomplete in some way, written in a way that allows for – in some cases, demands – being developed, or, at the very least, coloured, by improvising. This individualisation by the performers of what is written, whether it is a full melody or a single note, a scale, or a chord progression, is arguably the most important strength for a jazz composer, and developing this line of thinking has been a strong part of my development.

WHERE IT STARTS

Barnett Newman is a bow and arrow artist. The act of painting itself is what opens up the possibilities of making those decisions that create the image.[5]

I like that construct. It is the act of composing that makes things start to happen. And, for the jazz composer, it is the act of performing that allows *more* things to happen. Things that are, in some way, inherent in the piece, inherent in what's written down or developed during rehearsals.

When composing, my overriding idea is to try to make space for these things to happen, to write for *jazz* to happen, rather than writing to satisfy my own ego. That side of me gets fulfilled when I am on the stage directing the Jackson Pollocks, making something happen which is implied, rather than obligated, by what I have written.

This 'world view', which informs the direction of my writing, is fine in principle, but, as they say, it butters no parsnips. How *do* the ideas come? Where do the notes on paper come from?

When I start writing, quite often I have no clue what I am going to write, or how it will develop. Like most composers I will spend time just thinking, perhaps writing words, later to be discarded, about the piece, gradually immersing myself in the writing. What I'm looking for is an initial musical idea, something unique, something that represents 'me' and where I am at, something that 'breathes the right air'. This idea is the crux of the piece. From that – with work – everything else will develop.

I may be inspired to put a few notes down on the empty page at an early stage, but, usually, in a process I don't really understand, I go to the piano, and, 'feel' for the right musical shape. This could be a chord, a melody, or a bass line, that seems to fit in with my thinking (which at that stage I would certainly not be able to articulate clearly). By 'feeling' for an idea, I mean literally sitting there and moving the fingers above the keys until, almost like magic, they fall and something concrete is there. I don't really understand how it happens, I'm just glad that it works most of the time, and I'm very aware that the initial immersion in a project *has* to happen before I can get to this 'magical' stage.

Discovering the fertile idea, that specific melodic motif or a chord needed for a composition to start to develop, gives me what novelist Joyce Carey called 'the kick of a horse'. Once properly chosen, no other set of notes will do; even transposing them often seems incorrect. The idea breathes the right air, has a specific 'colour', inhabits a certain space, feels just right. This, and how I found the idea in the first place, is part of the mystery of creativity for which I have no explanation.

Once a 'way in' is found, the composition's DNA, that cell inside an organism that informs its growth, must be discovered. Once that is clear, the composition starts to achieve its own identity, a process I have likened to discovering a tiny thread and gradually tweaking it until something solid starts to emerge. As Barnett Newman said, 'It is as I work that the work itself begins to have an effect on me, just as I affect the canvas, so does the canvas affect me.'[6]

How that something is developed into a composition can be a mystery, but some inklings of how it can be done will be seen in the following notes, which deal with the initial ideas and the process which occurred during the writing of some of my compositions. Inevitably there is some discussion of the form of each piece, but this aspect – what I have called 'jazz form' – is looked at more fully in the next chapter 'PLAY A RAT PATROL SOUND'.

IDEA, PROCESS, FORM

The idea in *Three Simple Pieces* (later recorded on *The Third Colour* CD) was to feature four known soloists in their strong areas in a new, pre-titled, piece written to fit into a specific sixtieth birthday celebration programme of my works. As I wrote about the process at the time: 'a new "birthday" composition specially written for the concerts in London and Copenhagen . . . . One that isn't terribly complicated, but that shows me where I am now . . . . Shouldn't I just write something? The mature artist presenting a new piece for a special occasion? Sounds good. But how to start? – the usual question – and what form will it take? – or, again, as usual, what form will develop when the writing starts . . . . ?'

The form was pre-decided as three pieces to be played without a break. During the writing process these became slow, medium and fast with no obvious connections between them. The ballad called for a simple theme-solo-theme form, while the second piece developed from an open-form repetitive rhythmic pattern. The third piece, again open-form, is 'energy based', with ensemble fragments freely introduced against a strong tenor soloist. (Extracts from all three movements will be discussed below.)

For *Winter Oranges* (commissioned by the Danish Radio Jazz Orchestra) the initial idea came from my move to Spain in 1999, and the mature orange tree on our terrace, which had fruit throughout our first winter. The idea for the composition's development into a four part suite with loose biographical undertones ('Blue Spring', 'Eggshell Summer', 'Tinted Autumn', 'Winter Oranges'), came from realising that this was a time of my own 'winter oranges', the encouraging flowering of my career as I worked through my sixties.

From contemporary notes on the idea: "'Tinted Autumn' remains a good title, but it is perhaps less that than 'planting autumn', a time for things to develop, for my ideas to settle in, to articulate what I had been doing for a long time, but never clearly expressed. That expression comes in the final section,

'Winter Oranges', but the slow germination is in 'Tinted Autumn'
. . . . Is this kind of anthropomorphism true of the first two? 'Blue
Spring' is meant to be young, developing, full of energy and ideas
being thrown around, which sort of fits; 'Eggshell Summer' is
edgy, not yet knowing quite what's happening, neither young nor
mature.'

From contemporary notes on process: 'One route [in writing
for an established radio band] is to write an intellectual challenge
to the players – complicated melodies, odd times, difficult chords
– while the underlying ideas remain mine, and are directed by me.
Another route is to write something where good music can be created by them working together in a freer way than they are used
to. Quite possibly the latter will do them more good, but the former is what they will go for more . . . . I may be more than a little
worried about the situation. I shouldn't be. I know I have enough
ideas and have developed techniques which will produce good
music, and I need to be satisfied with the certainty that I can
make it work, although there may be a few in the band who resist
the new ideas . . . . [I'm happy now to report that there weren't.
Or, if there were, I wasn't told about them!]

'The DNA as I call it is generally some chord or set of chords
or melodic motifs, or rhythm . . . . What if I tried to find four
chords that summed up each of the titles . . . . This may have
cracked it: four three-note chords which make up the whole
twelve but also serve as launching off points for ideas – fairly
basic at this time, but they may work . . . . They seem to sit nicely; and I mustn't forget that above all my style rests on keeping it
simple . . . . '

In *Oxford Palms* (commissioned by George Haslam for his band
Meltdown and later recorded by The Collective in Perth,
Australia, for the CD *Bread and Circuses*) the idea came during the
early writing process as I decided to interweave two pieces,
inspired by the idea behind William Faulkner's *Wild Palms*, which
I was rereading at the time. In my notes I wrote, 'Each story grabs
you and then suddenly you're back in the other one . . . can this

be done musically? Yes, if the ideas are strong enough, and there's a sense of each part being unfinished, that something is going to happen when one strand stops.' (The title came from the connection between Oxford, England, where the piece would be premiered, and Faulkner's hometown of Oxford, Missouri.) The overall form came from the initial idea. The two juxtaposed musical ideas are an altered blues form and a ballad, each of which developed in interesting ways during the writing process.

From contemporary notes on process: 'Faulkner has two interlocking novels "each of which is informed by its juxtaposition with the other". Musically the idea could work well if each is altered by a sharp change to another mood, but, unlike Faulkner, I feel I have to connect the two more obviously – by using some common elements and linking the two ideas in the final section. A purer version might work but, as always, the composition takes over and decides its own structure. To deny that would be wrong.'

MAKING THINGS CLEAR

'Economy' here means happening on a moment when suddenly you realise as you are doing it (or better, you see) that enough is enough – that any more would destroy the openness to different (compatible) readings.... [7]

Normally in jazz, the starting point is a complete object, such as a standard song with its melodic line accompanied by a chord progression and some kind of pulse or rhythmic pattern. At times, one element may be stronger than the others, but, generally, they are played together and supply enough material for the complete performance.

However, some composers are not interested in looking at music in this way. There is less concentration on a melody, a rhythm, or a chord sequence as such, and more on building something within which these things exist, quite possibly in a more fragmented way. Rather than being the specific controlling idea they are *part* of the composer's palette.

In this respect, the thinking comes close to the way classical composers work. As Clement Greenberg said, Debussy 'would often present the mere texture of sound as the form itself of music', [8] and, as his biographer said of Polish composer Witold Lutosławski, 'the qualities of texture can take on thematic substance no less compelling than the more traditional thematic materials of melody, rhythm and harmony.' [9]

What is different, though, is the way the textures are created, the way the written elements are played. In a phrase: the involvement of the musicians themselves in the creative process. But before the musicians can do anything with what is given to them, they must understand the concepts and ideas behind the music. Whatever is written down, it has to be laid out in a way that informs the players without confusing them.

In orchestral music and the conventional big band, each player has his own part, extracted from a full score. In a jazz small group there may be no music, with each player working from memory. Or there may be a simple lead sheet, which, with a pre-set or improvised routine, is enough to make that lead sheet into a performance. This last approach is the one that I feel is best suited to the way I work. In the words of Duke Ellington, used above: 'Music saves time. It provides a basis for change.' In my world, as in his, both parts of the quote carry equal weight.

In its simplest form the players get what can be called universal parts, each with the same music, transposed when necessary for instruments of different pitches. There are some written instructions, but few if any dynamics. Depending on who is involved, the aim is that some of the music, some of the ideas, can be developed, even changed, during the rehearsal process – an obvious parallel to Ellington's 'thinking of a better way'.

Using these methods places a demand on the player's memory that orchestral or big band playing does not. It is closer to small group jazz practice, where the musicians have to remember routines and chord progressions, and be able to adapt quickly to changing circumstances. What appears on the paper may seem to be notes to be played by anybody, but the bandleader/director has to read the situation and decide who should play which part when. Much, then, is decided in rehearsal, using the parts as a guide, a process which echoes Billy Strayhorn's words about Ellington changing the parts in rehearsal because 'the part and the person weren't the same character'.

There are practical benefits, too, in each player having a shorthand version of the score. The music can be used by many different groupings, and be more quickly adapted than conventional written music when the expected instrumentation is not available.

Some colleagues have seen the universal parts approach as a pragmatic response to dealing with odd-shaped groups and missing musicians. Although this may be true, this way of presenting the music has developed as a by-product of my aim as a composer. That aim is to write relatively simple music that can be developed in performance by the musicians involved.

New notation ideas need to be developed, and, at times, working out ways to present these ideas on the paper has helped develop my ideas and techniques. Also needed is a set of signs and gestures to be used as reminders of the instructions written on the page, or of the instructions developed during rehearsal and performance. Such techniques are constantly being revised and adapted for new circumstances but the necessity has always been to keep them simple, to avoid confusion in what could be a strange situation for many musicians. (I should add that, unlike Butch Morris, I have not seen the necessity to patent my signs and gestures.)

Using such methods provides a way of writing interesting music for *any* large group. This could include the traditional big band but in today's climate such bands are few and far between. Many composers have a pile of music which, although some may have been recorded, is now gathering dust because of the difficulty of finding the circumstances, and perhaps the exact instrumentation, to ever play the charts again.

My answer to this has been to develop methods that are designed to use the creativity of the group playing them, and this has resulted in a set of scores that are playable by any instrumental grouping. They work in such a way that new angles are often revealed during a particular performance and that because of this and other 'open' factors, each performance is different. As a friend said during a composers' association dinner, 'You know, almost everyone in this room would give their eye-teeth to do what you do. To go around the world performing your own music.' To which I replied, 'But they would expect it to be more or less the same each time. I relish the opportunity for it to be different.'

I would also draw a parallel with this comment on sculptor Juan Muñoz from *Guardian* critic Adrian Searle: 'To keep things fresh and alive, full of the surprise of confrontation (both for himself, and for us), Muñoz treated works as material to be revisited according to circumstance.'[10] Searle's comment that 'without the spectator, the work is incomplete', provides a strong connection with my constant stress on *performance* as a vital factor in jazz composition.

What can happen with these methods is what we can call 'orchestration by accident'. Instrumental choices are made, textures are created, voicings developed, which could have been written down – but weren't. A melodic line that could, if orchestrated, have been given to a soprano saxophone because of its wide range, could, in these new circumstances, be given to a bass clarinet, thus changing the textural possibilities of that particular performance. Similarly, a group of musicians can, with some minimal instructions, develop an interesting, and constantly changing, textural background from a given idea – a chord progression, a pedal note or notes, a scale and so on. The way is left clear for creativity and for happy accidents to happen, like the formation of uncommon instrumental blends. Not setting out to copy Ellington's trademark of cross-section voicings, but using different means to achieve similar results.

There is no doubt that the end result loses some of the strengths possessed by pre-written music, in particular the ability to fine-tune textural densities. But that loss is replaced with something else, something very important for jazz – the ability of each musician to react to what is happening around him.

CREATING GOLD FROM ROLLED STEEL

Sociologist Howard S. Becker's comment that 'Writing is about discovering what you have to say. Then you go back and edit it to make it look as if you knew where it was heading all along', [11] is a clever conceit that has some application to the initial processes of jazz composition. But, unsurprisingly, it fails to take account of the importance of the musicians – who, at times, can thicken the composer's intentions more than he could have imagined. The composer or bandleader can put something on paper, suggest something in rehearsal or performance, which sets the stage, but what happens after that is up to the musicians. As Kip Hanrahan says, they can turn rolled steel into gold.

I should perhaps have been flattered when a reviewer said that I was 'a clever orchestrator who can use his palette of tone colours with assurance'. I may well *be* a good orchestrator, but in this case, the implication he took from what he heard was mistaken. As it said in the liner notes, the band were asked to create a 'carpet of sound' by improvising their way through a chord progression, behind a freely played melody. The players choose their own note or notes, not just to play organ-type long notes as in many written backgrounds, but in order to create what we could call a carpet of sound by re-attacking, colouring and thickening them in an individual way, making an individual 'textural' contribution to the whole. With these techniques, especially when instruments such as soprano sax, bass trombone, bass clarinet, and percussion are available to cut through the mix, a large group can create fascinating soundscapes, which are affected by the circumstances, and, crucially, will be different each time the piece is played. The end results almost always sound good, but I can only take credit for the method, not for the exact notes heard.

Such techniques have become an important part of my compositional thinking. Writing above about TEXTURAL IMPROVISING I described it as 'using various degrees of improvisation to interpret what is written down'. In doing this I am using the musicians themselves to help create *all* the music, not just the solos. They become part of the music rather than just foot soldiers, anonymous voices in the crowd. A stance supported by the comment of one Canadian musician that he 'felt like a colour in a paint box', and by the astute observation that I was 'directing 14 Jackson Pollocks'.

The piece 'misread' by the critic was the opening to Part One of *Three Simple Pieces*. As can be seen from the manuscript below, what the musicians worked from was very simple. What they did with it – 'in real time, once' – can be heard in the two audio examples referred to below. The first, by the *Jazz* Ensemble is from *The Third Colour*, was the one written about. The second, by the Danish Radio Jazz Orchestra from *Winter Oranges*, a different band on a different concert, is the one written about and shows a different 'real time' performance.

What is heard could all have been written out, orchestrated in the conventional way. But if it had been, it would have sounded exactly the same on each of these two performances, and every time the piece was played. The reality is that what may appear somewhat sketchy on manuscript paper becomes a fresh, new performance every time. It is this interface between the illusion and the reality that can be stimulating and exciting to performers and audiences. As saxophonist Geoff Warren, one of the musicians on *directing 14 Jackson Pollocks*, commented 'Finally got time to listen to the CDRs. Very nice. I'm afraid you're in danger of getting even more critical acclaim for your meticulous choice of voicings, and the funny thing is they'd be right.'

Three Simple Pieces: Part One

Graham Collier

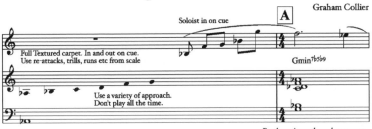

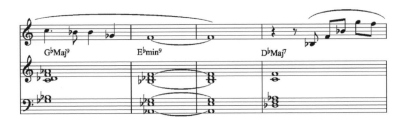

That each of the two examples is from a different band is interesting, but the same band working from that same music has
produced very different results also. *Three Simple Pieces* and the
three other long compositions on *The Third Colour* CD were each
played on three successive nights during the 1997 London Jazz
Festival. The compositions were still recognisably the same, but
the solos were different, the textural backgrounds were different,
and the structure of each piece found its own form *during the performance.* These are all 'hidden' elements of a jazz composer's craft.

§ *What may also be hidden are the costs incurred in recording three
consecutive performances of the same music. I felt it was an opportunity
too good to miss and hired the necessary engineers and equipment. At the
final accounting – taking those costs from the commission fee for* The
Third Colour *and the three gig fees – I made a profit of around £12. But
I was glad I did it, not only for the resultant CD, but for the opportunity
to compare the different versions of each composition. One of these,* The
Alternate Third Colour, *is now available on the CD* directing 14
Jackson Pollocks.

NB: The audio examples referred to here and in the next chapter can be
found on the audio page of *thejazzcomposer.com* website.

When you hear Gregorian chant in a cathedral, or the Bach
unaccompanied cello suites, you hear melodic lines seemingly
carving their own space in the air. This kind of melody writing,
this aspect of melodic thinking, is uncommon in jazz. But it can
be applied particularly appropriately when more than one soloist
interprets the melody in his or her own way, adding their own texture and timing to the written notes. As we have seen, Miles
Davis used this idea in most versions of 'Walkin'', and, very
prominently, in 'Nefertiti'. Mingus, too, used this technique, what
critic Andrew Homzy called 'loose-togetherness', as part of his
music. Something similar was seen in early New Orleans jazz,
where it could have been due to lack of musical skills in playing

together. Equally, though – and this would apply to some other occurrences – it may well have been the players' urge to express their individuality in all possible ways.

This technique, which I have called *shadowing*, has become important in my own work. In the following example, the opening of 'Blue Spring' from *Winter Oranges,* the melody is played freely by one player on the first pass, and then is shadowed by various others the second time through. Each musician, while paying regard to what his colleagues are doing, is free to make a strong independent statement of the motif or melody, and while doing this may well inspire the others to play differently. Other instruments create a carpet of sound similar to the first audio examples.

(*Another example of shadowing can be found in 'Mid' section from* The Third Colour *in the next chapter.*)

Blue Spring

Graham Collier

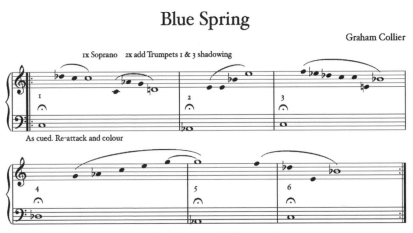

In many of my compositions the musicians are asked to *individualise a given note* or motif. In the example opposite from *The Miró Tile* the pedal notes that open the piece are individualised (coloured and articulated) by a close-knit group of low instruments. The players colour the note by varying the tone, use adjacent notes to move, possibly by smearing the sound, into and out of the given notes. The notes can be *re-attacked* at will, working with – or against – others. If needed, the amount of re-attacking can be specified as slow, fast, continuous, bell notes, sustained, rhythmic and so on. These individualised pedals became one of the compositional building blocks, recurring several times throughout the piece. (Given the effect of a low grouping of tuba, bass saxophone, baritone sax and bass trombone, the result, not surprisingly, became known as 'mud' when it came time to index the sections for the *Third Colour* CD.)

After exploring the pedals for some time the low instruments are given a motif to play freely. This technique, known as *motific improvisation* is discussed further below.

An example of how the mud is treated later in the piece can be found on the jazzcomposer website.

The Miró Tile: Opening

Graham Collier

Motific improvisation is an extension of the shadowing approach in that specific motifs can be freely interpreted by one or a group of musicians to create a textural background to a melody or solo. When appropriate they can also be given to the soloist to be used as reference points for a solo.

The following example, from the version of 'Aberdeen Angus' used in *Forty Years On*, starts with a *collective improvisation* over a bass line that soon moves to a heavy rock beat. On cue, the five given motifs are played freely until on a cue all the musicians gradually 'lock into' the written version of motif 5. This is then *thickened*, a technique which will be discussed further below.

Aberdeen Angus
from Forty Years On

Graham Collier

The reattacking and individualising of pedal notes seen in the *Miró Tile* example leads to an obvious thickening of the sound. Instead of a 'classical' pure note such as an orchestral unison, one gets what can be called a 'jazz unison' where the individuality of each player's sound can come through. When combined with *motific improvisation* it produces a technique which I have called *thickening*. Players are asked to make their own choice of notes using the rhythm of a given motif, and thus gradually 'thicken' it until, in some cases, it overwhelms whatever else is happening. For beginners this technique can teach them, collectively, that improvising on a simple idea can be effective, and can be fun. In a more advanced situation these ideas can be used to build a wall of sound against which a soloist can react.

In the examples below there are three versions of how a rhythmically strong one-bar motif can be thickened. The tension which is built up, is released each time by a strong ensemble written motif. There are, in the rest of the piece, other background ideas, all nominally there to provide a supporting level to the soloist, but at times they seem to become independent levels because of the strength created by the improvised approach. (The concepts of supporting and independent levels are a fascinating part of music, and are discussed further in 'PLAY A RAT PATROL SOUND'.) Overall 'Three Simple Pieces Part Three' illustrates *structural improvising*, what I have also called 'jazz form', where the complete form – and length of the piece – is determined during the performance by the soloist and the placing, and repetition, of the background ideas.

The thickening of this particular motif became a structural factor in the creation of Forty Years On, *recorded on* directing 14 Jackson Pollocks *and occurs at various times inside that composition. Other examples of thickening can be found on the jazzcomposer website.*

Three Simple Pieces: Part Three

Graham Collier

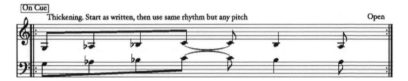

In the previous example, there is a constant pulse, but the form is open. At times, though, I work from a set pattern, possibly a blues form, possibly a repeating pattern such as the twenty-four bar Groove section from *The Third Colour* illustrated below.

The Groove is cued to be played at various times throughout the composition, with the overall idea being that it should be different on each pass. Both the audio versions are from the beginning of the piece, where, on the first pass, each of the Grooves is played, as written, by bass, guitar and piano respectively. On the second and subsequent passes the musicians are asked to add to it by these means:

1) Play the lines as written. In the earlier passes just the line given to your own section, then later, any of the lines.

2) Play fragments of any of the lines.

3) Play, and colour, the pedals. (The last note of each section is the underlying pedal of the next section.)

4) Thicken the melody by playing the rhythm of any of the fragments, but with your own notes.

5) Join in when you feel you should.

Third Colour Groove

Graham Collier

After its first performances in London I took the piece 'on the road' in a succession of workshops. Each time – possibly because of my increasing familiarity with the ideas expressed – the Groove sections got looser, culminating in the imaginative student performance heard in the second example.

(As will be seen in the next chapter, *The Vonetta Factor* uses similar ideas to thicken its groove patterns.)

Further versions of the Groove can be heard in The Alternate Third Colour *on the* directing 14 Jackson Pollocks *CD but, possibly because it was one of the first performances of the piece, the versions move very little from the paper.*

These ideas can be added to by the use of such concepts as space and levels, and by applying what I have often referred to as 'jazz form'. These areas are the subjects of the next chapter, where the meaning of the enigmatic title, 'play a rat patrol sound', will be revealed.

MORE ON TURNING ROLLED STEEL INTO GOLD

Finding examples of exactly what the musicians start from is still not easy in jazz circles, although collections of composer's scores and transcribed solos are increasingly available. However, there are examples here, and on my website, of just that. If you want to hear the full versions, all the music discussed in this and the next chapter is drawn from a series of recent recordings, all currently available on CD and digital download.

directing 14 Jackson Pollocks (a double CD on jazzcontinuum) recorded in London 2004 by Graham Collier's Celebration Band contains *Forty Years On*, a relook at many of my earlier compositions; *The Vonetta Factor*, discussed at length in the next chapter, plus *The Alternate Third Colour* recorded, like the original, during the 1997 London Jazz Festival.

The Third Colour (a double CD on jazzcontinuum), recorded in London 1997 by The *Jazz* Ensemble, contains four suites: *Three Simple Pieces*; *Shapes, Colours, Energy*; *The Miró Tile*; and *The Third Colour*.

Winter Oranges (jazzcontinuum), recorded in Copenhagen by the Danish Radio Jazz Orchestra in November 2000, includes the title suite as well as different versions of Parts One and Three of *Three Simple Pieces*.

16

'PLAY A RAT PATROL SOUND'

MOVING BEYOND THE NOTES

space: *somewhere in which incidents can happen*

levels: *the technique of divided attention*

jazz form: *thinking of a better way*

The enigmatic title of this chapter will become clear later, but at this juncture it acts as a reminder of how things happen in jazz. (Or how *some* things happen in some jazz, but that's an argument for the final chapter, RECOGNISING THE VIBRATIONS.) The quotation marks indicate that the instruction was a verbal one, not something written, and it could be implied that the instruction is for immediate action. In that phrase, and millions like it that went unrecorded, we have the essence of jazz composition. The reason why jazz composition relies on performance, and why it is a portmanteau phrase, having little or nothing to do with classical composition, and more than a little to connect it to the very apt phrase used about Duke Ellington's methods: 'thinking of a better way'.

This chapter deals with three areas of jazz composition which, in very important ways, move us beyond the notes. These are space – what poet and art critic Frank O'Hara called somewhere

'in which incidents can happen'; the concept of levels – beautifully summed up in Malcolm Lowry's phrase 'the technique of divided attention', and jazz form – what we can call the creation of a
complete performance using improvisational means. Although all
three concepts can be said to be somewhat amorphous and hard
to describe, they are important elements of the music, and often
turn up, as they did in the quote used as our title, by the process
of someone 'thinking of a better way'.

Whether all this improvising produces results that are better
than conventional music is up to the performers and listeners to
decide. If they genuinely believe that the resulting performance is
good, then it doesn't matter how it was written, or whether it was
structured in performance or not. There may well be the *illusion*
that all is written and pre-organised, but what has happened is
that the performance has taken what has been written or pre-
planned, and used that to direct the free spirits of the improvisers into making something that *sounds* finished. A whole that is
greater than the sum of its parts. As I said in *JAZZ HAPPENS IN REAL
TIME, ONCE*, what should come across to the audience is the excitement, the adrenaline rush from the musicians when 'something
happens'. That is the core of jazz, and making it happen is what a
jazz composer is for.

SPACE

The painter Yves Klein said, 'to paint space, I have to put myself
right into it, into space itself.'[1] That remark, and the O'Hara
quote used above, are phrases that could be applied to the famous
Miles Davis live version of 'My Funny Valentine' from *The
Complete Concert: 1964* (Columbia Jazz Masterpieces), where it
seems that the players allow the melody and its accompaniment
to unfold in their own, perfectly judged, time, placing them in
a vast cavern of space. In a different genre the same could be
said of Charles Ives' *Unanswered Question*, and of Gregorian
chant (which, as I have said above, I once heard memorably in the

vastness of Cologne Cathedral, where the melodic lines hung in the air until they slowly disappeared). This sense of space has been beneath the surface of many great jazz performances – there has been time for musical events to develop at the right pace.

However, the inevitable result of my unshakeable belief that 'jazz happens in real time, once' is that the concept of space, of incidents happening in their own good time, may be even harder to achieve in jazz than it is in other arts. Some jazz artists – Miles being the supreme example – have an inbuilt sense of space, an intuitive feeling for controlling the incidents that happen. In others, this sense is lacking and although the results can be interesting, the events lack space, seem to crowd in and overwhelm the senses. Listening to some jazz musicians I often feel that I'm eating too much chocolate cake. One slice is fine, two slices are just about manageable, but – if you stay for the full gig, listen to the whole CD – there's almost a plateful still to come.

Gil Evans' orchestrated works, the great triumvirate of *Miles Ahead*, *Porgy and Bess* and *Sketches of Spain*, are complex, and may, as I have said, include too many dips into the bran tub of orchestral colours, but they have a great sense of space in the writing and in the placing of the soloists. His later, more open, works, often just a scrap of an idea, possess a different sense of space, closer to what I – and Frank O'Hara – are talking about: a space in which incidents can happen. It is perhaps inevitable that such an open approach can lead to aimlessness at times, where, despite some good solos, things don't quite gel. As I said above, this accounts for my choosing the *Svengali* 'Zee Zee', rather than the *Public Theater* version as my classic performance in TAKING A CHANCE, but in both performances one can see the incidents happening, and great jazz being created.

There are many definitions of space. The one I like, the first in my dictionary, is particularly applicable to music: 'the limitless three-dimensional extent in which objects and events occur and have relative position and direction'. The second definition, 'physical space independent of what occupies it', applies on a more personal level. I think of it as room, room to breathe. I like that in scenery, I like it in my private life, disliking noisy places, needing every so often to get away and find some clear mental space. I dislike clutter, preferring to keep everything simple on the desk and other surfaces, hiding away the things that are not needed. This dislike of clutter is certainly part of my make-up as a composer and is a strong element of my reactions when I listen to music, look at art, or read a book.

Although no expert, I am very interested in art – as the many references to painters and art-critics in this project will have shown. My taste is fairly wide, but among my favourites are Klee, Van Gogh, Cézanne and Pollock. I would be hard-pressed to find a common denominator between them, but each in his own way appeals strongly to me, and forms part of my background culture. Even with Pollock, the more complex of the four, there is a feeling of control, that there is, despite the controversy of his methods, a direction. His work possesses what, in a different context, author and critic Martin Amis called 'the rarest quality known to any art – that of apparent inevitability'.[2]

Among the art movements I dislike is cubism. I keep trying, but, to be honest, I can't see what the artists are getting at. Sure, I understand the style is meant to represent the various planes of the objects simultaneously, but in asking 'why would they want to do that?' I come face to face with the problem. If the underlying motive of cubism is to represent everything, then it's going to produce a lot of clutter, and, coming from where I do in terms of an awareness of, and a liking for, space and simplicity, it's not surprising that I don't like the result. I don't want to represent everything, I want to be part of what the dictionary calls 'the limitless three-dimensional extent in which objects and events occur'. I relish the chance for events to interact, pictorially and musically.

One of the most interesting and influential periods in art for me is American abstract expressionism. There is a simplicity and depth of feeling in a Barnett Newman, or Clyfford Still, which appeals greatly. There is also a great sense of space. Even in

Jackson Pollock, on the surface seemingly very cluttered, there is a sense of order, and, the more one looks at his work, a sense of space emerges.

The sense of space I find in Pollock, and in *Kind of Blue,* is lacking in the work of many artists. Like the Cubists they are, for me, trying to express too much. One of these painters, the British abstract expressionist Howard Hodgkin, was the subject of a generally unfavourable review by critic Adrian Searle. 'However, two paintings stood out . . . . They make you realise how much can be done with very little, and how a bit of dirt from the palette, a small gesture, a sense of the internal dialogue between one mark and the next, can actually say something, and be extremely physical and at the same time highly suggestive . . . . The unstated counts. These two paintings are almost nothing yet there's something about their quiet presence, which is insistent and compelling.'[3]

Searle's point that two of the paintings 'make you realise how much can be done with very little . . . [yet there is] a sense of the internal dialogue between one mark and the next' is I believe as good a way of any of looking at jazz composition. And it goes some way towards telling us what space is.

Any discussion of space in jazz has to be somewhat vague – and tentative, but I believe that there are parts of jazz where space can be seen or felt. Though I am dividing these into specific areas there is, inevitably, a degree of overlap, and at times a need to draw attention to the spatial characteristics of ideas already discussed.

improvisational space

The promotion of the macho image of jazz, alongside the bebop roots of much contemporary playing, means that we can typify many, perhaps the majority, of present-day soloists as 'full' players who leave very little space in their solos. Somewhat surprisingly, perhaps, this intense approach is often the norm in free jazz, a genre where, although in theory space abounds, there can be such an unchanging density of sound that one wishes for the occasional long note, or, to paraphrase Miles, for the musician 'to stop by taking the horn out of his mouth'.

Such a full approach may be demanded by certain types of music but, as Miles, again, said about his *Porgy and Bess* album with Gil Evans, 'that other passage with two chords gives you a lot more freedom and space to hear things'. This kind of freedom is welcomed by those players who are more open in their approach. They use fewer notes, or alternate using lots of notes with silence or more sustained sounds. Some players use aural separation, Paul Desmond by alternating high and low register playing, Don Pullen by alternating Cecil Taylor-ish intense flurries of sound with more lyrical passages.

In his two interpretations of the music shown below the saxophonist Karlheinz Miklin acts as an observing soloist and demonstrates his take on *improvisational space*. He shows total control, using the space he has been given to work in, rather than showing off with a display of technique. This section from *The Third Colour* is one of the many spin-offs from the Grooves, discussed above, which occur as the piece is developed using structural improvisation methods. A repetitive one-bar figure, using the flat 9 interval, traditionally suspect because of its high degree of dissonance, is the sole accompaniment for the soloist before the introduction of two floating written lines. These lines are introduced consecutively, and are designed to be played on top of each other, but the fact that one is eight bars long, the other only three, produces a dislocation effect which serves to emphasise even more the space in which the soloist is working.

Third Colour: Mid

Graham Collier

compositional space

I was asked some time ago why I didn't transpose my motifs more. My answer was that 'I try to find a sound in the same way that a painter tries to find a colour . . . . I go to a lot of trouble to find the *compositional space* that a motif inhabits in sound. To transpose it would change that space.'

To put it another way, it feels right. I have found 'where it sits', and this is an implication of the inherent space I see in a melodic line, or a simple pedal note. When room is allowed for the individual musician to add something to what is written, that melodic line can be 'moved off the page', that pedal can be made to 'buzz'. Both can be given life.

The second version of the 'Mid' section of *The Third Colour*, which includes the melody that sets up the section, shows this well. The individual motifs, played at first by a lone trumpet, hang in the air, like Gregorian chant, and when the motifs are *shadowed* by the three trumpets that feeling is intensified. The improvised solo that follows develops this sense of space, and shows a synergy between what is composed and what is improvised. One could *write* music like this, but why, when the performance moves the music off the paper into a space created by the composer, and furnished by the musicians?

rhythmic space

Not surprisingly, the concepts of 'full' and 'spacious' discussed above in improvisational space, can be seen in the work of the rhythm section. In a full-on swing or jazz-rock performance it often seems as though there is little chance of space in the rhythm section because of the complex rhythmic interplay (if good) or the unrelenting density (if bad). Even a very good bebop rhythm section often feels closed, locked into a formula. However, experience has shown that, at times, 'space' can happen. The piece will open up, the tight rhythms have gone and the new approach gives a different dimension to the space that the tune and the performance previously inhabited.

In *Part Two* of *Three Simple Pieces* the rhythmic figure is written to be played throughout – rolled steel to support what happens around it. In some performances the repetition of the figure is all you get (but it should be realised that keeping something that simple absolutely steady for a long period is not easy). In other versions such as the one heard here, that simple idea is THICKENED and constantly developed to exciting heights by Roger Dean on piano, and John Marshall on drums. The soloist, here Ed Speight on guitar, but it could be any instrument, has no chords or given role to work from. He acts as an observer, developing his ideas over the underlying shifting figure, as well as the freely introduced melodic lines.

physical and aural space

Space can be, or seem to be, a physical thing. A soloist playing in front of a big band makes aural and visual sense. Moving certain players around because of the instrumental demands of the piece,

Three Simple Pieces: Part Two

Graham Collier

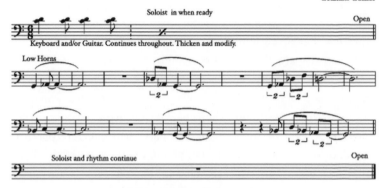

is more common in orchestras than jazz groups, but can be effective. The discovery that I could group instruments, and therefore possible textures, by range rather than by instrumental group, and that, where possible, I could even seat the players in a way that would maximise this effect, was very liberating in terms of texture.

Even if this cannot be done physically, arranging the available instruments in low, mid, and high groupings will produce interesting blends of sounds, and help to avoid the traditional clichéd section groupings. The aural separation of a very low line against a very high one, or, as traditional jazz knew well, a trumpet against a clarinet against a trombone, will achieve aural space. You can feel the same effect at work in the clarinet, piano and bass grouping of the Jimmy Giuffre trio. Or the trumpet, piano and drums grouping in Jøkleba. Both are uncluttered, very clean and sparse. Both exist in their own unique space.

The idea of 'instruments occupying their own space' is an interesting one. And for some reason Mark Murphy's voice, Harry Beckett's trumpet, come to mind: they are examples of individual jazz voices, very recognisable whatever the circumstances. Such musicians – and many others – exist in their own space, occupy their own distinctive level in the mix of sounds.

Think of Bennie Maupin's bass clarinet on *Bitches Brew*.

LEVELS

Taking advantage of the individual sounds of his musicians is one of the resources available to the jazz composer, something that Ellington knew well. But there are other aspects of levels that, once recognised, can be of great interest.

When listening to music, one's attention is usually focused on what we can call the foreground. In the most obvious situations this will be the melody or the soloist. In almost every case that foreground has *supporting elements:* the harmonies, the orchestration, the rhythms used, and, in the case of jazz, the underlying pulse and its development by the rhythm section. In other words 'texture which supports the main event'. A well-crafted melody such as 'Stella by Starlight' can stand on its own, but is enriched by the addition of its chord progression; a modal tune like 'Freddie Freeloader' could possibly work alone, but starts to live once the rhythm section begin to create the accompaniment, complementing the tune they are responding to. In cases like these, the whole becomes more than the sum of its parts. There seems no reason to do anything more.

At times, however, because the composer wills it, or the performance creates it, one or more of these elements is strengthened in a way that makes it, for a period of time, stand out. The creation of *aurally independent levels* means that one's attention is divided between two or more different elements. Supporting and independent levels can exist separately or together in a section of a piece or a whole piece. The change between them can be obvious or subtle, occasional or constant, distinct or overlapping.

While it is obviously true that music can exist simultaneously on different levels, whether supporting or independent, it was only when I came to write *The Vonetta Factor* that I came to understand the true nature of the beast. What happens in 'Vonetta', the track from *Sorcerer* (Columbia) by Miles Davis alluded to in my title, is that, surprisingly, Tony Williams accompanies a ballad with what has been described as a 'rat patrol' drum sound. Very staccato, very military sounding, this is an approach that could be regarded as the total opposite of what a ballad demands. Yet, even in its strangeness, it fits. (The fact that this approach was, as we will see, a decision of Miles in the studio is an interesting reflection on his role in such things. Rather than accept the normal way of doing things, he 'thought of a better way'.)

The discovery that the message underlying 'Vonetta' was not different levels, as I had first thought, but independence, unexpectedness, gave me much to think about and, eventually, led me into an interesting area of jazz composition. As well as becoming more conscious of what can be called supporting levels, where there is a common purpose, I became increasingly aware that, at times, independent levels are created where there is a sense of divergent purpose. At its best, as in 'Vonetta', these independent levels can be said to create a kind of parallel universe, and this, as I will show later, was what I tried to create with *The Vonetta Factor*.

supporting levels – levels of common purpose
The most prominent aspect of most music is the melody, which, in jazz, is normally followed by one or more solos. Underpinning both the statement of the melody and the solos is, almost always, a different *accompanying* level, played by the rhythm section with, perhaps, some ensemble backgrounds. Within that accompaniment, particularly in the rhythm section, there can be different levels, aurally different in terms of range and colour, rhythmically different such as a walking bass line against piano comping.

Normally, these are strictly accompanying roles, designed to complement the main strand, be it melody or solo, all working towards a common purpose. But at times an occasional flash of independence may come through – a pointer towards the fact that this separation of levels is not, cannot be, an exact science.

When orchestrating a passage, when working in a rhythm section, or when using the textural improvising ideas suggested above, decisions have to be made regarding textural levels. The simplest of these is making one instrument or group of instruments more prominent than the others, by reasons of presence or absence, range, volume or density of attack. The overall aim is to enhance what is written by making subtle changes of instrumentation, overall range, textural level, or dynamic level in the ebb and flow of a composition.

Supporting levels exist in a variety of other ways. In their most basic form they are decorative, supporting in its true sense of 'holding up', typified perhaps by the solid bass notes and string section arpeggios underpinning the melody in much classical writing. Jazz too has its filigree backgrounds, notes designed to fill a space rather than make any definite contribution but, as we can see in such music as Gil Evans' scores for Miles Davis, background writing can achieve much more. In 'Summertime', as we have seen, the repeating background riff accompanying Miles' solo has a constantly changing orchestration. This keeps it more in the foreground than we would normally expect.

At times the supporting elements achieve some kind of equality, where the melodic line is matched by one of equal or almost equal strength. Known as counterpoint, this can be seen in Bach's *Two Part Inventions*, as well as in the writing of Bill Holman, and the writing and playing of Gerry Mulligan. In fact, Mulligan's pianoless quartets, particularly the first with Chet Baker, exemplify the first two strands of this chapter – space and levels.

One can even see a kind of counterpoint in an unaccompanied solo line – a Gregorian chant, a Bach solo cello suite – where changes of register in the line may produce an effect of different aural levels, which can seem to be almost simultaneous. The line has moved away from a simple melody with one dimension, to something that can be seen from different angles, an effect which, as I have said, Paul Desmond and Don Pullen often achieved in their solos.

independent levels – levels of divergent purpose

Vonetta . . . is more than a stunning ballad because of Williams, who sustains an undercurrent of quasi-military rolls on his snare drum in the background. The effect is strange and tense, as if the peaceful mood of the ballad might be ripped apart at any moment. The contrasting elements work so impeccably that they seem to be a carefully calculated device but they came about spontaneously. As Hancock recalled several years later . . . Davis turned to Williams as they were about to start and said 'play a rat patrol sound'. [4]

The area of supporting levels is a large and fairly obvious one. What is not so obvious is the parallel universe and divergent purpose of independent levels. Whether this is created during a performance or during the writing process, it seems that one element of the event attracts, seemingly from nowhere, a very 'odd' new element, independent yet fitting with the other in some strange way. The realisation that Tony Williams seems to be in a parallel universe in the recording of 'Vonetta' was the springboard for my thoughts on this area of the music. The radical approach he demonstrates is surprising. The expectation that a ballad will be accompanied by the drummer 'stirring soup' with his brushes, while the bass plays a light walking line, has gone and the ground beneath our feet becomes unsteady.

I get a similar feeling from Charles Ives' *The Unanswered Question*, where the levels created are at times simultaneous and at times consecutive. In this piece, strongly independent levels are created against the strings by the repeating, hardly varying, solo trumpet line and the increasingly strident interjections from the four flutes. Ives achieves the same disorientating effect in the third of his *Three Places in New England*, and there are, of course, many more examples from classical music. In such music the effect has to be pre-planned, as indeed it can be in jazz. But it would seem that the opportunity for this effect, this factor, to happen spontaneously in performance, is an important strength of jazz, one which can reflect the music's real potential.

In the following example from 'Winter Oranges', the fourth section of the suite with the same name, what is immediately apparent is the independence of the trombone soloist, Vincent Nilsson, a huge contributory factor in the creation of independent levels. Part way through his cadenza he is accompanied by various improvised elements – a rhythmic bass figure, a cluster chord built up gradually from individualised notes, and a high brass chord. These elements are freely introduced and reintroduced against the soloist, and re-attacked as directed. There is a sudden change to a 12/8 repetitive piano figure, and the remainder of the piece has a strong sense of independence and space created by the individual solo voice working against the repetitive figure, and the lone clarinet melody and its echoing brass chords. The interjections of the guitarist, Anders Chico Lindvall, also create a different level.

Placing other elements freely against a soloist's contribution can be an important technique, but it is vital to remember that what the director does is influenced by what the soloist is playing, and what the soloist plays is influenced by the backgrounds which are introduced. This can be exciting but has its dangers. As I said in *I HEAR A SYMPHONY*, one soloist, in an aggressive piece where he couldn't see my cues because of the staging, commented afterwards that 'it was like walking through a minefield'.

Although it is not always that dangerous, it is hard, at times impossible, to forecast the outcome of many jazz compositions. Hence the necessity to recognise the existence of 'jazz form'.

Winter Oranges

Graham Collier

JAZZ FORM

He has largely given up the lateral thinking so common in jazz and in music generally, and replaced it with different sound structures which are often simultaneous and kept together in the frame of space.

Tension is built up by juxtaposition and superimposition of solo parts and ensemble, rather than by any routine principle of overall development.

The most characteristic thing . . . is not the thematic ideas, but rather the feeling of growth, which goes streaming through it. The way in which he creates a unity, in its plenitude of expressions – where hovering, free rhythmic passages stand both in contrast to – and mingle with – sharply drawn motifs, while a number of soloists are making their marks with individual contributions.

Those three critiques of my work, from the Finnish critic Thor Forsskåhl, the English jazz writer Barry McRae, and the doyen of Danish jazz criticism, Boris Rabinowitsch, come from different reviews over the past thirty or so years. They are encouraging support for my view that a composition should make its own form, that 'jazz form', rather than following a predetermined plan, arises in some way from the DNA discovered in the initial idea during the composing process. The 'act of composing' has opened up the possibilities. The act of performing has shown one of the possible paths.

As Jackson Pollock said, 'A picture is not thought out and settled beforehand. While it is being done it changes as one's thoughts change.' Or, as Miles Davis' biographer Ian Carr said about Gil Evans, the 'form originates from the spirit'.

Underlying this at times is the idea, common to jazz, of changing the form *in real time*. The form becomes flexible as the internal shape of individual sections, and even at times the total overall structure, changes from performance to performance. This concept of *structural improvisation*, touched on above, is unusual in more formal jazz composition, but mirrors what happens in small-group jazz, and demonstrates what jazz is – or can be – about.

Some of my early pieces, such as *Mosaics* and *Songs for My Father*, were movement based, but the order of the movements was determined during the performance by cues from whoever was soloing at the time or myself as bass player/bandleader. Other pieces were flexible in terms of who soloed on what and for how long. At that time – the late sixties and early seventies – I hadn't thought out any theory about these concepts, I just did it because it seemed a good idea to get away from the over-used theme-solos-theme jazz formula. Over the years I have developed these ideas, trying to keep the freshness of jazz within larger compositional forms, while attempting to contradict the generally held assumption that large-form jazz composition must mean lots of music paper.

Most composers predetermine the form of their pieces in the writing process, whereas with many of my own compositions I want to find ways of making the actual structure of the composition change. This can be done on what can be called the micro-level, and the macro-level.

In *micro-level structural improvising*, common in jazz, particularly in good live performances, the internal structure of a piece changes. All the elements of a composition can be controlled in an improvisatory way: the amount of time given to an open form piece, or the number of times a form such as the blues or standard song is played; the number of choruses that the soloist plays, or the length of solo in an open piece; at what point the backings come in; how those backings are created; when the final melody statement appears and so on. As can be seen in the example from 'Three Simple Pieces, Part Three' in the previous chapter soloists can be supported, inspired – and controlled – by such on-the-spot decisions.

'Colours', the conclusion of *Shapes, Colours, Energy*, combines structural improvising with textural improvising. Each of the three different levels is improvised from a given element. These roles are not allocated to specific instruments on the manuscript paper, and who plays what when can therefore be chosen with regard to the instrumentation available for each separate performance.

The first level, a pedal note, which continues throughout, is individualised, here by a designated group of low horns. Above this, the second level, here played by four reeds, each starting where he wishes, uses motific improvisation on a series of two-note motifs to create a 'shimmering' background. Once this is established, a third group, here three trumpet players, plays the given melodic motifs freely, each shadowing the other individual versions. Thus the piece, although based on written music, is almost totally improvised, texturally, in that the colours are not pre-decided, and structurally, in that the length of the section is entirely determined by the performance.

Another version of 'Colours' can be heard on the jazzcomposer website. This is from Forty Years On, *a composition where I took a fresh look at some of my compositions, where it is used as a background to a baritone solo.*

Colours

Graham Collier

Shimmering.......

On Cue. Enter anywhere

Intense, not loud. Re-attack and colour throughout

Repeat section freely

Melodies. When cued play freely, in order.

Macro-level structural improvising changes the form of the piece, often radically. While micro-level structural improvising changes are made within the form, macro-level structural improvising changes are made *with* the form. Separate sections of a suite can be played in a different order. Cues can be given by a director, or member of a band, even a soloist in a linking cadenza, which, as I said above, was the controlling idea in *Mosaics* and *Songs for My Father*. If the sections are flexible enough there is no reason why they shouldn't be played more than once, with a different soloist or a different background.

In *Mosaics* and *Songs* there was no musical idea linking the separate sections except the soloists' cadenzas. In some later pieces, a longer written section was incorporated and returned to throughout the composition, serving to hold the form together. In *The Third Colour* the opening 'Groove' section is the link, and, as we saw in the previous chapter, it has many textural devices built into it in order that it will change on each repetition. Cues given in any of the sections will end the groove at the end of that particular eight bars, and lead to an associated new page, as in the saxophone section illustrated above as an example of improvisational space. And within *those* pages cues are given to return to the Groove (always from bar one).

Thus the Groove, written to be extensively changed by *textural improvising* means, becomes the link between the sections of the whole composition, the final form of which is created afresh at each performance by *structural improvising* methods. Two completely different performances of *The Third Colour* are now available on CD and are discussed and compared on the jazzcomposer website.

THE VONETTA FACTOR

The simple narrative line is steadily overlaid and encrusted with levels of symbolism and descriptive parabolas, and the handling of time becomes less and less consecutive and linear. [5]

The composition I called *The Vonetta Factor* took the ideas of *The Third Colour*, and of earlier works such as *Mosaics* and *Songs for My Father* much further. I was interested in working with the band to produce a composition that holds together as a unified piece, but where something unexpected is happening most of the time. I was trying for subversion of the expected in compositional terms; subversion of the expected from what may appear to be a conventional big band (although they were not seated in any conventional way); subversion of the form, which is constantly changing; subversion of the melodies by ideas such as motif improvisation, shadowing and fragmenting; and subversion of the harmonies by creating them using 'carpet of sound' ideas.

Like *The Third Colour*, there are linking Grooves, each with its unique feel and associated with its own specific idea, as can be seen in the descriptive tags below. The rhythm section provides the base, and the remaining players use the given ideas to add unexpected layers above, seemingly random and each time different. To illustrate this the audio examples show two different passes of the same material.

Each of the Grooves can, at my discretion, be ended by going to an instrumental cadenza. This can return to the Groove, or go on to all or part of what I called the Extended Pages. A descriptive plan of what happened in one particular performance of *The Vonetta Factor* can be seen on the jazzcomposer website, along with some more of the score.

As we can see with *The Third Colour* and *The Vonetta Factor* the object of using structural improvisation methods is to create, at each performance, a different 'whole' from what is on the paper. Surprisingly, perhaps, given the amount of freedom and the changing parameters of different groupings and occasions, I have found that the overall timings, of separate sections or the whole composition, are often very close. This, we could say, is some justification for believing that there is such a thing as 'jazz form'.

In another interesting spin-off from this way of working, I have found that, when forced by pragmatic reasons, such as shortage of

The Vonetta Factor Grooves

Graham Collier

rehearsal time or restrictions on performance time, compositions constructed using macro-level structural improvisation methods can be reshaped, and can work well using only some of the parts. Which, waking the Ellington police from their slumbers, is somewhat akin to the way Ellington worked. We saw how most of his larger pieces are suites, and that some of the material used in the suites was borrowed from elsewhere. Yet the way he put them together created a 'whole' in a radical new way, and one that still works as a jazz composition. In the process, this way of thinking moves us even further away from the classical approach of one set version of a composition, seemingly written in stone. And lands us in the world where jazz composition, creating music using 'jazz form', is an accepted art.

Often in jazz, the form of a particular composition is something that has to be found *during* a particular performance. This applies to small group performances, but there can be places where the *possibility* of change has been written into a composition. When such options do exist, they are not the concern of the audience. They don't know the piece so they can't know what is 'supposed' to happen, or what 'can' happen when everything clicks. In such jazz compositions there is no one right answer. If what is written produces a good performance, then that is sufficient – until the next time.

What is also important is that the piece retains its identity. Musician John L. Walters, now a freelance editor and *Guardian* writer, was involved as a teenager in an initial workshopping of *Mosaics*. When he heard a subsequent broadcast by my own band he wrote: 'What makes it remarkable, knowing how loosely constructed it is, is the way your influence seems to extend over the improvisation, so that the end-result is a unified and well-balanced whole which at the same time sounds fresh and exciting.'[9]

To return to Charles Fox's felicitous comment that 'Aberdeen Angus' 'may be a different animal, but it still has the owner's name on its collar': no better metaphor exists for the role of the jazz composer.

MORE ON MOVING BEYOND THE NOTES

There is no book that I know of which covers these areas in
depth, but David Galenson's *Painting Outside the Lines, Patterns of
Creativity in Modern Art* contains some interesting comments on
form in painting that have a relevance to jazz.

'Jazz form' as used by the three major jazz composers is discussed
in 'Reflections on some of Duke Ellington's longer works', a typically trenchant article from Max Harrison in *a jazz retrospect;*
'Spontaneity: Mingus' "Plastic Form"' in Scott Sauls' *Freedom Is,
Freedom Ain't,* and various sections in Larry Hickock's *Castles Made
of Sound, the story of Gil Evans.*

17

THE FINAL WORD

RECOGNISING THE VIBRATIONS

JAZZ IN AN AGE OF DEEP PLURALISM

The matt black surface starts to sing: we recognise the vibrations given off by the inexplicably living surfaces of all authentic works of art. [1]

The word 'jazz' is still being used with great success, but I don't know how such great extremes as now exist can be contained under the one heading. [2]

Ours is a moment . . . of deep pluralism and total tolerance. Nothing is ruled out. [3]

There is a 'buzz', about certain films, books, paintings and pieces of music, a feeling that they 'breathe the right air'. They work. Looking at the lines of a painting by Joan Miró, for example, everything seems right. The works are simple, look playful but are serious in intent. And, importantly, Miró is recognisably present in all his art. This should be the aim of any jazz musician or jazz composer, and acknowledging that this aim is affected by the presence of other people should be seen as a strength, not a weakness.

We have discussed how Ellington *compiled* many of his arrangements, using the ideas, suggestions, strengths, even at times the tunes, of his musicians. And we have seen how he – and Miles –

'thought of a better way' while working, and how this led to the creation of what I have called 'jazz form', an element which, although it can seem intangible, is a distinguishing aspect of most good jazz.

We have seen how Miles Davis created magic with his – and Bill Evans' – ideas in *Kind of Blue*, as well as with his subsequent reworkings of standards such as 'Stella by Starlight', and how Gil Evans excelled in the same area with his orchestral recompositions of tunes such as 'Summertime' and 'Donna Lee'.

We have also seen how Gil Evans and Miles Davis found a new approach to jazz with 'Saeta', their collaboration based on the idea behind an Andalucían religious procession and how, in *The Black Saint and the Sinner Lady*, Charles Mingus created a masterpiece by using a different approach to jazz, making the final assembly, complete with overdubbed solos, in the studio. And we have seen how Gil Evans and others created jazz compositions from very little, or, at times, even nothing.

While demonstrating Ellington's point about the great extremes which now exist under the same heading, few would deny that these pieces are jazz, compositions that can hold their heads high in our 'age of deep pluralism'. But there is a lot more, an awful lot more (some of which is indeed awful) sold under the banner of jazz. To use some words that the novelist Robert Coover applied to what he called 'established American fiction', much of it is 'tediously conventional, imitative of the past, trite in its forms, and shallow in its ambitions'. [4]

How, to use Clifford Styll's comment again, 'can we live and die and never know the difference?'

I used to worry about this but, having learnt that, like banging your head against the walls of the Lincoln Center, such worry is pointless, I've managed to summon up a deeper tolerance for what goes under the name of jazz. Where my argument lies is that the part of jazz that still considers itself 'serious' is, in the main, ignored. Not recognised. Not even known about. As I said in DEEPENING THE GAME, 'The whole marketing and packaging

(Americanising) of jazz implies that there is an audience we should be looking for rather than an art we should be trying to work within. It could be argued that the "crisis in jazz" is not lack of record sales, but that sales, *per se*, are seen as important.'

What is important is recognising the creativity that is apparent all over the world. Not forgetting the past – the old masters are still with us on recordings, nor forgetting the traditions of jazz, which their music laid out for us. But realising in the words of Bill Evans, 'Jazz is not a what, it is a how. If it were a what, it would be static, never growing. The how is that the music comes from the moment, it is spontaneous, it exists in the time it is created. And anyone who makes music according to this method conveys to me an element that makes his music jazz.'[5]

My point throughout this book has been to look at the potential of the music rather than its marketability. And to constantly support the statement that has become one of my mantras: 'jazz happens in real time, once'.

For jazz to happen in real time once, it is essential that the music should, to repeat Clement Greenberg's words, 'determine, through its own operations and works, the effects exclusive to itself'. As is obvious, the effects peculiar and exclusive to jazz are not the written elements, the things that can be seen, but rather the things that can't be seen, what the musicians do with what they are given. In a word, improvising. There are certain stylistic fingerprints that can be used to identify the music, but the presence of improvisation – or, in some cases, the *appearance* of improvisation – is the determining characteristic.

There is another statement from Greenberg which is of enormous relevance to jazz: 'the acceptance, willing acceptance, of the limitations of the medium of the specific art'.[6] No one should deny that jazz has its limits. It's not classical music with its instrumental resources, its long history, its status, its subsidies. It's not pop music either, with its constant change, its huge audiences, its record company support. It's not Indian music, or Brazilian, or any other of the world musics that have their own defining ambience and sounds.

The above genres have their own identity and their own strengths and limitations. For good or ill, all have been intermixed with jazz at one time or another and, although I would not want to denigrate these trends, it has seemed to me that jazz has, in some way, usually lost out. In today's climate this puts me firmly in my place as an out and out Luddite, but, I would immodestly suggest, a radical one. Someone who believes that jazz has its limits but also its own particular strengths, strengths which are often forgotten, but which we should relish and develop.

To be specific about this: there is a potential in jazz and jazz composition that often goes unrealised.

In terms of this book, that potential can be easily seen when comparing the role of a classical composer and a jazz composer. In classical music the composer's role is to present music that tries to say something, reflecting in some way his or her view of the world. When the piece is performed there may be different interpretations, but the essential truth is contained in the score. The role of a jazz composer is also to present something original and individual, but, in doing so he also needs to encourage improvisation by using the skills of the musicians to enhance the given music. What is written down is only the starting point, the musicians' individual contributions are important, and because of this, and what is implicit in the writing, the composition should have the possibility of change from performance to performance.

This has, obviously, been a personal look at jazz and jazz composition. I have had some harsh things to say about other jazz composers. Some, like Thelonious Monk and George Russell, because, no matter how hard I try, I cannot like what they do. Some, like Jim McNeeley and Sammy Nestico, because I find that what they do has failed to take advantage of the potential of jazz which was opened up some fifty years ago.

I've had good things to say about some writers whose work may not be known to most of my readers. Paul Grabowsky and

Christian Mühlbacher were singled out in DON'T BE AFRAID . . . , and there are others such as Norwegians Geir Lysne and Jon Balke, Canadian Paul Cram, Italian Roberto Bonati and Austrian Christoph Cech, whose work I greatly admire. (More on these and other creative jazz composers will be found on the jazzcontinuum website.) There are undoubtedly many others working to extend the parameters of jazz composition while still retaining its traditions, but, like the ones I have named, their voices are more often than not drowned out by the market and the media.

When thinking about the prevailing situation, and the place of creative jazz composers in it, what comes to mind are two quotes. The first is Malcolm Lowry's description of one of his characters in *Under the Volcano*, the second is from the last letter, to a student fan, of Lowry's mentor, Conrad Aiken.

A madman passed, wearing, in the manner of a lifebelt, an old bicycle tyre . . . . He muttered to the Consul but waiting neither for reply nor reward, took off the tyre and flung it far ahead of him . . . . Picking up the tyre, he flung it far ahead again, repeating this process, to the irreducible logic of which he appeared eternally committed, until out of sight.[7]

If there is anything good in my poetry, people like you will find it. That's all we can hope for, and goodness knows it's enough. The effort alone is worth it.[8]

Or, as John Lewis said, 'The reward for playing jazz is playing jazz.'

NOTES

EPIGRAPHS

1 Paul Berliner, *Thinking in Jazz*, 802, n30.

2 Ted Gioia, quoted in Will Friedwald, *The Future of Jazz*, 75.

INTRODUCTION   *TAKE TIME OUT TO LISTEN*

1 James Isaacs, 'The BMI Jazz Composers Workshop', *Jazz Education Journal*, Volume 37, No. 1, 57.

2 Clement Greenberg, *Late Writings*, 182.

3 *Jazz Review*, Issue 51, 31.

CHAPTER ONE   *SOMETHING BORROWED, SOMETHING NEW*

1 Artist Terry Frost, speaking at the Serpentine Gallery, 1977.

2 T. J. Clark, *The Painting of Modern Life*, 220.

3 From a letter in *Jazz Changes*, Volume 1, No. 2, Autumn 1994, 4.

4 *Jazz Changes*, Volume 2, No. 2, Summer 1995, 18.

5 *http://forums.allaboutjazz.com/showthread.php?t=2452Quote:*

6 *http://forums.allaboutjazz.com/showthread.php?p=127233#post127233*

CHAPTER TWO   JAZZ HAPPENS IN REAL TIME, ONCE

1 Robert Walser, in Krin Gabbard, *Jazz Among the Discourses*, 178.

2 Clement Greenberg, *Essays Volume 4*, 86.

3 Gene Lees, *You Can't Steal a Gift*, 87.

4 Charles O. Hartman, *Jazz Text*, 10.

5 Duke Ellington, in Shapiro and Hentoff, *Hear me Talkin' to Ya*, 225.

6 Charles O. Hartman, *Jazz Text*, 14.

7 *ibid*, 73-4.

8 Jokleba's website is *http://www.musicfromnorway.com/default.aspx?music=11160&norwegian=album*

CHAPTER THREE   *WELL MAN, WE JUST BLOW*

1 Whitney Balliett, *Dinosaurs in the Morning*, 37-8.

2 Whitney Balliett, *The Sound of Surprise*, 10.

3 Gunther Schuller, *The Tanner Lectures*, 6.

4 Charlie Parker, in Shapiro and Hentoff, *Hear me Talkin' to Ya*, 405.

5 Cootie Williams, in James Lincoln Collier, *Duke Ellington*, 89.

6 Lee Konitz, in Whitney Balliett, *Jelly Roll, Jabbo and Fats*, 185-6.

7 Guitarist John Etheridge,in Geoffrey Smith, *Stephane Grappelli*, 182.

8 Miles Davis/Quincy Troupe, *Miles – The Autobiography*, 195.

9 Paul Berliner, *Thinking in Jazz*, 299.

10 James Lincoln Collier, *Duke Ellington*, 88.

11 Francis Davis, In *the Moment*, 180.

12 Bob Brookmeyer, *Jazz Educators' Journal*, Volume 36, No. 2

13 Francis Davis, *Bebop and Nothingness*, xvi.

14 Mike Heffley, *Northern Sun, Southern Moon*, 240.

15 Liner notes to *Mingus Dynasty* (Columbia/Legacy), 7-8.

16 *ibid*, 8.

17 Mark Tucker, *The Duke Ellington Reader*, 228.

18 Gunther Schuller, *Musings*, 86.

19 Robert Walser, *Keeping Time, Readings in Jazz History*, 213.

20 Ingrid Monson, *Saying Something*, 135-6.

CHAPTER FOUR   *WHO DOES WHAT WHEN*

1 Rex Stewart, *Down Beat* June 3, 1965, reprinted January 2005.

2 Quoted in Shapiro and Hentoff, *Hear me Talkin' to Ya*, 93.

3 Francis Davis, *Bebop and Nothingness*, 41-2.

4 Barry Kernfeld, *What to Listen for in Jazz*, 91.

5 Paul Berliner, *Thinking in Jazz*, 305.

6 Stanley Dance, *The World of Count Basie*, 107.

7 Barry Kernfeld, *What to Listen for in Jazz*, 74.

8 Gunther Schuller, *Early Jazz*, 244.

9 Gunther Schuller, *Musings*, 8.

10 Gunther Schuller, *Early Jazz*, 268.

11 Alyn Shipton, *A New History of Jazz*, 238-9.

12 James Lincoln Collier, *The Making of Jazz*, 184.

13 Alyn Shipton, *A New History of Jazz*, 328-9.

14 Gunther Schuller, *The Swing Era*, 20 n28-21.

CHAPTER FIVE   *ONE PLUS ONE MAKES THREE*

1 Billy Strayhorn, in Shapiro and Hentoff, *Hear me Talkin' to Ya*, 237.

2 Heinrich Wolfflin, in Arthur C. Danto, *After the End of Art*, 44.

3 James Lincoln Collier, *Duke Ellington*, 130.

4 Gunther Schuller, *Early Jazz*, 326.

5 Barney Bigard, *With Louis and the Duke*, 44.

6 *ibid*, 64.

7 Quoted in Shapiro and Hentoff, *Hear me Talkin' to Ya*, 238.

8 Mark Tucker, *The Duke Ellington Reader*, 502-3.

9   Mercer Ellington, in James Lincoln Collier, *Duke Ellington*, 48.

10 Quoted in Shapiro and Hentoff, *Hear me Talkin' to Ya*, 231.

11 Sidney Finkelstein, in Ken Rattenbury, *Duke Ellington, Jazz Composer*, 14.

12 Gunther Schuller, *Early Jazz*, 327.

13 Quoted in Shapiro and Hentoff, *Hear me Talkin' to Ya*, 225.

14 Mark Tucker, *The Duke Ellington Reader*, 229.

15 H. A. Overstreet, in Mark Tucker, *The Duke Ellington Reader*, 102.

16 Ken Rattenbury, *Duke Ellington, Jazz Composer*, 23.

17 Trumpeter Benny Bailey, in Paul Berliner, *Thinking in Jazz*, 309.

18 Quoted in Shapiro and Hentoff, *Hear me Talkin' to Ya*, 237.

19 Mark Tucker, *The Duke Ellington Reader*, 303.

20 Duke Ellington, *Music is my Mistress*, 452.

21 Mark Tucker, *The Duke Ellington Reader*, 135.

22 Ken Rattenbury, *Duke Ellington, Jazz Composer*, 23.

23 Mark Tucker, *The Duke Ellington Reader*, 366.

24 *ibid*, 217.

25 James Lincoln Collier, *Duke Ellington*, 52.

26 Quoted in Shapiro and Hentoff, *Hear me Talkin' to Ya*, 238.

27 James Lincoln Collier, *Duke Ellington*, 304.

28 Gunther Schuller, *Early Jazz*, 329.

CHAPTER SIX   *THINKING OF A BETTER WAY*

1   Producer Irving Townsend, in Mark Tucker, *The Duke Ellington Reader*, 322.

2   David Hajdu, *Lush Life*, 140-1.

3   Mark Tucker, *The Duke Ellington Reader*, 275.

4   James Lincoln Collier, *Duke Ellington*, 69.

5   Duke Ellington, *Music is my Mistress*, 88.

6   James Lincoln Collier, *Duke Ellington*, 234.

7   *ibid*, 145.

8   Critic Martin Williams, in Mark Tucker, *The Duke Ellington Reader*, 410.

9   Mark Tucker, *The Duke Ellington Reader*, 62.

10 The full text can be found in Tucker, 57-65.

11 Mark Tucker, *The Duke Ellington Reader*, 364.

12 *ibid*, 322.

13 *ibid*, 388.

14 *ibid*, 501.

15 David Hajdu, *Lush Life*, 160.

16 Gunther Schuller, *The Swing Era*, 142.

17 Mark Tucker, *The Duke Ellington Reader*, 203-4.

18 *ibid*, 351-2.

19 *ibid*, 389.

20 *ibid*, 394.

21 *Jazz Review*, 77, 19.

22 Quoted in Shapiro and Hentoff, *Hear me Talkin' to Ya*, 181.

23 Gunther Schuller, *Early Jazz*, 139.

24 *ibid*, 135-6.

25 Nat Hentoff, *Jazz*, 81.

26 Gunther Schuller, *Early Jazz*, 144.

27 Nat Hentoff, *Jazz*, 81.

28 Gary Giddins, *Visions of Jazz*, 253.

29 Walter van de Leur, *Something to Live For*, 100.

30 Gary Giddins, *Rhythm-a-ning*, 129.

CHAPTER SEVEN   *WHY WOULD WE WANT TO REPEAT IT?*

1 Eric Nisenson, *Blue, the Murder of Jazz*, 91.

2 Francis Davis, *In the Moment*, 29-30.

3 Gustav Mahler, *source unknown*

4 Eric Nisenson, *Blue, the Murder of Jazz*, 26.

5 *ibid*, 91.

6 *Jazzwise*, March 2005.

7 Walter van de Leur, *Something to Live For*, xviii-xix.

8 Eric Nisenson, *The Making of Kind of Blue*, 21.

9 Clement Greenberg, *Essays Volume 1*, 6.

10 Will Friedwald, *The Future of Jazz*, 102.

11 *ibid*, 100.

12 *ibid*, 104.

13 Francis Davis, *Outcats*, 202.

14 *ibid*, 200-2.

15 Will Friedwald, *The Future of Jazz*, 102.

16 Ashley Kahn, *Kind of Blue*, 177.

17 *New York Times*, May 12, 2006.

18 Benny Morton, Mark Tucker, *The Duke Ellington Reader*, 178.

19 Bill Laswell, unsourced.

20 Keith Jarrett, *Jazz Times*, May 1999.

21 Mark Tucker, *The Duke Ellington Reader*, 326.

22 *ibid*, 41.

23 Malcolm Lowry, author of *Under the Volcano*, from a letter to Robert

Giroux. Sherrill Grace, *Sursum Corda!, The Collected Letters of Malcolm Lowry*, Volume 2, 504-5.

24 Wynton Marsalis, in Francis Davis, *In the Moment*, 32.

25 Wayne Shorter, *The Guardian*, September 26, 2002.

26 *The Wire*, July 1993, 47.

27 Mark Rowland, *The Jazz Musician*, 159.

CHAPTER EIGHT   *INFINITE POSSIBILITIES*

1 Sidney Finkelstein, in Max Harrison, *a jazz retrospect*, 147.

2 Gary Giddins, *Rhythm-a-ning*, 83.

3 Nat Hentoff, *Jazz Review*, December 1958.

4 Ashley Kahn, *Kind of Blue*, 98-9.

5 *ibid*, 98.

6 *ibid*, 170.

7 *ibid*, 163.

8 Nat Hentoff, *Jazz Review*, December 1958.

9 *ibid*.

10 David Hajdu, *Lush Life*, 87.

11 Eric Nisenson, *Blue, the Murder of Jazz*, 134.

12 Alyn Shipton, *A New History of Jazz*, 697.

13 Ashley Kahn, *Kind of Blue*, 165.

14 *ibid*, 185.

15 Brian Priestley, *Mingus* 109-10.

16 Francis Davis, *In the Moment*, 145.

17 Brian Priestley, *Mingus*, x-xi.

18 *ibid*, 77.

19 *ibid*, 129.

20 Donald Judd, in Kirk Varnadoe, *Pictures of Nothing*, 92.

21 Krin Gabbard, *Jazz Among the Discourses*, 150

22 Dylan Evans, *Guardian*, June 7, 2005.

23 Sidney Finkelstein, in Max Harrison, *a jazz retrospect*, 147.

24 Clement Greenberg, *Late Writings*, 79.

25 *www.jazzhouse.org/bulletin/viewtopic*

CHAPTER NINE   *DEEPENING THE GAME*

1 Francis Bacon, in David Sylvester, *Interviews with Francis Bacon*, 29.

2 Novelist William Gass, *The Review of Contemporary Fiction*, Volume XI, No. 3.

3 *Jazz Review*, March 2002, 30.

4 William Gass, *ibid*.

5 Francis Davis, *In the Moment*, x.

6 Derek Bailey, *Improvisation*, 47.

7 Clement Greenberg, *Essays Volume 1*, 19.

8 Clement Greenberg, *Essays Volume 4*, 119.

9 David Sylvester, *London Recordings*, 195.

10 Michael Fried, *Art and Objecthood*, 220.

11 Personal correspondence with the author.

12 Jerry D'Souza, review of *Norrköping*, *All About Jazz* website.

13 J. Rose and R. Linz, *The Pink Violin*, 98.

14 James Lincoln Collier, *Jazz, the American Theme Song*, 262

15 Krin Gabbard, *Jazz Among the Discourses*, 114, n3.

16 *ibid*, 170.

17 *Selected Letters of Conrad Aiken*, 331.

18 Kirk Varnedoe, *Jackson Pollock New Approaches*, 245.

19 Critic Howard Mandel, found on *be-jazz.blogspot.com*

CHAPTER TEN   *IT AIN'T WHO YOU ARE*

1 John Surman, unsourced.

2 David Sylvester, *About Modern Art*, 322.

3 *ibid*, 324.

4 *Der Speigel*, 17 November 2006, quoted by Stuart Nicholson in *Jazz Times* May 2007.

5 Both from Alyn Shipton's liner notes to a repackaging by BGO in 2007 of *Down Another Road*, *Songs for my Father* and *Mosaics* as a double CD.

6 *Jazz Times*, undated.

7 Kirk Varnedoe *et al*, *Jackson Pollock*, 76

8 *Jazzwise*, September 2005.

9 *Jazz Review*, March 2002, 30.

10 *Atlantic Monthly*, March 2003.

11 Lee Hill Kavanaugh, bass trombonist with Diva, in a contribution to 'Women in Jazz', *Jazz Changes*, Volume 2, No. 1, Spring 1995.

12 A transcript of the seminar can be found at *www.najp.org/events/talkingjazztranscript1*

13 An anonymous gay black musician, in David Hajdu, *Lush Life*, 79.

14 *Vanity Fair*, May 1999.

15 *Vanity Fair*, June 1999.

16 *Jazz Journal International*, June 1999, 14-15

17 Mark Tucker, *The Duke Ellington Reader*, 368

18 *ibid*, 362.

19 Ingrid Monson, *Saying Something*, 201-2.
20 *ibid*, 203.
21 Ashley Kahn, *Kind of Blue*, 85.
22 Eric Nisenson, *Blue, the Murder of Jazz*, 176-7.
23 *ibid*, 177.
24 Mark Tucker, *The Duke Ellington Reader*, 232.

CHAPTER ELEVEN   *NO MORE BLUES?*
1   Clement Greenberg, *Late Writings*, 79.
2   Ekkehard Jost, *Free Jazz*, 140.
3   Ashley Kahn, *Kind of Blue*, 118.
4   *ibid*, 98.
5   *ibid*, 98.
6   *www.billevanswebpages.com/kindblue.html*
7   Ashley Kahn, *Kind of Blue*, 193.
8   *ibid*, 194.
9   Liner notes to the 1988 CD.
10 Ian Carr, *Miles Davis*, 112.
11 Interview with Michael Dwyer in *The Age, Melbourne*, May 11 2005.
12 Interview with Mark Gilbert, *Jazz Journal*, March 1996,7.
13 André Boucourechliev, liner notes, *The Orchestral Music of Debussy*
    (EMI), 4.
14 *ibid*, 4.
15 Ekkehard Jost, *Free Jazz*, 58.
16 Helen A. Harrison, *Such Desperate Joy*, 128.
17 Saxophonist John Handy, in Brian Priestley, *Mingus*, 103.
18 Eric Nisenson, *Blue, the Murder of Jazz*, 196.
19 Lewis Porter, Coltrane's biographer, in Ashley Kahn, *Kind of Blue*, 182.
20 Liner notes to *Let My Children Hear Music*. (Columbia Legacy).
21 Conrad Aiken, *a reviewer's abc*, 52
22 *ibid*, 203.
23 Charles Fox, *Jazz in Perspective*.
24 Unsourced.
25 Jimmy Giuffre, in Whitney Balliett, *The Sound of Surprise*, 40.
26 Maurice White of Earth Wind and Fire, in Ashley Kahn, *Kind of Blue*,
    143.
27 Ian Carr, *Miles Davis*, 136.
28 Doug Ramsey, *Take Five: The Public and Private Lives of Paul Desmond*.

CHAPTER TWELVE   *DON'T BE AFRAID*

1 Liner notes to *Mingus Dynasty*, 9.
2 Ashley Kahn, *Kind of Blue* 182.
3 Mike Heffley, *Northern Sun, Southern Moon*, 157.
4 Whitney Balliett, *The Sound of Surprise*, 35.
5 Liner notes, *Complete Verve Gerry Mulligan Concert Band Sessions, 3*.
6 *ibid*, 10.
7 Max Harrison, *a jazz retrospect*, 133.
8 Whitney Balliett, *The Sound of Surprise*, 89.
9 Francis Davis, *Outcats*, 29.
10 *date unknown*.
11 Max Harrison, *a jazz retrospect*, 141-2
12 Mark Gilbert, *Jazz Journal International*, August 1996,25.
13 Max Harrison, *a jazz retrospect*, 143-4.
14 Derek Jewell, liner notes to *Togo Brava*.
15 Walter van de Leur, *Something to Live For*, 25
16 *New York Times*, May 12, 2006.
17 John Gill, *Jazz Changes*, Volume 5, No. 3, Autumn 1998.

CHAPTER THIRTEEN   *I HEAR A SYMPHONY*

1 Ernst-Ludwig Petrovsky, in Mike Heffley, *Northern Sun, Southern Moon*, 193.
2 Brian Priestley, *Mingus*, 198-9.
3 *ibid*, 166.
4 Larry Hicock, *Castles made of Sound*, 90.
5 *ibid*, 112.
6 in Shapiro and Hentoff, *Hear me Talkin' to Ya*, 224-5.
7 Mark Tucker, *The Duke Ellington Reader*, 187.
8 Interview with the author.
9 Nat Hentoff, liner notes to *Sketches of Spain*.
10 Liner notes, *Complete Columbia Studio Recording*, 65.
11 Charles Mingus, in Brian Priestley, *Mingus*, 65.
12 Gunther Schuller, *Tanner Lecture*, 36.
13 Ekkehard Jost, *Free Jazz*, 35.
14 Brian Priestley, *Mingus*, 28.
15 *ibid*, 71-2.
16 Ekkehard Jost, *Free Jazz*, 38.
17 *ibid*, 38.
18 Brian Priestley, *Mingus*, 133.
19 *ibid*, 147.

20 *ibid*, 147.

21 'Riddle Me This', *Jazz Times*, December 2000.

22 Liner notes, *Creative Orchestra Music 1976* (Arista).

23 Paul Nash, *correspondence with the author.*

24 Robert D. Crowley, in Mark Tucker, *The Duke Ellington Reader*, 184.

25 Charles Mingus, *Beneath the Underdog*, 339-40.

26 Max Harrison, *a jazz retrospect*, 183.

27 unknown, possibly Clement Greenberg.

28 André Boucourechliev on Debussy's *La Mer*, from the *Orchestral Music of Debussy* box set.

29 Clement Greenberg, *Essays Volume Three*, 70-1.

30 Novelist Michael Ondaatje, interview on *The South Bank Show*, ITV.

31 *www.stylusmagazine.com/feature.php?ID=27*

32 *ibid.*

CHAPTER FOURTEEN *TAKING A CHANCE*

1 Steven Stucky, *Lutoslawski & his music*, Cambridge University Press (1991), 110.

2 Ekkehard Jost, *Free Jazz*, 182.

3 Bill Evans, liner notes to *Kind of Blue*.

4 Ashley Kahn, *Kind of Blue*, 134.

5 *ibid*, 135.

6 Ekkehard Jost, *Free Jazz*, 28.

7 Evan Parker, in Derek Bailey, *Improvisation*, 81.

8 Steve Harris, *correspondence with the author.*

9 Interview from 1987, reprinted in *DownBeat*, August 2005.

10 Ashley Kahn, *Kind of Blue*, 185.

11 Mike Heffley, *Northern Sun, Southern Moon*, 128.

12 *ibid*, 193.

13 *ibid*, 224.

14 Liner notes, *The Shadowgraph Series*, Spool records.

15 Brian Priestley, *Mingus*, 111.

16 Will Friedwald, *The Future of Jazz*, 83.

17 Mike Heffley, *Northern Sun, Southern Moon*, 315-6, note 40.

18 Playwright Alan Ayckbourn, unsourced.

19 Larry Hicock, *Castles Made of Sound*, 143.

20 Heard in passing in a documentary on Gil Evans.

21 Interview with Brian Case, *Melody Maker*, October 1984.

22 Interview with the author, 1994.

23 Interview with Brian Case, *Melody Maker*, October 1984.

24 Francis Davis, *Outcats*, 30.
25 Airto Moreira, in Larry Hicock, *Castles Made of Sound*, 183.
26 Francis Davis, *In the Moment*, 180.
27 Larry Hicock, *Castles Made of Sound*, 182-3.
28 Lew Soloff. *ibid*, 188.
29 *ibid*, 283.
30 Gil Evans, liner notes, *Where Flamingos Fly* (A&M).

CHAPTER FIFTEEN   *ROLLED STEEL INTO GOLD*
1 Kip Hanrahan, in liner notes, *All Roads Are Made of the Flesh*, (American Clave).
2 Thor Forsskåhl, *Huvvudstadtsbladet*, April 5, 1976.
3 Letter from Gill Fisher to mutual friends of the author, December 2004. Used by permission.
4 Malcolm Cowley, *And I Worked at the Writer's Trade*, 204.
5 Unsourced.
6 *Barnett Newman*, 63.
7 T. J. Clark, *The Sight of Death*, 126.
8 Clement Greenberg, *Essays Volume 2*, 20.
9 Steven Stucky, *Lutoslawski & his music*, 167. (See Chapter 14, Note 1.)
10 *www.guardian.co.uk/artanddesign/2008/jan/22/art*
11 Unsourced.

CHAPTER SIXTEEN   *'PLAY A RAT PATROL SOUND'*
1 Hannah Weitemeier, *Klein*, Taschen (2001), 28.
2 Used to describe Dame Judy Dench's performance in the film *Iris*, *Guardian*, 21 December, 2001.
3 *Guardian*, 17 July 2001.
4 Jack Chambers, *Milestones: The Music and Times of Miles Davis*.
5 Unsourced.
6 Letter to the author, 2 April, 1971.

CHAPTER SEVENTEEN   *THE FINAL WORD*
1 David Sylvester speaking of Ad Reinhardt, *About Modern Art*, 69.
2 Duke Ellington, *Music is My Mistress*, 453.
3 Harold Danto, *After the End of Art*, xiv.
4 Preface to John Hawkes *The Lime Twig*, xi.
5 Alyn Shipton, *A New History of Jazz*, 663.
6 Clement Greenberg, *Essays Volume 1*, 32.
7 Malcolm Lowry, *Under the Volcano*, 227.
8 *Selected Letters of Conrad Aiken*, 331.

BIBLIOGRAPHY

Aiken, Conrad. 1958. *a reviewer's abc, Collected Criticism of Conrad Aiken from 1916 to the present*. London: W. H. Allen.

_ 1978 *Selected Letters of Conrad Aiken*. New Haven and London: Yale University Press.

Bailey, Derek. 1992. *Improvisation, its nature and practice in music*. London: British Library National Sound Archive.

Balliett, Whitney. 1959. *The Sound of Surprise*. London: Penguin.

_ 1965. *Dinosaurs in the Morning*. London: Phoenix.

_ 1983. *Jelly Roll, Jabbo and Fats: 19 Portraits in Jazz*. New York: Oxford University Press.

Berliner, Paul F. 1994. *Thinking in Jazz, the Infinite Art of Improvisation*. Chicago: University of Chicago Press.

Bigard, Barney. 1985. *With Louis and the Duke*, London: Macmillan.

Carr, Ian. 1999. *Miles Davis, A Critical Biography*. London: HarperCollins.

Chambers, Jack. 1998. *Milestones: The Music and Times of Miles Davis*. Cambridge: DaCapo Press.

Clark, T. J. 1984. *The Painting of Modern Life, Paris in the Art of Manet and His Followers*. Princeton: Princeton University Press.

_ 2006. *The Sight of Death*, New Haven and London: Yale University Press.

Collier, Graham. 1973. *Inside Jazz*, London: Quartet Books.

_ 1975. *Compositional Devices*. Boston: Berklee Press .

_ 1976. *Cleo and John*. London: Quartet Books.

_ 1977. *Jazz a Students' and Teachers' Guide*. Cambridge: Cambridge University Press (Translated into German, Norwegian and Italian).

_ 1988. *Jazz Workshop the Blues*, London: Universal Edition.

_ 1995. *www.jazzcontinuum.com/writings/interaction/interaction.htm* book and CD package. Germany: Advance Music.

_ 2000. *'Are Chord Scales the Answer?'*. A paper presented at the Leeds International Jazz Education Conference, April 2000, revised November 2002. This and many other articles by Graham Collier can be found at *jazzcontinuum.com*

Collier, Graham, and Gill, John, eds. 1994–2000. *Jazz Changes, the magazine of the International Association of Schools of Jazz*. London: jazzcontinuum.com

Collier, James Lincoln. 1978. *The Making of Jazz, A Comprehensive History*. London: Granada.

_ 1987. *Duke Ellington*. London: Michael Joseph.

_ 1993. *Jazz, The American Theme Song*. New York: Oxford University Press.

Cook, Richard, and Morton, Brian, eds. 1992 (updated regularly). *The Penguin Guide to Jazz on CD*. London: Penguin Books.

Coover, Robert. 1995. Preface to John Hawkes, *The Lime Twig, Second Skin, Travesty*. New York: Penguin Books.

Cowley, Malcolm. 1978. *and I Worked at the Writer's Trade, Chapters of Literary History, 1918–1978*. New York: Viking Press.

Dahl, Linda. 1984. *Stormy Weather. The Music and Lives of a Century of Jazzwomen*. London: Quartet Books.

Dance, Stanley, 1980. *The World of Count Basie*. London: Sidgwick & Jackson.

Danto, Harold. 1997. *After the End of Art, Contemporary Art and the Pale of History*. Princeton: Princeton University Press.

Davis, Francis. 1986. *In the Moment, Jazz in the 1980s*. New York: Oxford University Press.

_ 1986. *Outcats, Jazz Composers, Instrumentalists, and Singers*. New York: Oxford University Press.

_ 1996. *Bebop and Nothingness, Jazz and Pop at the End of the Century*. New York: Schirmer Books.

Davis, Miles with Troupe, Quincy. 1989. *Miles The Autobiography*. New York: Simon & Schuster.

Dean, Roger T. 1992. *New Structures in Jazz and Improvised Music since 1960*. Milton Keynes: Open University Press.

Ellington, Edward Kennedy 'Duke'. 1974. *Music is My Mistress*. London: W. H. Allen and Co.

Evans, Gil. 1997. *Gil Evans Collection (Falk Symposium)*. Milwaukee: Hal Leonard.

Finkelstein, Sidney. 1948. *Jazz: a People's Music*. New York: Citadel Press. Reprinted 1964. London: Jazz Book Club.

Fox, Charles. 1969. *Jazz in Perspective*, London: BBC.

Fried, Michael. 1998. *Art and Objecthood*. Chicago: University of Chicago Press.

Friedwald, Will *et al*. 2002. *The Future of Jazz*. Chicago: A Cappella Books.

Gabbard, Krin ed. 1995. *Jazz among the Discourses*. Durham and London: Duke University Press.

Galenson, David W. 2001. *Painting Outside the Lines, Patterns of Creativity in Modern Art*. Cambridge: Harvard University Press.

Giddins, Gary. 1985. *Rhythm-a-ning, Jazz Tradition and Innovation in the '80s*. New York: Oxford University Press.

_ 1998. *Visions of Jazz The First Century*. New York: Oxford University Press.

Gill, John. 1995. *Queer Noises, Male and Female Homosexuality in Twentieth-Century Music*. London: Cassell.

Gioia, Ted. 1998. *The Imperfect Art, Reflections on Jazz and Modern Culture*. New York: Oxford University Press.

Greenberg, Clement. 1986. *The Collected Essays and Criticism, Volume I. Perceptions and Judgements, 1939–1944*.

_ 1986. *The Collected Essays and Criticism, Volume 2, Arrogant Prose, 1945–1949*.

_ 1993. *The Collected Essays and Criticism, Volume 3, Affirmations and Refusals, 1950–1956*.

_ 1993. *The Collected Essays and Criticism, Volume 4, Modernism with a Vengeance, 1957–1969*.

All edited by O'Brian, John. Chicago: University of Chicago Press.

_ 2003. *Clement Greenberg Late Writings*. Morgan, Robert. C, ed. Minneapolis: University of Minnesota Press.

Hajdu, David. 1997. *Lush Life, a Biography of Billy Strayhorn*. London: Granta Books.

Harrison, Helen A. ed. 2000. *Such Desperate Joy, Imagining Jackson Pollock*. New York: Thunder's Mouth Press.

Harrison, Max. 1991. *a jazz retrospect*. London: Quartet Books.

Hartman, Charles. O. 1991. *Jazz Text, Voice and Improvisation in Poetry, Jazz and Song*. Princeton: Princeton University Press.

Heffley, Mike. 2005. *Northern Sun, Southern Moon, Europe's Reinvention of Jazz*. New Haven and London: Yale University Press.

Hentoff, Nat and McCarthy, Albert, eds. 1977. *Jazz*. London: Quartet, Books.

Hicock, Larry. 2002. *Castles Made of Sound, the Story of Gil Evans*. New York: Da Capo Press.

Jost, Ekkehard. 1975. *Free Jazz*. Vienna: Universal Edition.

Kahn, Ashley. 2000. *Kind of Blue, the Making of the Miles Davis Masterpiece*. New York: Da Capo Press.

Kernfeld, Barry, ed. 1994 *The New Grove Dictionary of Jazz*. New York and London: Macmillan.

_ 1995. *What to Listen for in Jazz*. London and New Haven: Yale University Press.

Lees, Gene. 2001. *You Can't Steal a Gift, Dizzy, Clark, Milt and Nat*. New Haven and London: Yale University Press.

Leur, Walter van de. 2002. *Something to Live For, The Music of Billy Strayhorn*. New York: Oxford University Press.

Levine, Mark. 1995. *The Jazz Theory Book*. California: Sher Music Co.

Lowry, Malcolm. 1947 *Under the Volcano*. London: Jonathan Cape.

_ 1996. *Sursum Corda! The Collected Letters of Malcolm Lowry, Volume Two: 1946–57*. Sherrill E. Grace ed. London: Jonathan Cape.

Mandel, Howard. 1999. *Future Jazz*. New York: Oxford University Press.

_ 2007. *Miles, Ornette, Cecil*. New York and London: Routledge.

McKay, George. 2005. *Circular Breathing. The Cultural Politics of Jazz in Britain*. Durham and London: Duke University Press.

Mingus, Charles. 1991. *Beneath the Underdog*. New York: Vintage.

_ 1991. *Charles Mingus, More than a Fake Book*, ed. Andrew Homzy. New York: Hal Leonard.

Monson, Ingrid. 1996. *Saying Something, Jazz Improvisation and Interaction*. Chicago: University of Chicago Press.

Morton, Jelly Roll, 2005. *The Complete Library of Congress Recordings*. Rounder Records. A seven CD set of the famous 1938 recordings including Alan Lomax's biography, *Mister Jelly Roll: the Fortunes of Jelly Roll Morton, New Orleans Creole and 'Inventor of Jazz'*.

Newman, Barnet, 1963. *Barnett Newman*. London: The Tate Gallery.

Nicholson, Stuart. 2005. *Is Jazz Dead? (Or has it moved to a new address)*. New York and London: Routledge.

Nisenson, Eric. 1997. *Blue. The Murder of Jazz*. New York: St. Martin's Press.

_ 2000. The Making of Kind of Blue, New York: St. Martin's Press.

O'Hara, Frank. 1959. *Jackson Pollock*. New York: George Braziller.

Priestley, Brian. 1982. *Mingus: A Critical Biography*. London: Quartet Books.

Ramsey, Doug, 2008. *Take Five: The Public and Private Lives of Paul Desmond*. Seattle: Parkside Publications.

Rattenbury, Ken. 1990. *Duke Ellington, Jazz Composer*. London and New Haven: Yale University Press.

Rose J. and Linz R, 1992. *The Pink Violin, Portrait of an Australian Musical Dynasty*. Melbourne: NMA Publications.

Rowland, Mark and Scherman, Tony, eds. 1994. *The Jazz Musician*. New York: St Martin's Press.

Saul, Scott. 2003. *Freedom is, Freedom ain't. Jazz and the Making of the Sixties*. Cambridge, Mass., and London: Harvard University Press.

Schuller, Gunther. 1968. *Early Jazz. Its Roots and Musical Development*. New York: Oxford University Press.

_ 1986. *Musings. The Musical Worlds of Gunther Schuller*. New York: Oxford University Press.

_ 1989. *The Swing Era. The Development of Jazz. 1930–1945*. New York: Oxford University Press.

_ 1996 *The first of The Tanner Lectures on Human Values*. *www.tannerlectures.utah.edu/lectures/documents/schuller97*

Shapiro, Nat and Hentoff, Nat, eds. 1955. *Hear Me Talkin' to Ya. The Story of Jazz As Told by the Men Who Made It*. New York: Dover Publications.

Shipton, Alyn. 2001. *A New History of Jazz*. London and New York: Continuum.

Smith, Geoffrey. 1987. *Stephane Grappelli*, London: Pavilion Michael Joseph.

Smith, Hazel and Dean, Roger. 1997. *Improvisation, Hypermedia and the Arts since 1945*. Amsterdam: Harwood Academic Publishers.

Stucky, Steven. 1981. *Lutoslawski & his music*. Cambridge: Cambridge University Press.

Sturm, Fred. 1995. *Changes over Time: The Evolution of Jazz Arranging*. Germany: Advance Music.

Sylvester, David. 1993. *Interviews with Francis Bacon*. London: Thames & Hudson.

_ 2001. *About Modern Art (second edition)*. New Haven and London: Yale University Press.

_ 2003. *London Recordings*. London: Chatto and Windus.

Tucker, Mark, ed. 1993. *The Duke Ellington Reader*. New York: Oxford University Press.

Varnedoe, Kirk. 1998. *Jackson Pollock*, New York: The Museum of Modern Art.

_ 2006. *Pictures of Nothing, Abstract Art since Pollock*, Princeton: Princeton University Press.

Varnedoe, Kirk and Karmel, Pepe, eds. 1999. *Jackson Pollock New Approaches*. New York: The Museum of Modern Art.

Walser, Robert. 1995. 'Out of Notes: Signification, Interpretation and the Problem of Miles Davis'. In Gabbard *Jazz Among the Discourses*.

_ 1999. *Keeping Time, Readings in Jazz History*. New York: Oxford University Press.

Weitemeier, Hannah. 2001. *Yves Klein*. Cologne: Taschen.

Wickes, John. 1999. *Innovations in British Jazz, Volume 1 1960–1980*. Chelmsford: Soundworld.

Wilder, Alec. 1972. *American Popular Song, The Great Innovators 1900–1950*. New York: Oxford University Press.

Wright, Rayburn. 1982. *Inside the Score, a detailed analysis of 8 classic jazz ensemble charts*. Delevan, New York: Kendor Music.

INDEX

JAZZ BOOKS FROM NORTHWAY

Chris Searle,
*Forward Groove: Jazz and the Real World
from Louis Armstrong to Gilad Atzmon.*

Mike Hennessey,
The Little Giant – The Story of Johnny Griffin

Derek Ansell, *Workout – The Music of Hank Mobley*

Ian Carr, *Music Outside*

Alan Plater, *Doggin' Around*

Coleridge Goode and Roger Cotterrell,
Bass Lines: A Life in Jazz

Peter Vacher, *Soloists and Sidemen: American Jazz Stories*

Jim Godbolt, *A History of Jazz in Britain 1919–50*

Jim Godbolt, *All This and Many a Dog*

Ronnie Scott with Mike Hennessey,
Some of My Best Friends Are Blues

John Chilton, *Hot Jazz, Warm Feet*

Vic Ash, *I Blew It My Way: Bebop, Big Bands and Sinatra*

Digby Fairweather, *Notes from a Jazz Life*

Ron Brown with Digby Fairweather,
Nat Gonella – A Life in Jazz

FORTHCOMING JAZZ BOOKS FROM

NORTHWAY

Peter King,

Flying High: A Jazz Life and Beyond

Jim Godbolt,

A History of Jazz in Britain 1919–50 (paperback)

Leslie Thompson with Jeffrey P. Green,

Swing from a Small Island: The Story of Leslie Thompson

Join our mailing list for details of new books,
events and special offers: write to

Northway Books,

39 Tytherton Road, London N19 4PZ

or email *info@northwaybooks.com*

www.northwaybooks.com

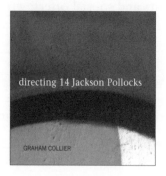

directing 14 Jackson Pollocks

GRAHAM COLLIER

Published at the same time as this book, *directing 14 Jackson Pollocks* is a double CD containing complete versions of two new compositions referred to in *PART FIVE: Forty Years On*, a re-look at pieces written throughout my career, and *The Vonetta Factor*, a major new composition. Also on the CDs is a different version of *The Third Colour*, a highly acclaimed earlier composition. Its inclusion is a marker to what I do as a jazz composer, which is to work with highly skilled musicians, the *14 Jackson Pollocks* of my title, to produce music with them that, like all good jazz, happens in real time, once.

The CD set is available from Amazon or direct from the composer. Alternatively the music can be downloaded from such companies as eMusic and iTunes, with liner notes (by Brian Morton) and artwork available from *www.grahamcolliermusic.com* where further information and more discussion of the music can also be found.